HOLDING

GOVERNMENT

BUREAUCRACIES

ACCOUNTABLE

HOLDING

GOVERNMENT

BUREAUCRACIES

ACCOUNTABLE

SECOND EDITION

BERNARD ROSEN

PRAEGER

New York
Westport, Connecticut
London

Library of Congress Cataloging-in-Publication Data

Rosen, Bernard, 1920–
    Holding government bureaucracies accountable.

    Bibliography: p.
    Includes index.
    1. Legislative oversight—United States.
2. Judicial review of administrative acts—United
States.   3. Bureaucracy—United States.   I. Title.
JK585.R67   1989   353.03   88–35731
ISBN 0–275–92981–7 (alk. paper)
ISBN 0–275–92982–5 (pbk. : alk. paper)

Copyright © 1989 by Bernard Rosen

All rights reserved. No portion of this book may be
reproduced, by any process or technique, without the
express written consent of the publisher.

Library of Congress Catalog Card Number: 88–35731
ISBN: 0–275–92982–5 (pb)
       0–275–92981–7

First published in 1989

Praeger Publishers, One Madison Avenue, New York, NY 10010
A division of Greenwood Press, Inc.

Printed in the United States of America

The paper used in this book complies with the Permanent
Paper Standard issued by the National Information Standards
Organization (Z39.48-1984).

10 9 8 7 6 5 4 3 2 1

JK
585
.R67
1989

Contents

Preface

The growth in power of government bureaucracies is one of the more profound developments of twentieth-century society. What we normally refer to as the bureaucracies have a daily impact on the quality of life of every person in this country and many millions outside our borders. The president, governors, mayors, legislators, judges, and many private citizens now find themselves increasingly concerned with how bureaucracies are using this power—with what they are doing or not doing. The underlying question persists: are government bureaucracies out of control?

Accountability is at the heart of these concerns. For what and to whom are bureaucracies answerable? How are they held accountable? This book discusses these questions, primarily in the context of the federal bureaucracy. While there are problems of accountability with regard to elected as well as appointed bureaucrats, the focus here is on accountability of nonelected bureaucrats.

In putting aside accountability for elected bureaucrats—congressmen, senators, state and local legislators, and elected chief executives at all levels—it is useful to recall a passage from James Madison's *Federalist 57*: "The House of Representatives is so constituted as to support in the members an habitual recollection of their dependence on the people. Before the sentiments impressed on their minds by the mode of their elevation can be effaced by the exercise of power, they will be compelled to anticipate the moment when their exercise of it is to be reviewed, and when they must descend to the level from which they were raised; there forever to remain unless a faithful discharge of their trust shall have established their title to a renewal of it."[1]

Throughout this book, the terms "bureaucracy" and "bureaucrat" are used in a neutral, non-pejorative sense. "Bureaucrat" refers not only to career civil service employees, including many of extraordinary competence, but also political appointees, many of whom are outstanding and come to government for relatively short periods after successful experiences in the private sector or academia. This book assumes that "politics" in a representative democracy is a necessary and honorable activity even though some politicians, just as is the case with some doctors, lawyers, engineers, and people in business, may not be a credit to their vocation.

The first two chapters deal with the substance of accountability: for what public administrators are accountable and to whom. The next five chapters are concerned with the processes of accountability, that is, how public administrators are held accountable—within the executive branch, by the legislative branch, through citizen participation and the news media, by the courts, and by some relatively new instruments. The last two chapters take note of several persistent problems and discuss new initiatives likely to improve the policies and processes for holding government bureaucracies accountable during the 1990s.

This revision retains the structure of the 1982 edition. However, every chapter has been updated to incorporate subsequent developments. Data from a new survey reveal the current views of ranking members of Congress and senior career executives in the federal government on the effectiveness of various accountability mechanisms. An important new law focusing on accountability, the Federal Managers Financial Integrity Act of 1982,[2] and resulting actions are discussed. There are wholly new sections also on the very significant work in accountability being done by the Public Integrity Section of the Department of Justice and by the independent counsels. The Iran-Contra affair is examined from an accountability standpoint. The Reagan administration raised to an intense level oversight and control by the Office of Management and Budget (OMB) of regulatory actions proposed by executive agencies, and that is described. Another important OMB oversight effort is directed to improving the productivity and quality of agencies' performance, and that is explained. This edition considers the adverse impact on accountability and citizen confidence in government of understaffing oversight organizations and permitting members of the permanent bureaucracy to engage in partisan political activity. Finally, special attention is given to the importance of competence, ethical behavior, and commitment to serving the public interest by those who accept the challenge of public service; these are bedrock requirements for responsible and responsive government bureaucracy.

The idea for this book was born after the author had served in the federal bureaucracy for more than 30 years and began teaching courses in public administration. Although the substance and processes of accountability grow large in importance for public administrators as their responsibilities increase, no single work focuses on the subject as a whole in terms of current policies and practices. I believe this book will help fill that need for students, teachers, and managers and other professionals in government. For courses in public management, politics of administration, public personnel administration, Congress, and the presidency, it would be a useful companion text to facilitate discussion and understanding of this overriding issue. Those studying business administration or in business and concerned with the relations between government and business will find that accountability policies and processes translate into opportunities for legitimate intervention in the decision-making processes of government.

With citizen expectations continuing to outrun funded governmental capacity, holding government bureaucracies accountable is a long-term, high-priority concern for the governed and the governors.

NOTES

1. James Madison, "The House of Representatives," in *Hamilton, Madison, and Jay on the Constitution*, ed. Ralph H. Gabriel (New York: The Liberal Arts Press, 1954), pp. 111–15.

2. 31 U.S.C. 3512.

Acknowledgments

The experience and insights of many outstanding practitioners in the arts of politics and public management are reflected in this book. Especially helpful for this edition were 37 members of Congress whose insights on accountability from the legislative vantage point were enriched by their roles as chairman or ranking minority member on standing committees or subcommittees in the House or Senate. Also of great help were 65 federal career executives who shared their views on the effectiveness of a wide range of methods for holding administrators accountable. Their judgments carry special weight because they had been recognized as distinguished career executives by the president based on nominations by the heads of their agencies and recommendation of a citizen review panel. These legislators and administrators shall remain nameless—they are too numerous to list.

An enormous contribution in research, editing, and typing for both the first and second editions was made by my wife Adele, a fellow student of the late Roscoe C. Martin. He was in good part responsible for our love affair—with each other and with public administration. His role must be acknowledged because writing the book in the first instance and now revising it was a labor of love.

Part I

The Substance of

Accountability

In a democracy the object is to keep the government subordinated to the people.

Public Administrators:

Accountable for

What?

"And now, if you will raise your right hand and repeat after me, I will administer the Oath of Office," said the Chief Clerk. The Oath of Office! The words were clear. Deceptively simple.

I, Bernard Rosen, do solemnly swear that I will support and defend the Constitution of the United States against all enemies foreign and domestic; that I will bear true faith and allegiance to the same; that I take this obligation freely, without any mental reservation or purpose of evasion; and that I will well and faithfully discharge the duties of the office on which I am about to enter. So help me God.

Participation in a nationwide competitive examination, interviews, forms filled out, the Oath, and now I was an employee of the United States Government—the Executive Branch!

During more than 30 years in the federal civil service, the duties to be "well and faithfully" discharged spanned a series of necessary and often exciting assignments that ranged from recruiting workers for Pearl Harbor in order to help rebuild the fleet that was destroyed by Japan's surprise attack, to White House meetings on issues related to improving the effectiveness of government—meetings that on some occasions included even the president. Along the way, I wrestled with management policies and practices of federal agencies as they operated in all 50 states and in many other countries. This involved discussing problems and possible solutions—testifying before congressional committees, listening to and talking with congressmen, senators, governors, agency officials, news media reporters, union leaders, veterans' organization officials, civil rights leaders, and representatives of numerous other interest groups as well as individual citizens, all of whom had views on the duties that I was charged to perform "well and faithfully." They all had a claim on me. In one respect or another, they felt I was accountable to them. I shared that feeling, although not always with joy.

Accountability in the executive branch of the federal government starts with the president. The President's Oath of Office, specified in the Constitution, is even briefer than that taken by all other officers and employees:

I, _____, do solemnly swear (or affirm) that I will faithfully execute the Office of President of the United States, and will to the best of my ability, preserve, protect, and defend the Constitution of the United States.[1]

With an oath of similar intent, if not identical words, elected and appointed officials at all levels of government in the United States officially undertake their duties and thereby become accountable. Accountable for what?

In our national government overall executive responsibility is vested in the president, whose specific powers and duties are rooted in the Constitution. The clause "he shall take care that the Laws be faithfully executed"[2] establishes the need for a bureaucracy and the president's role as its head. Similar provisions in many state constitutions and charters for local governments give legitimacy to executive-branch bureaucracies.

The substance of accountability places at least four requirements on elected chief executives and public administrators throughout the bureaucracy:

1. Make laws work as intended with a minimum of waste and delay.
2. Exercise lawful and sensible administrative discretion.
3. Recommend new policies and propose changes in existing policies and programs as needed.
4. Enhance citizen confidence in the administrative institutions of government.

Each of these merits separate discussion.

MAKING LAWS WORK AS INTENDED

This appears perfectly clear, and one might assume it can lead to a prompt and decisive action. However, many laws are the product of compromises in ideas and languages. Often the crucial agreements are achieved through deliberate ambiguity, and the conflicting forces then merely shift the field of battle from the legislative halls to the administrators' offices. Rowland Egger's essay on "Responsibility in Administration" describes the reality:

A public servant who is really convinced that his every official action is fully informed by incontrovertible legal sanctions, instructed by clear policy directives, and supported by objectively demonstrable fact is a dangerous person. He requires to be confined in a straightjacket.[3]

On the issue of determining the intent of laws and dealing with deliberate or accidental ambiguity, the architects of the Constitution offer little guidance for public administrators whose roles have changed enormously in two centuries. A grand total of less than 800 employees constituted the executive branch of the United States government in 1789. The laws to be "faithfully executed" were few in number, quite specific in content, and related almost entirely to collecting revenues, moving the mail, providing for a miniscule military force, and carrying on relations with a small number of countries. The president, and department heads appointed by him, made virtually all significant decisions involving administrative policy. There were few doubts about who was accountable for what.

In the final decade of the twentieth century, the federal government's executive branch, with over two and a half million civilian employees, is engaged in executing tens of thousands of laws by doing almost every conceivable type of work. Federal employees propose laws, and develop the implementing policies and programs for those that are enacted, on subjects that weren't even thought about when the nation was founded: laws dealing with environmental pollution, space exploration, abortion, unemployment compensation, neutron weapons systems, occupational health and safety, cancer research, control of pesticides, minimum wage, subsidized housing, deregulation of regulated areas, and hundreds of others. As for accountability, in our twentieth decade as a nation, a president found it impossible to fulfill a campaign commitment that heads of agencies would personally review and approve their regulations—regulations that have the effect of law. The Carter administration quickly learned that agency heads do not have the time to consider personally the numerous issues and conflicting interests that constitute the essential background for every regulation.

Several examples will illustrate the complex and difficult problems that confront public administrators as they seek to fulfill the first requirement of accountability: make laws work as intended with a minimum of waste and delay.

A critically important statutory responsibility of the U.S. Secret Service is to protect the President of the United States. During the administration of President Reagan, the Director of the Secret Service cited one of numerous situations where protecting the president must be balanced with other needs. Security at the White House complex was his example: "The White House is the residence of the Chief Executive, an office building where the affairs of state are conducted, and a national monument open to the public. So far as the Secret Service is concerned, a basic conflict exists from the start—the need for maximum *access* on the one hand—and the need for maximum security on the other."[4]

The Secretaries and staffs of the Department of Health and Human Services (HHS) (formerly the Department of Health, Education, and Welfare [HEW], renamed in 1979 when a separate agency was created for education) in the Ford and Carter administrations worked for almost six years to develop policies for implementing a law designed to strengthen the civil rights of handicapped people. The unfinished task then became the responsibility of the Reagan Administration. The long delay reflects the many controversial provisions of the law. For example, it calls for public transportation to be accessible to handicapped people. Does this mean that all buses in interstate commerce, and all other bus transportation that is financed in part with federal funds, must be accessible to people in wheelchairs? Powerful forces with primary concern for the handicapped argued "yes." Other powerful forces which estimated the costs of such a conversion in the billions of dollars, argued that this was not the intent of the law, and that alternate forms of transportation could assure equal or greater mobility at significantly less cost.

Then there was the matter of timing. Regardless of the approach, enormous expenditures would be required. Over what period were these to be made? The adversaries included those who believe that because civil rights are the foundation of our democratic society, as soon as a major shortcoming is identified it should be corrected; those at the other end of the spectrum hold that additional expenditures for such purposes should be made at a speed and level that will not adversely affect the economy; and there were many in between. To reach a consensus to enact legislation it was necessary to avoid being specific in these matters, even though this presented a serious problem for the administrator charged with carrying out the law as intended. The intent was not clear.

Another example relates to action by the Congress to attach riders to appropriation bills for the Department of Health and Human Services that restrict the use of federal funds for abortions. The language finally adopted after major struggles within the House and the Senate and between the two was subject to a range of interpretations, any one of which would be contrary to the position of some individuals who found the language in the law acceptable. The fact is that if Congress had insisted on eliminating all ambiguity, it is doubtful that agreement would have been reached on some appropriation bills. Yet the administrator is charged with carrying out the law as intended with regard to the use of funds for abortions.

Across the board it is certainly the intent of Congress and the president that laws be carried out in the most efficient and economical manner. Effective implementation of public policy requires not only comprehensive planning and competent execution but also systematic evaluation to facilitate timely corrective action. When implementation involves massive contracting out, assuring efficiency and economy may be more complex. Some policies and programs are particularly vulnerable to inefficiency and corruption during their implementation. New programs that involve spending large sums of money in relatively short periods of time to achieve goals that are quite general provide fertile ground for poor productivity, inefficiency, and even dishonesty.

The strongest signals sent to administrators by the president and Congress at the beginning of such programs call for moving ahead quickly. Often in the first year a key question is whether the money is being spent at the anticipated rate. There is little or nothing in most legislation authorizing and funding new multibillion dollar social and defense programs to evidence a clear concern on the part of either the president or Congress that the need for speed should be balanced against the need for integrity, efficiency, and high productivity. Rarely are there specific provisions for early, continuing, and systematic review by legislative bodies or within the executive branch. Yet administrators of civil and military programs can testify from firsthand experience that years after the programs were launched, they were held accountable on these grounds.

EXERCISING LAWFUL AND SENSIBLE DISCRETION

In his excellent book *Discretionary Justice*, Kenneth Culp Davis recognizes that administrative discretion is indispensable to effective government; but he argues that public officials now have too much discretion, and that a great deal needs to be done to confine, structure, and check this discretion to assure a more just society. Davis holds that some of this excess discretion should be restricted by legislators but most need to be defined and limited by higher-level administrators. In general, he favors administrative discretion when it is not practicable to lay down a rule that will permit fair consideration of unique situations.[5] Of course, to the degree that public administrators have unnecessary discretion, accountability is diminished.

One of the virtues of bureaucracy is that its very nature contributes to a *lawful* exercise of administrative discretion. Max Weber discussed three characteristics of bureaucracy that help in this regard:

1. Fixed and official jurisdictional areas, which are generally ordered by rules, that is, by laws or administrative regulations.

2. The regular activities required for the purposes of the bureaucratically governed structure are distributed in a fixed way as official duties.

3. Methodical provision is made for the regular and continuous fulfillment of these duties and for the execution of the corresponding rights; only persons with the generally regulated qualifications to serve are employed.[6]

But these elements may also work against the *sensible* use of administrative discretion. They have a tendency to encourage a narrow rather than broad responsiveness to problems; there are obvious risks for administrators who deal responsively with situations that do not fit the established rule.

"Responsiveness" is a complicated idea in the context of administrative discretion. It may involve action, or even inaction if today's decision reduces tomorrow's options. Public administrators are urged to be flexible; but they must also keep in mind the precedential power of each decision. They can become so responsive that they are not responsible. The basic question is always present: responsive to whom and with what consequences for the broader public interest? To illustrate:

The Federal Trade Commission may or may not choose to regulate in a particular area. This decision may be made for reasons of policy, priority, or resources. In any event, its decision is likely to be applauded by some as a sensible use of its discretion, and it is also likely to be condemned by others as being unresponsive to the problems. As expected, the chairman of the Commission came in for lavish praise and sharp criticism on his proposal to prohibit advertising so-called "junk food" on television programs that cater to small children.

In another instance, President Jimmy Carter's secretary of HHS and many governors and mayors were given high marks by some and denounced by others for conducting antismoking campaigns. In the last year of the Reagan administration, the surgeon general of the United States was caught in a similar crossfire. He issued a report which declared that not only were cigarettes a health hazard with regard to cancer, but also that nicotine in cigarettes is as addictive as cocaine or heroin and should be labeled accordingly.

Several secretaries of Transportation have been buffeted by conflicting forces on the issue of requiring all new automobiles to have airbags or seat belts that automatically lock into place.

In these and many other examples, the central issue relates to whether the administrator used discretion lawfully and sensibly in carrying out the government's responsibility.

How administrators exercise their discretion within the framework of law is subject to many forces. Higher-level supervisors have powerful influence on the exercise of discretion by subordinates. President Gerald Ford caused HHS to reverse quickly the decision of one of its civil rights officials who cast doubt on the tax-exemption status of a nonprofit organization because it allegedly discriminated based on sex by sponsoring a mother-daughter luncheon. Although the decision of the HHS official was probably a correct literal application of the civil rights law, it was not politically feasible. Subsequently, there was no difficulty using administrative discretion "sensibly" in responding to a query from a school administrator as to whether federal funding would be jeopardized by continuing to hold father-son breakfasts for the football team.

There are almost unlimited numbers of conditions and circumstances where laws and rules do not fit the situation and where discretion must be used. Many of the most controversial proposals for applying significant administrative discretion are debated and decided at the point where political and career officials interface. Political appointees often consider the use of discretion in terms of action that will produce results *soon*, recognizing that on the average their tenure is about two years—accountability in the short term. On the other hand, senior career officials are likely to weigh the use of discretion in longer terms, including history of the policy or program, and the need for continuing relations with interest groups, legislators and staff, central management agencies, and the news media.

Decisions of the courts also guide the exercise of administrative discretion on a wide range of issues such as the granting or revocation of licenses, the immigration or deportation of aliens, approval or rejection of claims for social security or disability pensions, and the interpretation of the Constitution and laws in thousands of other situations where the executive branch agencies provide or deny benefits.

Legislative institutions as well as individual legislators and their principal staff influence the use of discretion by administrators. A proposed amendment to a bill or statute, or merely a phone call from a legislator or staff director of a committee expressing dissatisfaction with an agency policy can result in immediate reconsideration.

Along with a proper respect for supervisory, legislative, and judicial restraints on using discretion, there is also a need for public administrators to take reasonable risks in exercising discretion in order to achieve the intent of legislation "with a minimum of waste and delay." In developing policies (including legislative proposals), interpreting laws and executive orders, planning policy implementation by deciding among options regarding strategy, priorities, means, ends, and providing for appropriate evaluation, the public administrator is constantly confronted with the need to exercise discretion.

The decisions made are not risk-free, nor should they be. There may be varying degrees of risk for those directly impacted by the policy being implemented, risks for the organization and staff carrying out the implementation decisions, and risks for the public manager who made the decisions. To minimize the possibility of abuse in the exercise of administrative discretion, ethics and values must be a significant, at times even the compelling consideration. In *Moral Obligations of Public Officials*, Donald Warwick suggests ethical principles that can provide guidance for the exercise of administrative discretion by a public official. The essential elements are these:

1. *Discretion should be exercised in the public interest.* While discretionary choice need not be empty of personal, agency or constituent interests, the public interest must be paramount.

2. *The process of exercising discretion should include reflective choice.* This involves being clear that the ends sought are not in conflict with our basic values; being reasonably certain that the information used is adequate and

reliable; and being consciously persuaded that there is a plausible link between the action to be taken and the problem to be solved.

3. *The exercise of discretion should be grounded in veracity.*

4. *The exercise of discretion should include a fundamental respect for established procedures* because they are probably the single most important factor in promoting fairness and accountability.

5. *The exercise of discretion should include the exercise of restraint on the means chosen to accomplish organizational ends.* Means that violate law or civil liberties are unacceptable; means that entail unfairness in application of public policy are unacceptable; means that undermine trust in government are unacceptable.[7]

Warwick notes that the key question for ethical administrative discretion is responsibility in the generation and use of power. Power need not corrupt; and lack of power can be quite as corrupting and as deleterious to the public interest.

Irving Kristol suggests that: "The major intellectual problem facing the American polity in the decades to come might well be: How can we realize the potentialities of big government without surrendering ourselves and our goals to the mercies of little men."[8] In terms of accountability the dilemma can be stated this way: more administrative flexibility increases the possibilities for abuse of administrative discretion while less administrative discretion breeds excessive uniformity.

INITIATING CHANGES IN POLICIES AND PROGRAMS

Daily immersion in the operation of public programs provides the competent administrator with a unique opportunity for understanding the usefulness of particular policies. No one else has as good information about the effectiveness of policies, or can get it as quickly. No one else is in a better position to ascertain as soon as it is discernible that a program should be curtailed or ended because it can not do what was intended or has outlived its usefulness. No one else is in a better position to identify needed changes in law or administrative policies that would enhance the possibilities of fulfilling the goals of the law and the chief executive's policies. And no one else is better equipped to determine that there is a greater need for the resources in other parts of the same organization.

Nevertheless, the close-to-unanimous complaint of elected officials remains: government bureaucracy does not initiate and does not innovate; and too often it uses its enormous capacity to destroy new ideas that involve change. Is this the reality or is it the rhetoric of frustration and demagoguery? Does truth fall somewhere in between?

A major difficulty in holding administrators accountable for initiating change—for innovation in organizational structure, policies, and operations—is that often there is a wide gap between the citizens' expectations and perceptions, and the reality.

As to expectations with regard to innovation in organizational structure, there is little doubt that taxpayers want efficient and effective government organizations; they want smaller and less expensive government structures.

What do they perceive they are getting in the way of movement in that direction? In the United States, there is a widely held impression that no one from inside the government bureaucracy ever changes the organization; only outsiders have the ideas and the will to change it. This idea is kept shiny and bright by many of those seeking elective offices every two, four, or six years: they flail the "unimaginative" bureaucracy; they promise to reorganize it to cut out waste; they feed the popular perception that *reor-*ganizations are good and the bureaucracy denies them to us.

The reality about innovating with regard to structure is that at least some parts of larger agencies are *always* in a state of reorganization. In most instances there is recurring internal pressure for organizational change. It originates with agency heads, program managers, and their management analysts who are devoting full time to examining and solving organizational and procedural problems. Structural changes do result; some are major and many are only incremental but still significant. Almost always people inside the bureaucracy play a key role in initiating and implementing the changes.

Generally, these internally initiated reorganizations have been undertaken for such good reasons as establishing clearer accountability, giving visibility to a new program, eliminating duplication, or consolidating like functions—all intended to improve government operations. Sometimes, reorganizations are launched for purposes other than to achieve better government: to diffuse criticism, to create a diversion, to provide the appearance of new leadership "taking charge," or simply to make room for a political crony.

Administrators need to be held accountable for making proper and timely use of their power to reorganize. For taxpayers the bottom line is smaller and fewer government agencies; but the fact is that government structures cannot disappear or shrink very much unless programs authorized and funded by law are cut back, eliminated, or contracted out. These are very difficult political decisions, and the direction and speed of such actions are the business primarily of elected officials, not the bureaucracy.

The situation is quite similar with regard to policy innovations by bureaucracies. Taxpayers want policies that work well universally—everywhere and at all times; they want good policies put in place and let stand so they can avoid the uncertainties that accompany changes in policies. In other words, they want the stability and continuity that bureaucracies are uniquely suited to provide. When policies do not work well, taxpayers want them changed promptly; they also want necessary new policies and programs launched without increasing the overall cost of government.

The general perception of many taxpayers is that their policy expectations are being ignored or thwarted at every turn by the bureaucracy. It is now an article of faith with many of our citizens that the government has lots of poor policies and they cannot be eliminated or changed largely because of the bureaucracy. Taxpayers see problems all around, and many feel that the bureaucracy is not changing or initiating policies to solve these problems. They perceive the bureaucracy as mindlessly applying policy, waffling on the need for change, engaging in endless negotiations, and making compromises that too often result in policies too weak to be useful.

How do these perceptions of policy innovation in public bureaucracies square with the reality? Even though there is some truth in these perceptions, for the most part they miss the mark. In an atmosphere of frustrated expectations, citizens give little weight to the complexity of problems and the difficulties in making policy changes. There is only modest awareness of the fact that changes in public policy usually create new winners and new losers, and therefore while proposed changes are debated internally they are also strongly contested from outside the bureaucracy.

In a democratic society, to govern requires a consensus. Developing a consensus on the broad elements of public policy is the business of political leadership. Reaching agreement on the details of public policy also involves negotiation and pragmatic compromises by political leaders and among government bureaucracies. Within this framework there is considerable policy change advocated from inside the bureaucracy, but undoubtedly there is great unevenness and room for improvement.

As for initiating changes in operations, taxpayers want government to do well and quickly what needs to be done. Taxpayers want government employees to be competent, hardworking, and courteous; they want managers in the bureaucracy to be decisive, to make good decisions, and to be willing to take risks in dealing with policy, people, and program problems; they want operations free of failure. The inherent conflict between some of these expectations merely indicates that there is no Newtonian rule that commands harmony among the "wants" that we taxpayers have.

How do the taxpayers see these expectations being met? Most see government operations as neither effective nor efficient. Public employees are perceived by many as moderately competent to incompetent, lacking ambition, interested primarily in job security, overpaid, underworked, and even arrogant. Government bureaucracies are considered wasteful. Certainly, taxpayers do not perceive the strong suit of public bureaucrats as innovation to make government operate better and more economically.

What are the facts? By law, federal employees may receive cash and honorary awards for contributing beyond their job requirements to improving efficiency, economy, and effectiveness of government operations. Since 1954, when this governmentwide program was started, employees have been recognized on more than six million occasions for their adopted ideas and performance beyond job responsibilities. Collectively, these employee contributions produced *first-year* savings in government operations of over $14 billion. There were also many other improvements in government operations in medicine, science, and national security where the benefits could not be measured in dollars.

In 1986 alone, federal employees formally contributed 181,900 ideas to improve the operations of our national government, and 44,800 of these ideas were adopted with resulting changes in operations that produced first-year benefits to the taxpayers of over $348 million. Such changes have an average life of five years. Therefore, the tangible benefits from these 1986 employee innovations exceed $1.7 *billion*.[9] On a smaller scale most state and many city governments have similar experiences. All this is in sharp contrast with the widely held perception that government bureaucrats simply go on doing what they have been doing, unthinkingly and unyieldingly.

Effectively holding the individual administrator accountable for initiating change calls for a sensible sorting out of expectations, perceptions, and reality, even while we recognize that in political terms what people perceive *becomes* their reality.

It is the nature of bureaucracies to try to survive. Clients and suppliers promote the continuance because they have a strong interest in the status quo. Woe to the administrator who recommends policy changes that diminish or eliminate services or benefits to clients. Bureaucrats know that clients are interested in more, not less, and they therefore behave in ways that will gain support to help them achieve overall goals.

The intensity of the bureaucrat's search for change and degree of determination to achieve it, reflects not only professional competence in identifying the need for change and feasible alternatives but also a consideration of *values* and *risks*.

—Which changes are really important? A matter of values.

—What is the cost-benefit relationship of the change where intangibles are involved? A matter of values.

—Change implies criticism of architects of the present policy. A matter of risks.

—What if the change is not adopted? Will the administrator be tagged as having bad judgment, and if so, what are the implications? A matter of risks.

—What are the rewards if the change is adopted? A matter of values.

—Is the political climate, internal and external, *conducive* to change? (For example, the months and year preceding an election may be viewed in some political quarters as a very favorable time to initiate the particular change, while that time may be viewed in other quarters as completely inappropriate.) A matter of risks.

—What if the adopted change generates major unexpected criticism? A matter of values and risks.

These are difficult questions. Only the ablest of bureaucrats can deal with them satisfactorily and avoid being immobilized by the inherent inertia of bureaucracy which carries with it the virtue of stability.

Among the more powerful forces that motivate public administrators to achieve needed change are (1) inner compulsion to do well, and (2) self-preservation. The first involves such qualities as commitment, professional pride, and eagerness to advance. The second is concerned more with survival. Operating separately and together, they have much to do with determining whether individual public administrators meet a major requirement of accountability by recommending and making policy and program changes in a timely manner.

ENHANCING CITIZEN CONFIDENCE IN THE ADMINISTRATIVE INSTITUTIONS OF GOVERNMENT

Simple logic dictates that citizen confidence in public institutions is vital in a society where government is based on consent of the governed. This goes hand in hand with the fact that a democratic society depends greatly on the willingness of citizens to obey laws, from paying taxes to observing speed limits; and this willingness is related to the citizen's confidence in the government. Citizen confidence is hard to define and still harder to measure. But this much is clear: there is significance in major shifts of public opinion relating to citizen confidence and such shifts are often discernible.

In 1980, pollster Louis Harris provided some shocking information about the confidence of the American people in the leadership of institutions in both public and private sectors of the United States. He concluded that in less than 15 years, the proportion of adults having confidence in this leadership had slipped sharply. A 1986 poll reveals very little improvement as evidenced by the following:

the feeling that "what you think doesn't really count very much anymore" had gone up from 37 percent in 1966 to 61 percent in 1980 and stood at 60 percent in 1986;

the idea that "people running the country don't really care what happens to you" had gone up from 26 percent in 1966 to 60 percent in 1980 and stood at 55 percent in 1986.[10]

The Watergate scandals and corporate bribery of public officials in the 1970s no doubt account for part of these shifts. "Restoring confidence in government" *was* a major issue in the 1976 presidential campaign, and it continued as a central concern for the remainder of the decade as various proposals for dealing with problems of inflation and energy failed to achieve a consensus for government action. The Reagan administration sought to build citizen support for a smaller, more efficient federal government. However, in the late 1980s, subsequent to the 1986 Harris poll, revelations from the Iran-Contra Affair, indictments of former White House officials, and a military-procurement fraud and bribery scandal probably caused a further decline in citizen confidence.

The confidence of citizens in their government is affected by many other conditions. One legacy of the Revolutionary War is a continuing distrust of the power of government. By definition, a constitutional democracy is committed to protecting the people *from* the government. The Declaration of Independence and the first ten amendments to the Constitution make this clear. And if further evidence is desired we need only look at provisions in the Constitution relating to the three branches of government: carefully structured systems of checks and balances were designed to place restraints on the power of each branch of government.

There is continuing tension, usually of a low grade, between the people and the bureaucracies, because bureauracracies make demands throughout life: register the baby's birth, attend designated public schools, take a driving test, obey traffic regulations, answer questions from the census taker, sign up for tax withholding, get a social security number, fill out tax and other forms, pay for a marriage certificate, file an environmental impact statement, observe zoning requirements, use a five-digit zip code in addition to a correct address, and submit to investigations by inspectors for compliance with laws pertaining to wages, health, safety, and income tax. This is only a very small sample of the interactions between the citizen and governments engaged in promoting the "general welfare."

Citizen confidence hinges in part on whether these legal demands and limitations appear necessary or useful. Are they reasonable requirements? Citizen confidence also hinges on how fairly and sensibly requirements of law are applied and how well authorized services and benefits are provided. Is there honesty as well as competence in the performance of essential services? Confidence further hinges on whether law and administrative action contribute to the citizen's unending search for identity and personal fulfillment. Clearly the administrator has an important role in earning and retaining the citizen's confidence in government, and especially in its administrative processes.

Statutes normally contain provisions authorizing agency heads or the chief executive to issue implementing regulations. The resulting policies would appear to reflect an exercise of major administrative discretion with the law serving as the only restraint. In fact, the power of the administrator to make policy is limited by the kind and quality of citizen participation in the decision-making process. The nature of this participation has important accountability implications. For example:

Have the principal officials of an agency developed such a cozy relationship with a special group of citizens—those they are called on to regulate or assist—that as a practical matter they may have become more accountable to them than to other citizens who will also be affected by the agency's decisions?

Does the agency seek out the views of representatives from all citizen groups that may have an interest in its actions and give them careful and impartial consideration in the course of developing policies and programs?

Does the agency establish mechanisms that will encourage representatives from a wide spectrum of interested citizens to contribute their views on the operations of its programs to facilitate necessary and timely changes?

Do agency officials recognize that secrecy is the archenemy of accountability, and that citizen participation and confidence in government are more likely to result from openness, with secrecy as the exception?

Although the views of different citizen groups are rarely in complete harmony, administrators operating on a presumption that openness is *good* are likely to be more successful in obtaining productive citizen participation in policy formulation and program administration and thus enlarging citizen confidence in the operations of government. This reduces the possibility of a citizenry alienated from its government, and increases the likelihood of more effective, more responsive, and more accountable government.

Finally, citizen confidence in the administrative institutions of government is profoundly affected by evidence of the administrator's commitment to the most fundamental values in a democratic society. Citizen confidence is enhanced when the policies and decisions of the bureaucracy provide for equal treatment under the law, when they support each person's right to life and liberty, when they respect individual privacy, when they honor due process, and when they move us toward a more just society. When our government bureaucracies behave in this manner they help preserve our noblest ideals and enlarge the consent of the governed.

NOTES

1. U.S., Constitution, Art. 2, Sec. 1.

2. U.S., Constitution, Art. 2, Sec. 3.

3. Rowland Egger, "Responsibility in Administration," in *Public Administration and Democracy*, ed. Roscoe C. Martin (Syracuse: Syracuse University Press, 1965), p. 303.

4. John R. Simpson, Director, U.S. Secret Service, *Roger W. Jones Lecture*, Washington, March 7, 1988.

5. Kenneth Culp Davis, *Discretionary Justice* (Chicago: University of Illinois Press, 1976), pp. 3–161.

6. *From Max Weber*, trans. and ed. H. H. Gerth and C. Wright Mills (New York: Oxford University Press, 1946), pp. 196–244.

7. Donald Warwick, "The Ethics of Administrative Discretion," *Public Duties: The Moral Obligations of Government Officials*, ed. Alan Fleischman et al., 1981, pp. 115–125.

8. Irving Kristol, "Big Government and Little Men," *The New Leader*, November 26, 1962, p. 14.

9. *A Report on The Federal Incentive Awards Program*, U.S. Office of Personnel Management, 1987, p. 5.

10. *The Harris Survey*, "Alienation Sharply Rises," September 8, 1986.

2

Public Administrators:

Accountable to

Whom?

Experienced public administrators know that, aside from power to hire and fire, lines of accountability are strongest to those who control the administrator's responsibilities, authority, and resources. Without these there is nothing to administer. In the national government, basic accountability relationships have their origins in checks and balances created by the Constitution. James Madison put it succinctly: "You must first enable the government to control the governed; and in the next place oblige it to control itself."[1] In *Myers* v. *United States*[2], Justice Louis Brandeis, writing for the majority, stated the issue in another way but with equal clarity: "The doctrine of the separation of powers was adopted by the Convention in 1787, not to promote efficiency but to preclude the exercise of arbitrary power."

The separate branches of government are not isolated from each other. Equally important, they are not isolated from political, economic, and social forces of the nation. The administrator is part of a hierarchy, and while hierarchy is important in helping to establish lines of accountability, there is more to accountability than chain of command.

For example, an administrator, appointed by the chief executive to head a major program within a department based on the strong recommendation of a powerful interest group or the chairman of an appropriations subcommittee that deals with that agency, will very likely view his accountability as going beyond simple administrative hierarchy. To do otherwise carries substantial risk, as the head of an agency quickly learned during the Nixon administration. Traditionally, recommendations of veterans organizations have been pivotal in the president's decision to appoint an administrator of the Veterans Administration. Consequently, the administrator who proposed a reduction in the agency's budget, in response to strong pressure from the White House, saw his support from veterans organizations evaporate and shortly thereafter lost his job.

Economic and social forces impact on administrators in a variety of ways, causing them to consider in a political context information that reflects the diverse conditions, attitudes, and values of a pluralistic society. It is in this political process, as individuals and groups exercise the right of access to the decision makers with resulting adjustments and compromises, that the accountability of public administrators in a representative democracy is put to the most sophisticated tests; because it is *then* that the definition of the "public interest" is honed.

THE PUBLIC ADMINISTRATOR AND THE ELECTED CHIEF EXECUTIVE

Hierarchy as a basis for accountability is as old as bureaucracies. And, as William McNeill notes in *The Rise of the West: A History of the Human Community* (Chicago: University of Chicago Press, 1970, p. 53), bureaucracies were well-developed in the time of Hammurabi, about 1700 B.C. The line of accountability was clear—to the Emperor; and so it has continued for each sovereign down through the ages. Hierarchical accountability in the U.S. government is established by the Constitution. It vests executive power in the president. With the advice and consent of the Senate, the president is authorized to appoint "Officers"—the heads of executive departments and agencies. Appointment of "inferior Officers" is in the hands of the president or department heads, as provided by law.[3] The Supreme Court, in *Marbury* v. *Madison*,[4] made clear that power to appoint also included power to remove, unless it was otherwise limited by the Constitution or statute.

With minor variations, this framework for accountability in a hierarchy, based on power to appoint and remove, also prevails in the executive branch of most state and local governments. Principal exceptions take the form of constitutional provisions or statutes that call for popular election of heads of certain departments, or for their appointment by boards or commissions that are largely independent of the elected chief executive.

Newly elected chief executives—presidents, governors, mayors, county executives, and the key officials they appoint—almost always come into office convinced that they will have problems "controlling" the bureaucracy. Where strong merit systems exist, chief executives and their principal assistants generally express concern about their ability to direct and be accountable for work of the bureaucracy when they are free to appoint persons of their own choosing to only a very limited number of positions. For example, the president and his principal officers are free to bring about 3,000 people into a workforce of 2.8 million.

For decades, at all levels of government, there has been a fashionable suspicion among many top political appointees, especially in the first year or two of a new administration, that senior and sometimes even midlevel career employees are firmly committed to policies of the previous administration and will not change. Therefore, they reason, these career professionals at best cannot be expected to carry out enthusiastically the policies of the new administration; and at worst, they will try to scuttle them.

The breadth and importance of these feelings are reflected in two personal experiences.[5]

In the summer of 1961, several key people in the Kennedy administration visited me in San Francisco and indicated that high officials in the administration felt that senior civil servants in Washington and the field, "holdovers" from the Eisenhower administration, were not supporting the president's efforts to change policies, program priorities, and emphases. I told them that I was well acquainted with the top career people in federal agencies in that western region, having been the United States Civil Service Commission's Regional Director for three years, and that I saw no evidence of any foot-dragging.

To the contrary, I had heard a number express concern that they were receiving no significant changes in policy or program direction from their headquarters. In a meeting with some of these career executives later in the day, this point was underscored for the officials from Washington by a comment from one career executive to the effect that after seven months of the Kennedy administration, he had received no new policies from his headquarters, and the only clear evidence he had of a new president was what he read in the newspapers and saw on television.

Eight years later, in the summer of 1969, I had a repeat of that experience with high officials in the Nixon administration. This time it was at a meeting in the White House where the judgment was expressed by undersecretaries from five or six departments that Johnson administration "holdovers" in important career positions were behaving as if there had not been an election nine months earlier. Based on my then current contacts with career executives in Washington and the field, I expressed the same opinion I had voiced in 1961.

Further, I related the 1961 episode and remarked that undoubtedly some of the people considered in 1969 as Johnson administration "holdovers" were viewed in 1961 as Eisenhower administration "holdovers." No one challenged my statement and, in fact, one presidential appointee agreed. Nevertheless, in the intervening years and subsequently, the myth continued to be replayed—and always without supporting facts.

In part out of similar concerns, the Carter administration in 1978 initiated major civil service reforms, including the establishment of a senior executive service that would give the president and his appointees more control over the bureaucracy. The Carter administration also issued new guidelines and standards to be followed by state and local governments when they fill positions in programs funded by the national government. These revised standards have the effect of shifting more such positions from open competitive to political appointment; and here again the primary reason given for making changes was to permit more political control of the bureaucracy.

In seeking to reduce the federal government's role, the Reagan administration further limited the application of national standards of merit for employment in federally funded state and local programs. At the same time, the Reagan administration demonstrated its distrust of the bureaucracy by increasing the number of political appointees and reducing the role of career executives in policy development and program leadership. Opponents of these changes charge that they opened the civil service to more political patronage.[6]

During the Carter administration, some actions of the Department of Health and Human Services (HHS) with regard to funding abortions, antismoking campaigns, and civil rights enforcement were widely criticized as evidence of a bureaucracy out of control; yet these administrative actions accurately reflected decisions of the president's own secretary of HHS.

The bureaucracy of the Department of Energy (DOE) was often flailed for being unresponsive; here again the highly criticized actions or inactions reflected decisions of the president's appointees. Investigations of the causes of the gasoline shortage of 1979 is a case in point. On May 25, 1979, the president directed the Departments of Energy and Justice to "jointly conduct a comprehensive investigation of the apparent gas shortage situation, using all available and appropriate authority and resources at your disposal, to determine whether there is a reason to believe that the apparent shortfall is a result of concerted activity by firms at the refining and/or marketing level, or of excessive stockpiling or hoarding of supplies." *Ten days after* this strongly worded memorandum was issued, the presidentially appointed Deputy Secretary of Energy convened a meeting that set in motion an effort by the department that ignored the president's call for a "comprehensive investigation." Instead, about two months later, the president's appointees provided the White House with a 53-page report that summarized the information available within the department or readily obtainable from the oil industry's Washington representatives.[7] Clearly, this report was not the product of a bureaucracy out of political control.

The views of federal career executives on the subject of political control of the bureaucracy are quite revealing. Most think that their top politically appointed bosses are on the whole in reasonably good control of their operations. In a survey I conducted in spring 1988 of 65 senior career executives in the most responsible positions in 15 federal agencies, 56 percent stated that the agency head or deputy is very effective in holding agency administrators accountable; another 33 percent rated them moderately effective in doing so; 11 percent rated them as rarely effective in this regard.

If there is a real problem in democratic political control of the bureaucracy, the primary cause may well be the short tenure and lack of government experience of political appointees. This is quite evident at the national level. Despite significant achievements in nongovernment sectors, most new political appointees come to Washington knowing very little about operations of the federal government; most know practically nothing about the particular program they will be heading or advising on; and often they are virtually ignorant of the legislative and executive processes for getting things done in government. The problem becomes even clearer when one considers the range of knowlege most higher-level political appointees need before they can function effectively. They must develop an understanding of

agency programs overall and their own specific programs;

administration policies as they impinge on relevant agency policies and programs;

relations with key people in the three branches of government;

organization of the executive branch;

relationship of own agency to the president;

relationship of own agency to other agencies;

relevant governmentwide policies as to personnel management, financial management, procurement, etc.;

roles of the central management agencies;

relation of federal government to state and local governments on pertinent matters;

role of the career staff and role of noncareer appointees in own agency;

government's ethical standards;

key people in the organization—what they do, and their strengths and weaknesses; and

institutional history.

Too often political appointees leave government before they have become effective. The average length of time that assistant secretaries of departments remain in office is less than two years. The resulting cost from nonperformance and poor performance during successive transitional learning periods cannot be determined, but it is substantial.

Major problems in the accountability of agencies arise when interagency coordination or cooperation is essential to achieving results. This is particularly so when "coming into agreement" on a matter requires one or several agencies to alter their behavior significantly. The problem becomes very serious if an agreement can be achieved only by reducing the organizational autonomy of even one of the agencies. Interagency negotiations designed to establish conditions governing the accountability of one agency to another in a specific program area can be protracted and resulting operations may be ineffective. (For a more detailed discussion see James Q. Wilson and Patricia Rachal, "Can the Government Regulate Itself," *The Public Interest* [Winter 1977]:3–14.)

Accountability also becomes a problem when administrators report to multiheaded commissions or boards. While the chairman of such a multiheaded body may be legally designated as chief executive officer, the fairly common practice of annual rotation of the chair and the need for agreement by a majority to make many decisions often result in complex communications patterns and unclear relationships between the administrators and board members.

THE PUBLIC ADMINISTRATOR AND THE LEGISLATURE

Although it had long been accepted that oversight is a necessary function of Congress, not until the Legislative Reorganization Act of 1946[8] was a specific requirement placed on all standing committees of Congress for "continuous watchfulness" over how the agencies under their jurisdiction carry out the laws. States have been equally slow in defining and assigning clear responsibility for legislative oversight. Failure to move comprehensively and systematically in this area has not been due to any serious doubts about the right to do so. But for most legislators, service to constituents is first priority and legislating second; oversight ranks last. The legality of oversight has been established repeatedly. Chief Justice Warren Burger, speaking for the Supreme Court in *Eastland* v. *United States Servicemen's Fund*,[9] affirmed the constitutionality of legislative oversight by referring to a 1927 decision of the Court: "This Court has often noted that the power to investigate is inherent in the power to make laws because 'a legislative body cannot legislate wisely or effectively in the absence of information respecting the conditions which the legislation is intended to affect or change.' *McGrain* v. *Daugherty*, 273 U.S. 175 (1927)."

In 1974, the National Academy of Public Administration recommended that Congress "give major attention to strengthening its capacity to perform the oversight function, with particular emphasis on evaluating the performance of executive agencies."[10] Hearings held in the House that same year indicated that numerous congressmen and senators support this view.[11] During the second session of the 100th Congress, I conducted a survey of 14 senators and 24 representatives, *each with significant oversight responsibility* as chairman or ranking minority member of a committee or subcommittee. In response to the question "In your judgment, how well is the House, overall, holding administrative agencies accountable for carrying out the laws as intended," *only one* of the 24 representatives rated the House as doing very well; 63 percent as doing quite well; and 33 percent as not well enough. Of the 14 senators asked the same question applicable to the Senate, none rated it as doing very well, 50 percent as quite well, and 50 percent as not well enough. An earlier survey of members of state legislatures by Rutgers' Eagleton Institute of Politics[12] also evidenced a low regard for their oversight activities. The percent of legislators in six states rating their own legislature's oversight as excellent or good ranged from a low in one state of 20 percent to a high of 32 percent in another.

Many federal administrators also believe some improvement in congressional oversight is needed but, overall, they are not as critical as the members of Congress. The survey of senior career executives revealed that 47 percent believe that the authorization process is very effective in holding agency administrators accountable, while 37 percent thought it was moderately effective, and 16 percent thought it was rarely effective. The first two sets of figures change significantly with regard to accountability through the appropriations process: 67 percent believe it is very effective, 19 percent moderately effective, and 14 percent rarely effective.

Legislative oversight is most often directed to getting answers on a few issues; and specific inquiries may deal with rather minute items. The big questions that generate oversight are these. Are the purposes of the laws being fulfilled? Are the agencies being administered honestly and efficiently? Is administrative discretion being exercised in the public interest? Of course, legislative oversight may also be initiated for less noble reasons, such as to secure favorable publicity, to embarrass the political opposition, to demonstrate support for a constituent that is not warranted, or to harass an administrator who did not grant a favor.

Legislative bodies experience many difficulties in holding administrative agencies accountable. Major problems encountered by Congress include the following: "(1) imprecise definitions of program goals, (2) lack of adequate staff, (3) lack of time required to do adequate oversight (since most staff time is used to prepare new legislation), (4) nonobjectivity resulting from the mutually reinforcing relationships that develop between legislative committees and federal agencies, and (5) lack of established patterns of cooperation among authorizing, appropriations, and government operations committees in sharing information relevant to agency and program oversight."[13]

Nevertheless, Congress has an impressive array of resources to carry on legislative oversight. In addition to the excellent data collection and analysis activities of the Congressional Research Service of the Library of Congress and the Office of Technology Assessment, there is the General Accounting Office (GAO), which conducts hundreds of on-site audits and evaluations of federal agencies every year and makes reports to the Congress. The General Accounting Office audits and investigations rate quite high with Congress as a mechanism for holding administrators accountable. My 1988 survey of senators and representatives showed that 34 percent believe GAO is very effective, 61 percent moderately, and only five percent rarely effective. Senior career executives have a lower regard for GAO's performance in holding administrators accountable. My survey showed 17 percent believe it is very effective, 59 percent moderately so, and 24 percent rarely effective.

Furthermore, the Congress itself has a variety of methods and techniques to oversee administrative agencies. Among the more widely used are committee and subcommittee investigations and hearings, reporting requirements, confirmation hearings, casework, and the authorization and appropriations processes. These will be discussed in Chapter 4. At the state and local levels of government, the legislative bodies generally use similar methods and techniques.[14]

THE PUBLIC ADMINISTRATOR AND THE CITIZEN

Individual citizens hold public administrators accountable on two levels. First, citizens are inclined to focus on performance of an agency when they are not satisfied with what it is doing to them or for them. Their evaluation comments are legion:

—It costs too much to send a letter.

—My property is assessed too high.

—The income tax form is too complicated.

—I have to stand in line for over an hour to register for unemployment compensation.

—The pot holes in the street still have not been filled.

—The stoplight at Fourth and Main is not working again.

—The trash collectors left a mess in front of my house.

—It takes too long to get a building permit.

—I wrote to the agency in Washington three weeks ago, and still no answer.

—He really didn't make any effort to help solve the problem; in fact, he was even a little arrogant.

—The letter doesn't answer my question; now I am more confused than I was before.

—The phone rang and rang. After they answered, they put me on "hold," and after five minutes I was disconnected. It happened twice; and when we finally did begin to talk, he said another office handles these questions.

Citizens personally affected by an agency in a way they believe to be unfair, improper, or inefficient do not always call to account the responsible public official or someone higher in that organization. When they do, an explanation and/or corrective action usually concludes the matter. Sometimes a citizen remains dissatisfied with the action of the agency and seeks a more favorable decision by enlisting help from citizen groups and legislators. In some situations, a citizen holds the administrator accountable by seeking a court order to compel the administrator to act as the citizen believes is proper.

The other level on which citizens hold administrators accountable relates to agency performance in a more general sense: performance that does not directly and immediately affect the individual citizen. Reports of waste, inefficiency, misdeeds or "no deeds" may cause citizens to question to competence, devotion, and even the honesty of administrators and those they supervise.

While this occasionally generates communication with the administrator by a concerned citizen, accountability more often is initiated in less direct ways. These take the form of letters or personal comments to the news media, legislators, and elected chief executives. To the extent that the problem is easily identifiable, and a solution is readily available, such citizen initiatives may produce early and positive results. However, if the problem and a solution cannot be easily isolated because they are part of another problem, then the evaluative information obtained from citizens becomes part of the record to be considered when the larger issue is up for decision.

Individual citizens rarely have time, information, and resources to hold a public administrator accountable for action taken or failure to act, except in fairly simple situations that directly affect the complaining citizen. Determining the adequacy of agency policies and the effects of its programs, and then pressing for desired changes, require considerable expertise, resources, and persistence. Therefore, citizens with common interests often band together and hire staff, who in turn may organize volunteers from members of the group to oversee and influence the performance of both legislative bodies and executive agencies on issues in which they are interested.

The power of such citizen groups is not necessarily related to size or the breadth of their interests. In serving the interests of their members on specific issues before the legislative body or an executive agency, smaller organizations may be more influential than those with much larger memberships. What counts is access and political clout with influential legislators on the relevant committees and key people in the executive branch.

Often administrative agencies are confronted by interest groups whose views are in conflict. Before deregulation it was common for different airlines to take opposite sides as approval of the Civil Aeronautics Board was sought on route or rate proposals. Each argued that if the board did not rule as it proposed, the public interest would not be served. Consumer groups and business organizations have presented diametrically opposed views to federal and state regulatory agencies, each claiming that adoption of its position would best serve the public interest.

Business and labor organizations often take opposing positions in dealing with administrators of occupational safety and health policies. Right-to-life and family-planning organizations are adversaries when they beseech and threaten HHS administrators with regard to the use of federal funds for abortions. Other interest groups in favor and opposed to busing children to schools monitor and seek to influence the actions of officials in the Department of Justice as well as HHS. The ultimate purpose of these efforts is to influence administrators to adopt policies favored by a particular interest group and then hold the administrator accountable for performing as promised.

Interest groups are cultivated by public administrators, not only to obtain the varied views of our pluralistic society but also to develop constituencies. They can be helpful in obtaining funds or changes in law that the administrator desires. They can criticize proposals adverse to the agency even when such proposals are advanced by the chief executive or the legislative committees. The dilemma that inevitably faces the administrator is how to nurture these constituencies without becoming their prisoner—accountability in the extreme.

Legislators find interest groups a valuable source of information in alerting them to policy and operational problems in the agencies of the executive branch. In the survey of senators and representatives, 35 percent rated interest groups as very helpful in this regard and 62 percent rated them moderately helpful. Somewhat lower, but still very positive, are ratings by senior career executives: 36 percent rated interest groups as very helpful and 35 percent saw them as moderately helpful in alerting agency officials to policy and operational problems.

THE PUBLIC ADMINISTRATOR AND THE COURTS

At all levels of government, constitutions and statutes empower courts to act as a brake on arbitrary action or inaction of executive agencies. In the national government, to assure ability, integrity, and independence in the judiciary, the Constitution provides life tenure for judges, subject to their good behavior. Alexander Hamilton justified life tenure in this way: "And it is the best expedient which can be devised in any government, to secure a steady, upright, and impartial administration of the laws."[15]

On the other hand, in many state and local jurisdictions, judges are elected for specified terms of office and must be reelected if they choose to remain a judge in subsequent terms. While elected judges in some jurisdictions compare favorably to the best on the federal bench, on the whole they do not enjoy as good a reputation as federal judges either because of the initial selection process or because of limited tenure.

Individuals and organizations seek judicial intervention to cause executive agencies to act in a specified manner. Judicial decision in a particular case may take the form of refusing to review because the administrative process has not been exhausted, or the plaintiff lacks standing (has not been adversely affected), or the agency, not the court, has jurisdiction. The court may need to decide whether there was due process (did the agency follow proper procedure?), whether the agency interpreted correctly the applicable law, or, in some cases, whether the facts justified the decision of the agency.

In deciding appeals from decisions of government agencies, most federal and state courts tend to concentrate on questions of law and rely on agency-created records for the facts. However, courts have not been reluctant to examine facts when the record raises significant doubts in this area.[16]

Judges do very well at holding bureaucracies accountable in specific problem situations that come into court. Because courts deal only with *cases*, they are not very good at holding agencies accountable for overall performance. The process and effectiveness of judicial review are discussed in more detail in Chapter 6.

THE PUBLIC ADMINISTRATOR AND THE
NEWS MEDIA

Incompetence, dishonesty, indifference, and arrogance in agencies of government make good copy, and therein lies the news media's basic power for holding government bureaucracies accountable. The promise of a free press is guaranteed by the First Amendment to the Constitution, and that promise is zealously protected by the news media and the courts.

Every administration is embarrassed by some appointees or nominees. So it was in the Eisenhower administration with Chief of Staff Sherman Adams and the gift of a vicuna coat; Richard Nixon with his White House aides and their Watergate coverups; Jimmy Carter with Office of Management and Budget Director Bert Lance and his pre-government service banking practices; and Ronald Reagan with an unusually large number of appointees and nominees about whom serious legal and ethical issues have swirled.

Lack of qualifications for a position sometimes arouses the attention of the news media. In the spring of 1981, major newspapers, television, and radio focused on Max Hugel, selected by William Casey, Director of the Central Intelligence Agency (CIA), to head the agency's clandestine operations. What made the appointment so newsworthy was the fact that for the first time this extremely sensitive and difficult position was being filled by a person without significant experience in the field of covert operations. Casey and Hugel were beginning to be held accountable by the news media.

On July 14, 1981, the accountability process ended with the resignation of Hugel and the appointment of a career CIA officer to the post. While the resignation was prompted by allegations published in the Washington *Post* that same day of improper or illegal stock-trading practices and threats of blackmail related to these practices that were not revealed to the CIA during Hugel's security investigation, his lack of qualifications for the position appeared to be a major underlying reason for strong interest on the part of the news media and members of the Senate Intelligence Committee.

The survey of senators and representatives showed that 22 percent consider the news media very helpful in alerting them to operating and policy problems in the agencies; 56 percent see the news media as moderately helpful; and 22 percent rate them rarely helpful. Like the courts, the news media are especially effective in holding administrators accountable on specific problems.

Citizens are eager to learn about misfeasance, malfeasance, and nonfeasance in government, and the press and electronic media work hard to satisfy this desire. Investigative reporters have given the news media vastly increased potential for holding administrators accountable. Generally, the news reports are factual. But since the libel laws offer little protection to public officials, rumors and speculation about unsatisfactory or improper actions by administrators are often highlighted and reported as fact, with corrections or retractions receiving considerably less attention than the initial report.

The news media serve as instruments of accountability in additional ways. Occasionally, they focus the public's attention on a controversial issue being considered by an agency, with the result that more citizens and groups likely to be affected are encouraged to become involved by taking positions and presenting their views.

The news media also report on some of the significant routine actions of administrative agencies, thereby contributing to greater public understanding of important developments. Unfortunately, in the competition for readers, viewers, and listeners, the news media find such reports often lack wide appeal and therefore coverage is minimal unless the administrative action seriously affects the poor or the powerful or is otherwise newsworthy.

Probably the most important continuing actions taken by the news media that enhance accountability are reports made about activities of individuals or groups who seek to influence public policy and the controversy they generate. Wide publicity about significant differences over policy, program, and performance between agency administrators and other executive agencies, legislative committees, interest groups, and courts alerts and educates the citizenry.

AN OVERALL VIEW

Individual citizens and all of the institutions discussed in this chapter have some capacity for holding public administrators accountable. At various times their actions are redundant, intimidating, harassing, costly, and ineffective. More often they are constructive and productive. Strengths and weaknesses of these accountability agents will be apparent as we discuss specific policies and processes.

NOTES

1. James Madison, "Checks and Balances," in *Hamilton, Madison, and Jay on the Constitution*, ed. Ralph H. Gabriel (New York: The Liberal Arts Press, 1954), pp. 72–77.

2. 272 U.S. 52 (1926).

3. U.S., Constitution, Art. 2, Sec. 2.

4. 1 *CRANCH* 137 (1803).

5. Bernard Rosen, *Monograph on the Merit System in the United States Civil Service*, prepared for the U.S., Congress, House, Committee on Post Office and Civil Service, 94th Cong., 1st sess., 1975.

6. *Report on the Presidency*, Washington: National Academy of Public Administration, 1988, Chapter 4.

7. Washington *Post*, August 12, 1979, sec. 1, p. 1.

8. 60 Stat. 132, Sect. 136 (1946).

9. 421 U.S. 491 (1975).

10. *Watergate: Its Implications for Responsible Government* (Report prepared by a panel of the National Academy of Public Administration at the request of the Senate Select Committee on Presidential Campaign Activities, 1974), pp. 71–72.

11. U.S., Congress, House, Select Committee on Committees, *Hearings on Committee Organization in the House*, 93d Cong., 1st sess., 1973.

12. Alan Rosenthal, *Legislative Performance in the States* (New York: Free Press, 1974), p. 12.

13. U.S., Congress, Senate, Committee on Government Operations, *Legislative Oversight and Program Evaluation*, 94th Cong., 2d sess., 1976, Committee Print, p. 29.

14. Edgar G. Crane, Jr., *Legislative Review of Government Programs* (New York: Praeger, 1977).

15. Alexander Hamilton, "The Nature and Power of the Federal Judiciary," in *Hamilton, Madison, and Jay on the Constitution*, ed. Ralph H. Gabriel (New York: The Liberal Arts Press, 1954), pp. 168–77.

16. Kenneth Culp Davis, *Administrative Law and Government*, 2d ed. (St. Paul: West, 1975), p. 463.

Part II

The Processes of

Accountability

Laws reflect governments' promises, and executive bureaucracies produce the most visible evidence of governments' performance; the gap between the two is determined in good part by the effectiveness of accountability processes.

3

Accountability

Processes within the

Executive Branch

The newly elected chief executive—president, governor, county executive, mayor—and the managers inside the bureaucracy begin their relationship with considerable tension. During part of the first year, each side has varying degrees of skepticism, doubt, and even some fear as to the intentions and ability of the other. Questions that loom large in the mind of the chief executive relate to the bureaucrats' loyalty, ability, and willingness to change. Will they support my policies? Will they really try to make my policies work or will they sabotage them through poor action and inaction? Are they competent? Are they willing to work hard? Will they be open to change? Will they help me move in the direction I promised the citizens by coming forward with proposals for change based on their more intimate knowledge of the operations of government?

No less important are questions that managers in the bureaucracy have about a new chief executive and that executive's own ability, priorities, commitments, new appointees, and views on the purpose of government. Were his criticisms of the bureaucracy during the campaign largely political rhetoric, or does he really view us as the enemy? Does he care about the programs we are managing, or are they rather low on his list? Will he have an open mind about what it will take to have the programs produce what the laws promise? Is he appointing first-rate people to head each agency or does he consider these jobs as political plums for campaign supporters who may know little and care even less about the long-term effectiveness of government? Will he and his appointees assume we are competent and dedicated professionals, or do we start with two strikes?

It is in this atmosphere of periodic and sometimes continuing uncertainty and suspicion that accountability operates within the executive branch. Fortunately, the vast majority of people working in the bureaucracy experience little of the resulting tension. The strain is greatest at the point where political officials and career employees interface and it decreases with the organizational distance from that point.

In theory, the individual government employee, the unit, the institution, and ultimately the whole system are accountable. The actual process of accountability within the executive branch takes many forms. It ranges from supervisory direction and review, through internal audit, to evaluation by an external group that is still within the executive branch.

In addition, the process must be adjusted for special problems in accountability that arise because of unique arrangements for accomplishing the work of government—sometimes referred to as government by proxy or third-party government. These include contracts for government services, grants to individuals and public and private organizations for research and related services, agreements with companies to operate government-owned plants, and government-financed privately run "think tanks."

SUPERVISORY DIRECTION AND REVIEW

The simplest and most straightforward accountability occurs when the public manager, in the role of supervisor at whatever level, directs a subordinate to perform a task and then personally reviews what was done. If the task was not done as directed, the supervisor promptly initiates corrective action related to both the task and the employee. It involves a 100 percent review of all work performed.

This form of accountability is undesirable and impracticable in most circumstances. It destroys employee initiative. It costs too much. The supervisor may simply not have sufficient time or may be physically separated from the employee—across town or even in a foreign country. For these reasons alone, it is evident that in general it makes little sense to try to achieve accountability by checking all the work of each employee as it is completed.

Achieving accountability as a normal part of supervision is neither easy nor certain because accountability is, among other things, a state of mind. Do the individual employees—technicians, professionals, managers—find their work meaningful? Do they take pride in their own work? If so, they are more likely to feel accountable and have a strong desire to understand what is expected and then fulfill those expectations. A 1986 survey of 21,620 federal employees in the 22 largest agencies revealed that 81 percent find that "The work I do on my job is meaningful to me."[1]

Supervisors who encourage employees to this end by explaining the importance of the work, developing performance standards in consultation with the employees, making certain the employee possesses the necessary knowledge and skills to meet the standards, and providing recognition to those who perform in a superior manner, contribute enormously to both individual and institutional accountability.

Supervisors can enhance accountability in many other ways. One is by frequent, informal, personal contact with the employee (face-to-face or by telephone or letter), wherein the supervisor evidences in a constructive and confident style a continuing interest in the work and the worker. Table 1 shows how senior career executives rated this and other methods for holding accountable those reporting to them. Better than three out of four executives consider frequent informal personal contacts and regularly scheduled one-to-one oral discussions very effective methods for holding subordinates accountable. Written reports are less effective, but still quite helpful. Self-evaluation reports are largely ineffective.

THE BUDGET PROCESS

How much money will you use this year to run your program? How does that amount compare with last year's? What about the year before? What accounts for the difference? How much do you need for the next fiscal year? Why the increase? Granted that without a 12 percent increase we will have major problems, how would you manage with a 15 percent *decrease*? In priority order, which programs would have to be curtailed or terminated? As a minimum could you carry out all requirements mandated by law? How would you manage with a "no-change" budget—no increase, no decrease?

These are the initial anxiety-provoking questions, strong in accountability implications, asked periodically by agency managers at higher levels of those who report to them. These questions are central in discussions and decisions related to planning policy changes and program operations, preparing and revising budgets to fund them, allocating and reallocating funds, and assigning and adjusting personnel ceilings. It is all part of the business of managing in an environment where accountability for past performance and estimating future needs merge to a rhythm and timing that is dictated by the budget process.

For the federal government, and in most state and many local governments, the budget process requires individual agencies to determine their financial requirements within limits and guidelines established by the chief executive at least 18 months in advance of the fiscal year. In this *pre-preparation* phase, the chief executive and the central budget office are engaged in a rationing and conserving process. After agencies prepare their budgets, the central budget office and, as necessary, the chief executive scrutinize and revise their estimates. This leads to a budget for the entire executive branch in a time frame designed to permit the legislative branch

Table 1
Effectiveness of Various Methods for Holding Accountable Those Who Report to You

Method	Ratings by 65 Senior Career Executives (in percentages)		
	Very Effective	Moderately Effective	Rarely Effective
Frequent informal personal contact	88	12	0
Regularly scheduled one-to-one discussion on progress & problems	72	23	5
Staff meetings	25	60	15
Ad hoc written reports per your instructions	35	51	14
Periodic written reports on progress & problems	20	58	22
Copies of required periodic self-evaluation reports	6	29	65
Ad hoc evaluations directed at specific problems by a special staff that reports directly to you	40	31	29
Regularly scheduled program evaluations and internal audits by a special staff that reports directly to you	31	40	29
Evaluations by central unit that reports to the head of the agency	11	50	39
Budget process	27	45	28

Source: Compiled by the author.

to make decisions that will result in appropriations for agencies before the fiscal year begins.

In the federal government, sharp differences between the president and Congress over spending priorities frequently prevent timely completion of the appropriation process. To continue obligating and spending in the new fiscal year, agencies are given temporary authorizations, usually at the same rate as in the preceding year.

Except when a budget is being prepared for new and different functions, the costs of current and past agency operations constitute the primary basis for justifying the "next year's" budget. Since "new and different functions" are rarely more than a very small percentage of the total executive-branch budget in governments that have been operating for some time, history and experience dominate the budget process. Does this history reflect good or poor management? Do those making budget decisions *know* that is was good or poor? These are questions that have great significance in the matter of accountability. The budget process provides unique opportunities for holding managers accountable.

Whether the budget is built from the bottom of the organization up within a framework of policy assumptions established by the agency head, or developed centrally by the agency's comptroller and imposed on subordinate managers with the approval of the agency head, the proposed budget and backup papers carry estimates of what the organization proposes to do during the budget year and at what cost. These performance budgets provide tools within the hierarchy for holding managers at every level accountable for work units accomplished at a given cost and within a given period.

Many state and local governments have adopted performance budgets. In the national government this budget system was applied widely beginning in 1951 as a result of the Budget and Accounting Procedures Act of 1950.[2] Performance budgeting made possible a continuous process of holding managers accountable, from inside and outside the organization, for improving the efficiency and economy of operations—for doing things right. It did not, however, focus hard on whether the right *things* were being done.

To increase the possibility that the right things would be done, the budget process was widened to include planning the future. This was called *program* budgeting. It involved establishing clear goals and identifying programs, subprograms, and program elements for achieving the goals. While program budgeting gave additional assurance of the relevance of work performed to goals, it did not deal with the equally fundamental question of allocating resources among governmental activities to achieve the goals best.

The gap was closed by adding systematic consideration of alternatives throughout the process, by using cost-benefit analysis to compare program elements, and by projecting costs for more than a single year—usually five years, thereby creating the Planning-Programming-Budgeting System (PPBS). This placed in the hands of executives a powerful new tool for rationally allocating resources and for holding subordinate managers accountable.

As a system, PPBS has not survived—it was too complex, rigid in structure and procedure, and time-consuming. On the other hand, certain features have been retained: emphasis on goals, multiyear cost projections, a search for program alternatives, and a concern for accomplishment in relation to goals.

In the 1970s, zero-base budgeting (ZBB), which originated in the private sector with Texas Instruments, was introduced in a number of public jurisdictions, including the national government. Despite the name, zero-base budgeting does not reduce the importance of knowing about the cost and significance of past performance. Rather, it puts a premium in analysis and evaluation of relative need, performance, and consequence. Establishing clearly defined policy and program objectives, performance standards and measurement, and time frames for achieving results is given a high priority. Management by objectives fits easily and naturally with ZBB. All these management techniques can be useful in the process of holding government bureaucracies accountable.

Zero-base budgeting requires each manager, starting at the lowest level where decisions about priorities and use of resources are made, to justify why money should be spent for a specific purpose (often termed a "decision unit")—an excellent way to begin underscoring accountability. This first step in ZBB—which involves identification of decision units, followed by an analysis of purposes, functions, and procedures of each—also compels the manager to explore how each unit can achieve the desired results in a more efficient and economical manner. This includes establishing alternative decision units at three or four possible levels of funding: (1) at a predetermined percentage below current costs, (2) halfway between that point and current costs, (3) at current costs, and (4) at a predetermined level above current costs.

The second step in ZBB requires this same manager to group the decision units into "decision packages" by priority. The first decision package contains all those decision units or parts of units to which the manager assigns the highest priority. Those considered to be of lesser importance are grouped in succeeding packages at lower levels of priority. The third major step in ZBB is for managers at successive higher levels to establish their priorities by ranking the packages of their subordinates. Thus one manager's top priority may become a second priority with his superior when the needs of all managers are considered. The priorities established at the highest agency level become the basis for the agency's appropriation request and subsequent allocation of funds.

The zero-base budgeting process is being debated and changed as it is applied in public jurisdictions. While it was introduced as a bottom-up decision-making process, this is being seriously questioned by those who believe that at the outset and throughout the process there must be major input from the *top* concerning priorities on policies and programs, both ongoing and proposed, in order to avoid unnecessary work. Another area of concern is the increased paperwork that ZBB generates in the budget process. This is troublesome on several counts: it is expensive and time-consuming to prepare, and the increased paper makes it easier for valuable program information to escape the attention of higher officials. These considerations plus an apparent lack of significant results led the Reagan administration to abandon ZBB procedures while urging agencies to improve evaluation methods and productivity measurements.

A third area of concern is the misleading title. As practiced in the public sector and many private organizations, there are few reexaminations that result in building the budget from zero. It would be wasteful as well as foolish to disregard at the national level the reality of a continuing commitment to defense, social security, air traffic control, and many other programs; it would be equally indefensible at the state and local levels to ignore the continuing necessity for education, roads, public health, and numerous other services. There is a credibility problem in the catchy term "zero-base budgeting."

Whatever the title—PPBS, ZBB, or some new acronym—it is clear that the budget remains central to accountability. In evaluating policies, programs, and structures in order to consider alternatives and then set priorities for funding, executives and managers at all levels are engaged in a process that inevitably makes them more accountable within and outside the organization.

INTERNAL AUDIT

The purpose of internal audit is to provide the agency's top executives and lower levels of management with an independent and objective evaluation of the effectiveness of policies and programs and the legality and efficiency of operations, systems, and procedures. The report on the internal audit identifies problems and makes recommendations for remedial action.

Internal audits are most effective when they are conducted by a well-trained professional staff within the agency that is independent of the managers whose operations will be reviewed. This arrangement is necessary to help assure that the inquiry, reasoning, and recommendations of the auditors will be impartial. Such independence can usually be achieved by making the audit unit directly responsible to the head or deputy head of the agency.

Internal audit is not a substitute for controls, requirements, and reviews that managers find necessary as part of their supervisory function. Rather, internal audit provides an independent evaluation of the adequacy of these management processes and practices for sound and economical operations.

In the national government, the Budget and Accounting Procedures Act of 1950, as amended in 1982 by the Federal Managers Financial Integrity Act (FMFIA),[3] makes clear that the head of each federal agency is obliged to have internal systems of control for proper accountability of the agency's "funds, property, and other assets for which the agency is responsible, including appropriate internal audit." The act also directed the comptroller general of the United States, who heads the General Accounting Office (GAO), to lay down principles for internal auditing. The principles and standards issued by GAO are also considered appropriate for internal auditing in state and local agencies.

In fact, as a result of requirements laid down for federal grants-in-aid programs including technical assistance, state and local governments are beginning to apply these principles in their internal management. The principles and standards are also appropriate for any external auditing that agencies are required to do with regard to activities carried on through grants, contracts, and related means.

The FMFIA of 1982 requires federal managers to determine whether internal control systems have weaknesses that can lead to fraud, waste, and abuse in government operations. The act also requires heads of federal agencies to report annually to the president and the Congress on the status of these systems and plans to correct identified weaknesses. Agencies are directed to make their evaluations and reports in accordance with guidelines established by the Office of Management and Budget (OMB) in consultation with the GAO.

The OMB guidelines call on agencies to provide "adequate coverage of their programs as an aid in determining whether information is reliable; resources have been safeguarded; funds have been expended in a manner consistent with related laws, regulations, and policies; resources have been managed economically and efficiently; and desired program results have been achieved." To comply with this very broad charge, the guidelines specify that agencies should determine audit priorities in terms of frequency and coverage based on statutory and regulatory requirements, adequacy of internal control systems, newness and sensitivity of the program, current and potential dollar magnitude, and a number of other considerations, including the availability of audit resources.[4]

Central to a sound program for internal audit are effective internal control systems. Internal control weaknesses identified in recent years by the agencies and GAO "impair the effectiveness of federal programs and result in the loss or waste of billions of dollars. . . . These weaknesses are not limited to certain 'problem areas' but rather span a broad range of government activities and affect a variety of programs."[5] The FMFIA requires the comptroller general to establish standards for agency internal control systems. GAO states that the purpose of such systems is to reasonably ensure that the following objectives are achieved:

Obligations and costs comply with applicable law.

All assets are safeguarded against waste, loss, unauthorized use, and misappropriation.

Revenues and expenditures applicable to agency operations are recorded and accounted for properly so that accounts and reliable financial and statistical reports may be prepared and accountability of the assets may be maintained.[6]

Standards issued by GAO in 1984 define the minimum level of quality acceptable for agency internal control systems. There are three categories of standards:

General Standards

1. *Reasonable Assurance.* Internal control systems are to provide reasonable assurance that the objectives of the systems will be accomplished.
2. *Supportive Attitude.* Managers and employees are to maintain and demonstrate a positive and supportive attitude toward internal controls at all times.
3. *Competent Personnel.* Managers and employes are to have personal and professional integrity and are to maintain a level of competence that allows them to accomplish their assigned duties, as well as understand the importance of developing and implementing good internal controls.
4. *Control Objectives.* Internal control objectives are to be identified or developed for each agency activity and are to be logical, applicable, and reasonably complete.
5. *Control Techniques.* Internal control techniques are to be effective and efficient in accomplishing their internal control objectives.

Specific Standards

1. *Documentation.* Internal control systems and all transactions and other significant events are to be clearly documented, and the documentation is to be readily available for examination.
2. *Recording of Transactions and Events.* Transactions and other significant events are to be promptly recorded and properly classified.
3. *Execution of Transactions and Events.* Transactions and other significant events are to be authorized and executed only by persons acting within the scope of their authority.
4. *Separation of Duties.* Key duties and responsibilities in authorizing, processing, recording, and reviewing transactions should be separated among individuals.
5. *Supervision.* Qualified and continuous supervision is to be provided to ensure that internal control objectives are achieved.
6. *Access to and Accountability for Resources.* Access to resources and records is to be limited to authorized individuals, and accountability for the custody and use of resources is to be assigned and maintained. Periodic comparison shall be made of the resources with the recorded accountability to determine whether the two agree. The frequency of the comparison shall be a function of the vulnerability of the asset.

Audit Resolution Standard

Prompt Resolution of Audit Findings. Managers are to (1) promptly evaluate findings and recommendations reported by auditors, (2) determine proper actions in response to audit findings and recommendations, and (3) complete, within established time frames, all actions that correct or otherwise resolve the matters brought to management's attention.[7]

To facilitate agency compliance, GAO provides a more detailed description for each of these internal control standards.

The internal control weaknesses in federal agency operations that are revealed in GAO reports deal with procurement, grant/loan and debt collection management, eligibility and entitlement determinations, cash management, automated data processing, property management, financial management and accounting systems, and personnel and organizational management. A GAO report[8] that focused on this issue offers a range of examples.

—Following a Defense Department report on problems in its procurement control systems, GAO identified specific deficiencies in the Department's program to ensure the quality of major weapons purchases. Offices responsible for the Department's in-plant quality assurance program were not performing all mandatory inspections and inappropriately delegated some of their inspection responsibilities to contractors who were building the weapons. Also, because data to identify recurring supply and service problems were not collected, the offices were often prevented from taking timely action to correct quality assurance deficiencies.

—In fiscal year 1986, Defense awarded about $82 billion in contracts without price competition. Defense did not have adequate internal controls to assure that negotiated prices, absent competitive bidding, were reasonable. GAO examined contractor estimates totaling $244 million in prime contracts and found that over half of them were innaccurate or unreliable.

—After reviewing the Department of the Interior's Minerals Management Service activities in five states, GAO reported that, as of September 30, 1986, over $12.6 million in royalties and rent on coal leases had not been collected from lessees. GAO found a number of internal control weaknesses which contributed to the inadequate collection practices, such as the lack of an adequate system to identify the nonpayment or underpayment of rent.

—In July 1987, GAO reported that the Health Care Financing Administration (HCFA) of the Department of Health and Human Services (HHS) did not have adequate controls to assure that Medicare outpatient rehabilitation services claims were paid only to those eligible to receive them. HCFA records indicated that Medicare paid about $1 billion in one year for such services. GAO found that in 96 percent of 346 randomly sampled beneficiary cases, claims-processing contractors had insufficient documentation to determine whether a beneficiary was eligible for those services and that many of these cases were of types that indicated the beneficiaries were, in fact, not eligible.

—In August 1986, GAO reported that, on a governmentwide basis, federal agencies had not complied fully with the provisions of the Prompt Payment Act. They had paid about one-quarter of the government's bills late, thereby incurring millions of dollars in interest penalties annually. Another problem was that agencies had paid close to a quarter of their bills too early, thereby costing the government at least $350 million annually in lost interest.

—GAO reported in March 1987 that Treasury's Custom Service and Justice's Drug Enforcement Administration unnecessarily held millions of dollars in cash seized from drug traffickers and organized crime figures in vaults and safety deposit boxes instead of expeditiously depositing this money with the Treasury. Deposit delays ranged as high as four years, with one-third of the delays in the audit sample exceeding one year.

—In October 1987, GAO reported poor physical security controls at five of the nine Army ammunition storage sites visited. Missiles, such as the Stinger, were stored in lightweight corrugated metal sheds with the type of weapon stenciled on the side. Similar sheds, containing antitank rockets, had doors with broken locks. Other missiles were stored in tractor trailers and open concrete pads easily observable from the perimeter of the storage facility.

There is no reason to believe that the kinds of internal control weaknesses identified by federal agencies and the GAO do not also exist in many state and local governments.

Often the root cause of weak internal management controls is the failure of federal agencies to establish accounting systems that meet the standards of the General Accounting Office. Four decades afer the 1950 Budget and Accounting Act required all federal agencies to establish and maintain accounting systems that meet GAO standards, many of the agencies are not in compliance. Inadequate accounting systems simply fail to provide the information needed for effective management.

In addition to establishing standards for internal control systems, the comptroller general issued standards governing internal audits conducted by agencies on their own *financial management* and *program performance*.[9] The standards are built on these major premises: public officials are responsible for applying resources efficiently, economically, and effectively to achieve the authorized purposes; such officials are accountable to the public and to other levels and branches of government for resources provided; they are responsible for complying with applicable laws and regulations; and reports of audit are in the public domain unless prevented by legal restrictions or ethical considerations.

Financial audits cover such matters as financial statements and related information, contracts, grants, internal control systems, computer-based systems, and fraud. Performance audits focus on economy, efficiency, and program results. To perform effectively across this range of duties, the audit team must know a good deal about the policies and programs of the agency, sound management practices, statistical sampling, economics, and operations research. From time to time, the audit staff may have to be reinforced by outside experts in order to have all the skills and knowledge needed to meet its responsibilities.

A key requirement for a successful internal audit program is that the reports of audit be timely as well as factual, clear, concise, and constructive. Any delay in providing management with a report and recommendations for action that should and could be taken promptly diminishes the value of the audit.

The usefulness of the audit is also affected by the quality and timeliness of follow-up to encourage decisions and action on the recommendations. Periodic reports for top management on the status of recommendations and the resolution of difference between operating officials and auditors is essential for an effective internal audit program.

In the national government, all large agencies and many small ones have internal audit units that report to the agency head or a principal assistant, such as an assistant secretary or assistant administrator for management. As a result of legislation enacted in 1978, the audit function in some agencies has been made part of a new Office of the Inspector General (fully discussed in Chapter 7).

The size of federal nondefense agencies' audit staffs varies from less than ten to more than 1,000. Audit staffs in the median group have from 50 to 150 employees, of which more than three-fourths are professional personnel as distinguished from support staff. In 1988, among nondefense agencies, the Department of Health and Human Services had the largest audit staff— 1,205. The Defense Department had 12,412 military and civilian people in its audit, inspection, and investigations activities.

Audit methods used also vary, depending on the nature of the audit and skills of the staff. Analysis of policy and program effectiveness requires different methods than analysis of management efficiency. A first-rate evaluation, using analytical tools most appropriate to the problem, can do much to bring about improvements in policies and program management. Almost always, such analyses show that better program management depends in part on improving accountability.

Good audits involve a number of sequential steps. First, problems for study must be identified. A continuous, systematic inventorying of problems normally produces a workload that exceeds capacity. Deciding on priorities reflects considerations of urgency, possible benefits, likelihood of a successful evaluation, the probability that recommended improvements can be implemented and the estimated cost of the study.

Once a problem is programmed, an audit plan is developed. It covers such matters as a clear statement of the problem, a list of assumptions, the nature of the product (one report, or interim reports and a final report), timetable for various stages of the study, staff required, and estimated costs. The analytical methods selected should meet these combined requirements and conditions.

When the audit plan is established, resources earmarked, and staff assembled, the study begins. Data collection is the first step, with a strong concern for relevance, reliability, time, and cost. Data are acquired from knowledgeable sources in many ways: interviews, on-site observations, questionnaires, program records and reports, and comparative statistics from government agencies. Determinations as to data desired and sources to be tapped become integral details of the overall audit plan and are critical to the analytical methods used.

After data are analyzed and tentative conclusions subjected to intense examination, a report is prepared. If the report is clear, concise, relevant, timely, and offers the decision maker feasible choices, there is a reasonably good chance that some positive action will take place. Making such a report to the accountable official, the one that can take appropriate action or see that others take it, is essential. (For a more detailed discussion, see *Evaluation and Analyses to Support Decision Making*, U.S. General Accounting Office, 1976).

In recent years, internal audit has contributed significantly to effectiveness, efficiency, and honesty in government operations. However, the overall results fall far short of their potential in large measure because agencies frequently fail to follow up and resolve audit findings.

In testimony before a congressional committee, the comptroller general of the United States said the "government is losing billions of dollars because agencies are not acting on audit recommendations to recover funds, avoid costs, and improve operations."[10] While some audit findings have been rejected for valid reasons by program managers, the failure to resolve audit recommendations promptly and properly is costing the taxpayer dearly. A survey of federal agencies in 1981 showed 11,000 unresolved audit findings in 71 agencies representing potential savings of $6.7 billion. Many had been pending for several years. These conditions were recognized as part of the larger problem of weak internal control systems and the fact that federal managers were not being held sufficiently accountable for this essential management responsibility. A 1987 report by the comptroller general shows that while there has been significant improvement, much remains to be done if we are to secure optimum benefits from audit recommendations. Several examples from that report[11] are illuminating.

—GAO first reported control problems in identifying abuses of Medicaid in 1978, when it was noted that states administering the program did not effectively use their management information systems for this purpose. Since then, although the Health Care Financing Administration (HCFA) has implemented a program to review the effectiveness of states' control systems, those who may improperly receive Medicaid funds are still rarely identified and investigated. In a September 1987 report, GAO estimated that Medicaid recipients and providers of Medicaid services abusing the system may have cost the federal government at least $54.5 million and possibly as much as $400 million during 1985. Such abuse continued because HCFA's reviews of states' systems, a principal control feature, were inadequate and because HCFA did not provide sufficient technical assistance to states having problems using their information systems.

—In 1987, the Department of Agriculture reported that it had not yet completed 70 corrective actions related to automated data processing weaknesses reported from 1983 through 1986.

—In its 1986 Financial Integrity Act report, the Defense Department said that inventory and supply management problems represented the largest number of uncorrected weaknesses reported by its components. These problems, most of which date back to the 1960s and 1970s, were exacerbated by the large-scale military buildup in the 1980s. Although Defense has attempted to strengthen controls in this area by initiating an inventory control improvement program that includes proposed actions through 1990, widespread problems remain.

New initiatives[12] for strengthening internal controls and improving action on audit recommendations are discussed in Chapter 8.

EXTERNAL EVALUATION

In accordance with responsibilities assigned by statute and executive order, the central management agencies hold other agencies accountable with varying degrees of effectiveness for a wide range of management actions.

Personnel Management

In the federal government and some state and local governments, the central personnel agency evaluates the personnel management of agencies for compliance with governmentwide policies. The United States Office of Personnel Management (OPM) is responsible for evaluating the personnel management of federal agencies for legality, effectiveness, and efficiency. Until the early 1980s, OPM and its predecessor, the United States Civil Service Commission, carried out this responsibility with specially trained staff located in Washington and each of its regional offices by making periodic on-site inspections at both headquarters and field activities. At times, inspection teams included employees of the agency under evaluation. This provided valuable training for agency personnel who were or would be assigned subsequently to internal audit. On completion of an inspection, the team prepared a report which included its findings, conclusions, and recommendations. The report was directed to the head of the agency or field activity covered. Agencies were required to report to the inspecting office within a specified number of days on the action taken or planned for each recommendation. OPM has the authority to compel agencies to correct clearly illegal actions.

Despite its substantial authority, the effectiveness of OPM as an instrument for accountability is inadequate. In good part this is due first to a decision of the director during the Carter administration to reduce significantly the number and scope of evaluations, and second, a decision by another director during the Reagan administration, to end OPM's comprehensive on-site inspections of agency personnel operations. He replaced them with a new approach to evaluating personnel management that is far less effective for determining agency compliance with civil service laws and related policies.[13]

Money Management

The processes for preparing and administering executive-branch budgets in federal, state, and local governments constitute the primary means used by chief executives to hold agency administrators accountable in a systematic way. Most chief executives have a special organization and staff whose major concern is preparation and execution of the budget in accordance with existing laws and policies. This entails much interaction between the central budget arm and the agencies.

Chief executives and their budget staffs can predict with reasonable certainty that agencies will seek increases in appropriations to carry out existing responsibilities. If new initiatives are to be undertaken, still larger increases will be requested. Although administrators strive to be responsive to directives and pleas from their chief executive to reduce expenditures by eliminating low-priority activities, cutting waste, and operating more efficiently and economically, the central budget office usually finds that such "jawboning" does not result in significant reductions in either current or proposed expenditures. With rare exception, agency and program administrators feel they are underfinanced and understaffed to do adequately what is expected of them.

Faced with constantly rising costs for existing operations, strident demands for more services and benefits, and a citizenry restive about increasing taxes, chief executives are making even greater use of their central budget offices to hold down expenditures. In a variety of ways these budget offices transmit and interpret the chief executives' concerns and priorities to agency administrators. They question, usually on a highly selective and ad hoc basis, the efficiency and effectiveness of current agency policies, procedures, and practices. They examine proposals for new legislation and programs in terms of need, compatability with the policies of the chief executive, workability, and estimated costs.

In all of these contacts and relationship with the agencies, there is little doubt in the minds of the administrators that on behalf of the chief executive the central budget offices are engaged in an accountability process that deals with past performance and places limits on plans for the future. At no time has this been demonstrated more convincingly than in the first months of the Reagan administration when the director of the Office of Management and Budget was point man in reducing President Carter's proposed budget for fiscal year 1982 for civil agencies by $36 billion.

Regulatory Management

The Reagan administration was successful also, beyond any previous administration, in using OMB to hold executive branch agencies accountable for taking regulatory action in harmony with the philosophy of the president. Control of agency regulatory programs is a recent area of presidential concern. In good part, this is a late entry on the presidential agenda because the rule-making authority of many agencies, executive branch as well as the independent regulatory commissions, is specifically granted to these agencies by Congress and may be exercised only by them. In establishing rules, which have the force of law, agencies are governed by statutes and principles of due process.

In the 1970s, criticisms about the cost to business of applying government regulations, especially those issued by the Environmental Protection Agency (EPA), Consumer Products Safety Commission (CPSC), and the Occupational Safety and Health Administration (OSHA), caused a president of the United States for the first time to initiate a strategy for controlling regulatory bureaucracies. Convinced that unnecessary economic regulations "impose too many hidden and inflationary costs on our economy," and that they "must be identified and eliminated," President Gerald Ford ordered agencies to analyze the costs of each *major* proposed regulation and submit an "Inflation Impact Statement" to the Office of Management and Budget.[14] While OMB was charged with administering the program, the Council on Wage and Price Control was designated to assist since it was the president's prinicipal agency for controlling inflation. Uncertainty about the extent of presidential authority in this area resulted in authorizing OMB to issue guidelines for agency preparation of cost-benefit analysis and to secure compliance "to the extent permitted by law."[15] The unique legal status of the independent regulatory commissions won them a "voluntary compliance" status. None complied.

OMB's primary leverage in dealing with proposed rules that it considered cost-excessive involved forcing the agencies to continue to reexamine and rework their economic impact statements. Rules could not be published until OMB approved the analyses. The resulting delays often led agencies to revise the proposed rules along lines more in keeping with OMB's views.

Before leaving office, President Ford authorized continuance of the cost-benefit analysis program with one important addition: agencies would also be required to estimate the cost of feasible alternatives to the proposed rule.

The Ford initiative was the start in holding agencies accountable within the executive branch for their regulatory activities. However, the impact of OMB's role was limited by several conditions. Agencies decided which of their proposed rules were major (estimated cost of $100 million) and there-fore required an Inflation Impact Statement; cost-benefit analyses were fre-quently of poor quality; and OMB lacked effective incentives and disincentives to secure *prompt* compliance.[16]

Building on President Ford's program, President Carter established the Regulatory Analysis Review Group (RARG), an interagency body, to help executive agencies apply cost-benefit analysis. High-level representatives from OMB and the Council of Economic Advisors (CEA) dominated the executive comitttee of RARG. "Authority to carry out the cost-benefit policy evaluation program officially resided with OMB. However, OMB delegated authority for the conduct of day-to-day management to RARG. Consequently, RARG's stated goal was to make certain that the costs of each proposed rule had been fully considered so that the least costly means might be identified."[17]

Inevitably, this involved informal discussion on proposed policies between RARG staff and the regulatory agency. The propriety of such communi-cation, with its attendant influence, was debated in Congress and litigated in the courts—both inconclusively. The cost-benefit analysis process con-tinued to produce results favorable to the business establishment despite the fact that the process was opened up to the views of nonbusiness interests.[18] Estimating the value of benefits from regulation to reduce adverse conse-quences for health and safety was particularly complex and contentious.

In the final month of the Carter administration, EPA, OSHA, and other agencies released over 200 rules in both proposed and final form. The rules were responsive to the concerns of nonbusiness interests regarding hazardous waste control, air quality, consumer fraud, access for the handicapped in public transportation, and the regulation of nursing homes.[19]

President Reagan lost no time in declaring regulatory reform essential to sustained economic growth. In his state of the union address and speeches thereafter, the president "consistently indicted inefficient regulatory practice as a counterproductive force, which erected 'barriers to investment, pro-duction and employment'; a 'very significant factor' in the rise of inflation; and, in general, a major factor causing the 'retardation' of economic growth. . . . The position advocated by Reagan stressed the feasibility of a substantial reduction in the cost of economic regulation to business 'without signifi-cantly affecting worthwhile regulatory goals.' "[20]

In the days and weeks following his inauguration, the president made a series of decisions that translated philosophy and concepts into action. He established a cabinet level Presidential Task Force on Regulatory Relief chaired by the vice president to lead the effort on reducing the government's role in decisions affecting the economy. The Task Force was supported primarily by the staff in OMB's Office of Information and Regulatory Affairs (OIRA). The Regulatory Analysis Review Group established by Carter was abolished and its cost-benefit analysis work was assumed by

OIRA. All rules pending in executive-branch agencies were frozen for 60 days with the stated purpose of eliminating as many as possible. Executive Order 12291[21] was issued extending the cost-benefit analysis program and giving OMB the authority to determine the significance of a proposed rule, thereby permitting *it* rather than the agencies to decide on the applicability of such analysis.

This new OMB influence over the analysis agency was delegated to OIRA. The OIRA staff could now initiate contact with the agencies at any time and exercise important leverage at the formative stages of rule making. While the OIRA staff could be contacted by both business interests and non-business interests, the latter knew that the goals of the former were the primary concern of the president and OMB. Executive Order 12291 was "formulated to enable the evaluation staff to stop the policy process any time the staff judged an executive-branch agency was moving to produce economically inefficient rules. Staff at OIRA was encouraged to assume an adversarial relationship vis-à-vis the regulators. . . . The staff was to move any time it found it necessary to further the administration's course of action."[22] The OIRA used "cost-benefit analysis to determine the timing and to alter the substance of executive-branch policy-making, particularly in health, safety, and consumer affairs. . . ."[23]

In addition, the president's appointive power was used to place business-oriented executives in key positions in EPA, OSHA, and other executive-branch and regulatory agencies. The budgets of the regulatory functions were cut, thus reversing the trend in the Carter years. Less money meant fewer regulators and fewer regulations.[24] The high profile Task Force on Regulatory Relief was abolished in 1983 with a positive self-evaluation that it had achieved its objective—correcting regulatory excesses.

For his regulatory thrust in the second term, the president issued an executive order[25] calling for the development annually of the "Administration's Regulatory Program." The information required would be used to create a statement of the regulatory policies, goals, and objectives of each agency, and a description of the administration's significant regulatory actions underway or planned. OMB explained the purposes as follows: "Development of this regulatory policy document is intended to create a coordinated process for developing on an annual basis the Administration's Regulatory Program, establish Administration regulatory priorities, increase the accountability of agency heads for the regulatory actions of their agencies, provide for presidential oversight of the regulatory process, reduce the burdens of existing and future regulations, minimize duplication and conflict of regulations, and enhance public and congressional understanding of the Administration's regulatory objectives."[26]

OMB's control of rule making was made much tighter by requiring agencies to identify any important *pre*-rule-making action "taken to consider whether to initiate, or in contemplation of, rule making; . . . or dissemination of draft guidelines, policy proposals, strategy statements, and similar documents that may influence, anticipate, or could lead to the commencement of rule-making proceedings at a later date."[27]

OIRA was authorized to require agencies to prepare detailed cost-benefit analysis of initiatives considered potentially significant even though still in the pre-rule-making stage. OIRA was authorized also to return to agencies any draft regulatory program that was *not consistent* with administration policies and priorities. If modification would make it consistent, OMB could indicate changes needed. Disagreements between an agency and OIRA could be raised for further review by the president or such forum as the president designated. With the addition of the pre-rule-making requirement, for all practical purposes, executive-branch regulatory organizations had become completely accountable to OMB acting for the president except where statutes prescribed otherwise.

As OMB's control increased in the regulatory area, criticism from Congress and elsewhere intensified, largely with regard to alleged secret influence of business interests on its review of proposed rules. In response, OMB announced important changes in its procedures effective August 1986, among which were the following:

1. At the request of any federal agency, OIRA will send the agency copies of all written material concerning that agency's rules that OIRA receives from persons outside the federal government; advise the agency of all oral communications concerning the agency's rules, such as meetings, telephone calls, that OIRA has with persons outside the federal government; and invite agency representatives to all scheduled meetings with such persons concerning agency rules.

2. As soon as it completes its review action, OIRA will place in its public reading room all written material received from persons outside the federal government concerning rules of any agency; and for those agencies requesting OIRA actions in "1" above, OIRA will place in its public reading room a list of all meetings and all other communications with persons outside the federal government pertaining to the rules of those agencies.

As of June 1988, only five agencies requested OIRA to apply the new procedures when OMB reviews their proposed rules.[28]

From March 1981 until June 1988, agencies submitted 17,863 proposed rules. Of this, 14,342 were approved as submitted; 2,781 were approved after agencies made changes; 381 were withdrawn by the agencies; 83 were returned because they were incomplete; and 276 were returned because they were not consistent with administration policy. The average elapsed time for OMB review of agency submissions was 19 days. The shortest elapsed time was one day and the longest exceeded two years.*

---

*Information obtained from James MacRae, Acting Administrator, Office of Information and Regulatory Affairs, OMB, June 15, 1988.

SPECIAL ACCOUNTABILITY PROBLEMS IN GOVERNMENT BY PROXY

In the last half of this century, governments in the United States have turned increasingly to outside organizations to perform a wide range of functions and services. Through contracts, grants, loans, loan guarantees, and related legal means, public funds are being spent to achieve public purposes by using the talents and capacities of universities, business and industry, private nonprofit institutions, quasi-public organizations, and governments within and outside the federal system. Dispensing public funds in these ways has given rise to new problems in accountability.

One basic issue cuts across most of the problems: how to allow maximum possible independence while assuring adequate accountability. In an essay entitled "Independence and Accountability," Harvey Mansfield looks at this issue in terms of legal independence, fiscal independence, and political independence. Legal independence is sought, he states, to gain freedom from hierarchical control and procedural constraints in such matters as setting intermediate goals, establishing and applying standards, selecting and paying personnel, and procurement. "This independence, being formal, may be real or only nominal. Its nature and latitude are influenced by a variety and often a mixture of motives. It may be broad because the contractor can be trusted or because he can be closely watched—making the risk minimal in either case—or because he is in a bargaining position to demand latitude, risky or otherwise; or because the goals and methods of the enterprise are in conflict and consequently ambiguous, or must be adaptable to unpredictable conditions and emergencies and so are too uncertain for specification in advance."[29]

As for fiscal independence, Mansfield sees two broad types. One provides access to the public Treasury, with fewer of the controls normally applied to appropriated funds, for example, the right to borrow money directly from the Treasury. Block grants, while different in some respects, also illustrate freedom from controls normally applied to appropriated funds. The second type of fiscal independence relates to the ability to acquire and use funds without going through the Treasury or the appropriations process. The Federal Reserve Banks have this capacity; they pay their expenses from the money they earn and turn the profits over to the Treasury.[30]

Mansfield's comments on political independence are equally cogent. "Political independence for a contractor or grantee consists in the possession of political support in some quarter not under the control of either the central budgetary authorities or the contracting agency, sufficiently potent to make the apparent obligations of the contract largely unenforceable in practice, or to win such a conceded degree of discretion for itself as to leave little in the way of obligation to be enforced."

He illustrates the point by referring to the shipbuilding industry's "subsidy contracts, apparently immune to repeated criticisms that allege failure to protect the government's interest." The strongest form of political independence occurs, he points out, when a state or local government is interposed "between the federal mission and funds and the contractor or grantee," as for example, some local antipoverty organizations, or the "Soil Conservation Service District Committees and the farmer's committees that pass on the eligibility of borrowers from the Farmers Home Administration."[31]

Contractors, grantees, and their advocates seek independence in the interest of encouraging initiative and creativity, and "to get the job done." All would agree that, having signed the contract or accepted the grant, contractors or grantees are accountable for performance, "to get the job done" in accordance with the terms of the contract. Since public funds are involved, accountability must include honesty, effectiveness, and efficiency.[32]

Now the dilemma is clear: how to strike a balance between requirements for standards, reports, on-site audits, etc., in order to assure accountability for honesty, effectiveness, and efficiency, and at the same time permit the independence needed to mobilize the required talents and resources outside the particular government agency; that is, how to achieve and preserve the best possible combination of accountability and independence. This dilemma was discussed by Elmer Staats, former comptroller general of the United States, in an essay entitled "New Problems in Accountability for Federal Programs."[33] His insights are reflected in the next seven paragraphs.

The magnitude and importance of the dilemma becomes evident by identifying some major contract operations of executive-branch agencies in the national government. Many private nonprofit organizations, including such organizations as the Rand Corporation, the Aerospace Corporation, the Systems Development Corporation, the Johns Hopkins University Applied Physics Laboratory, the Urban Institute, and the Logistics Management Institute, have contracts to perform scientific research, systems engineering, strategic analysis, and related research. Annual public funds for these research centers have exceeded $1 billion since the early 1960s, and some of these centers were initially created to perform work solely for the government. Here the accountability dilemma comes into even sharper focus: can these research centers have freedom from the accountability caused by marketplace competition as well as independence from normal accountability in government?

Federally funded research and development in colleges and universities, also exceeding $1 billion annually, present related problems if not the identical dilemma. How can evaluations be made and accountability assured without controls that impact adversely on academic freedom and initiative?

Different problems in accountability arise when the government decides to make certain goods by building or buying facilities and equipment and then using private contractors to operate the government-owned plants. Contracts with these government-owned contractor-operated (GOCO) industrial plants, primarily in support of our defense and nuclear-energy programs, run in the billions of dollars annually. Accountability problems arise because profit is not an incentive to efficiency and effectiveness—the contractors are paid a fee above costs. What kind and how much evaluation should the government require and provide for to serve the public interest adequately and at the same time avoid unnecessary infringement on the independence of the management for which the government contracted?

Negotiated procurement contracts, especially when they involve a sole source, present still other kinds of problems in accountability. Tens of billions of dollars are spent annually by the federal government on such contracts, and the problem is how to assure that the government is paying a fair price, not only in relation to actual costs but also with regard to reasonable efficiency, without intruding unduly on the independence of the contractors.

Some quasi-public organizations, financed or otherwise supported in part by government, present unique problems in accountability because they do compete in the marketplace. These profit or nonprofit organizations, established to help fulfill a public purpose, include the Communications Satellite Corporation and the Corporation for Public Broadcasting. Again the central issue is how much accountability is appropriate, by what means it should be ensured, and to what extent limitations on independence should be tolerated. Similar questions arise in considering another type of quasi-public corporation, one that is chartered by the national government, and is now privately owned and no longer included in the federal budget. Such organizations include the Federal National Mortgage Association, Federal Home Loan Banks, Federal Intermediate Credit Banks, Federal Land Banks, and Bank for Cooperatives.

In his essay, Elmer Staats comments as follows on the difficulties encountered as the government attempts to achieve simultaneously several public purposes:

The accountability issue is clouded and made more difficult by the fact that the government, in the various forms of delegation or contracting..., is seeking to accomplish, in most cases, more than one public purpose.

In most if not all of these arrangements, the government has the option of direct operations. Its decision not to do so may be influenced heavily by the fact that other—and frequently conflicting—objectives are sought by the use of external organizations:

—Strengthening private enterprise.
—Supporting educational institutions.
—Fostering international cooperation.
—Encouraging private investment as a means of lessening public expenditure requirements.

I would not argue, as does Peter Drucker, that government is inherently incapable of efficient management, and thus should limit itself to a policy role, but many thoughtful students of government argue that pluralism in carrying out government programs, like pluralism in the private sector, may in and of itself be an objective which should be encouraged. It would be difficult to conceive of a situation where we attempted to carry on all federal activities through direct federal operations.

There must be a balance between accountability and delegation. We now realize the Defense Department's total package procurement concept, for example, which resulted in Lockheed's problems with the C_5A aircraft and the Cheyenne helicopter, is not a viable arrangement. We now recognize that the government must have a continuing, intimate, day-to-day relationship in monitoring development and production problems when a weapons system is being purchased which pushes the "state of the art."[34]

The emerging problems in accountability that Elmer Staats alerted us to in his 1975 essay are very visible now. Investigations and reports of the U.S. General Accounting Office provide clear evidence of such problems as banks, industrial corporations, hospitals, states, cities, and nonprofit organizations serve as government proxies in carrying out federal programs.

For example, the U.S. Department of Energy exercises little control over the procurement activities of its nuclear weapons operating contractors and therefore has little assurance that they "(1) are adequately stressing competition in subcontracting, (2) are reasonably protected against the occurrences of kickbacks, and (3) are following federal payment procedure. Significant violations were found in all three areas."[35]

In another instance, Professional Review Organizations (PRO) contract with the U.S. Department of Health and Human Services' Health Care Financing Administration (HCFA) "to review the necessity, appropriateness, and quality of inpatient hospital services received by the Medicare program's beneficiaries." GAO found that HCFA routine monitoring was not identifying and correcting PRO performance problems. This means that "Medicare and its beneficiaries may not have been receiving all of the protection intended under the programs."[36]

As a further example, "Under the Guaranteed Student Loan Program about 13,000 lenders provided more than $9 billion in loans to 3.7 million students for postsecondary education in fiscal 1986." When borrowers default on loans, the federal agencies which guarantee the loans pay the outstanding principal and accrued interest. From 1965 to 1987, the Department of Education, through 47 loan guarantee agencies (federal), paid over $4 billion to lenders for defaulted loans. In 1986 alone, such payments exceeded $1 billion. "The guarantee agencies are required to set and enforce procedural standards approved by the Department of Education requiring lenders to (1) make all reasonable efforts to collect delinquent loans and (2) promptly file claims for reimbursement when they are unable to collect a loan so that interest paid by the federal government stops accruing." GAO found that not all the guarantee agencies developed standards for lenders' use in collecting loans and filing claims; the Department of Education never reviewed or approved most of the standards that were developed; these standards were frequently not followed by lenders; and they were poorly enforced by the guarantee agencies. Thus, GAO estimated that in 1984, the six guarantee agencies reviewed paid $83 million for claims they could have rejected because the lenders' collection actions fell short of what was required.[37]

Operating government programs by proxy or third party involves sharing government authority. While the means for sharing this authority and the kinds of third parties exercising the authority have increased greatly in mid-twentieth century, the capacity for government agencies to hold third parties accountable effectively has not kept pace. Project grants, formula grants, loan guarantees, and regulation are quite different tools in the operation of this shared authority. "What makes the existence of different tools so important . . . is that each instrument has its own characteristics, its own procedures, its own network of organizational relationships, its own skill requirements. . . . each of these tools is really a complex system of action and actors. Each has its own personality and its own internal and external pressures."[38]

Thus, there are great differences in the kinds of organizations exercising the shared authority. Other governments, for-profit and not-for-profit organizations vary widely in size, competence, and culture. While a government agency can share its authority with one or more proxies, it can not relinquish its responsibility for achieving the purposes for which it was authorized and funded.

Similar problems in accountability, but further complicated by issues of sovereignty, arise in connection with the national government's expenditures through contributions to international organizations. The key issue that needs to be addressed in each instance is how much and what kind of accountability should be established to protect the public interest while permitting the degree of independence required to achieve desired results.

Another dimension of this problem was highlighted by the General Accounting Office when it reported the results of a study on contracting by federal agencies. Evidencing concern about the pervasive influence of consultants on government functions, GAO noted that contractors' advisory role may become so extensive that it "limits agencies' ability to develop options other than those proposed by the contractor."[39] This would impair an agency's ability to control policies and programs and thereby weaken accountability.

Government by proxy complicates the process for holding government bureaucracies accountable because "it fragments power, obscures who is doing what, and severs lines of control."[40] In addition, there is considerable evidence of agencies failing to define precisely the requirements placed on third parties and related estimates of costs. These are fundamental to developing and applying specific strategies that will obtain desired performance as to quality, quantity, timeliness, and cost from third-party government.

NOTES

1. *Working for the Federal Government; Job Satisfaction and Federal Employees*, U.S. Merit Systems Protection Board, October 1987.

2. 64 Stat. 832.

3. 31 U.S.C. 3512.

4. *Audit of Federal Operations and Programs*, Office of Management and Budget, Circular No. A–73 Revised, June 20, 1983.

5. Report of the U.S. General Accounting Office, AFMD–88–10, December 1987, p. 12.

6. *Policy and Procedures Manual for Guidance of Federal Agencies, Title 2, Accounting*, U.S. General Accounting Office, May 1988, p. 121.

7. Ibid., pp. 123–24.

8. Op. cit., 88–10, pp. 14–16.

9. *Government Auditing Standards*, Comptroller General of the United States, 1988.

10. U.S., Congress, House, Committee on Government Operations, Subcommittee on Legislation and National Security, Statement of the Comptroller General, U.S. General Accounting Office, February 25, 1981, 97th Cong., 1st sess.

11. Report of the U.S. General Accounting Office, AFMD–88–10, December 1987, pp. 20, 21.

12. *Management of the U.S. Government*, U.S. Office of Management and Budget, Fiscal Year 1989, pp. 33–51.

13. *Report on the Significant Actions of the Office of Personnel Management During 1983*, U.S. Merit Systems Protection Board, Washington, December 1984, p. 51.

14. Executive Order 11821, November 29, 1974.

15. Edward Paul Fuchs, *President, Management, and Regulation* (Englewood Cliffs: Prentice-Hall, 1988), pp. 21–28.

16. Ibid., pp. 31–44.

17. Ibid., p. 53.

18. Ibid., pp. 70–80.

19. Timothy B. Clark, "Outgoing Carterites Rush to the Printer with a Flood of Rules," *National Journal* 13 (January 24, 1981), p. 154.

20. Op. cit., Fuchs, p. 87.

21. Executive Order 12291, February 19, 1981.

22. Op. cit., Fuchs, p. 90.

23. Ibid., p. 118.

24. Staff Report, "Regulatory Agencies Get Double Whammy in Reagan Budget Cuts," *National Journal* 13 (March 21, 1981), pp. 425, 502–3.

25. Executive Order 12498, January 4, 1985.

26. U.S. Office of Management and Budget, *Bulletin 85–9*, January 10, 1985.

27. Ibid., pp. 2–3.

28. The five agencies are Environmental Protection Agency and the Departments

of Labor, Transportation, Treasury, and Housing and Urban Development. The new procedures with additional details were communicated to heads of departments and agencies in an OIRA memorandum of August 8, 1986.

29. Harvey Mansfield, "Independence and Accountability for Federal Contractors and Grantees," in *The New Political Economy*, ed. Bruce L. R. Smith (New York: Wiley, 1975), p. 321.

30. Ibid., pp. 322–23.

31. Ibid., pp. 323–24.

32. Ibid., p. 324.

33. Elmer B. Staats, "New Problems in Accountability for Federal Programs," in *The New Political Economy*, ed. Bruce L. R. Smith (New York: Wiley, 1975), p. 46.

34. Ibid., pp. 62–63.

35. Report of the U.S. General Accounting Office, RCED–87–166, August 28, 1987, pp. 2–4.

36. Report of the U.S. General Accounting Office, HRD–88–13, October 8, 1987, pp. 2–3.

37. Report of the U.S. General Accounting Office, HRD–87–48, August 20, 1987, pp. 2–3.

38. Lester M. Salamon, "Rise of Third Party Government, Part I," *The Bureaucrat—The Journal for Public Managers*, Summer 1987, p. 28.

39. Report of the U.S. General Accounting Office, FPCD–81–43, June 19, 1981.

40. Lester M. Salamon, "Rise of Third Party Government, Part II," *The Bureaucrat—The Journal for Public Managers*, Fall 1987, p. 26.

4

Accountability
Mechanisms and
Methods Used by the
Legislative Branch

By making laws that establish what administrative agencies are expected to do and by appropriating money to do it, legislative bodies have the ultimate power to hold administrators accountable. At all levels of government, legislators and legislative institutions call on agency administrators to account for their actions or failure to act. This is known as legislative oversight. Most often it is conducted on an ad hoc basis, less frequently as part of a well-defined systematic process.

While much of the discussion that follows relates to the mechanisms and methods used by Congress, many state and larger local governments operate in essentially the same way with a few significant exceptions. State and local legislative bodies have not yet gone as far as the national government in establishing professional support staffs for members as well as committees; that, together with the fact that state and local legislators serve part-time, has slowed the development of their accountability processes.

Current congressional oversight is based on major decisions taken in 1946, 1968, 1970, and 1974. As mentioned in Chapter 2, the Legislative Reorganization Act of 1946[1] requires all standing committees of Congress to exercise "continuous watchfulness" over agencies under their jurisdiction. The Intergovernmental Cooperation Act of 1968[2] called on legislative committees to review grants-in-aid programs without expiration dates to determine whether the programs are meeting their intended purposes, whether further federal assistance is needed to meet the objectives, and whether any changes should be made in the programs.

The Legislative Reorganization Act of 1970[3] requires the Congressional Research Service to make experts available to committees to evaluate legislative proposals and to provide each committee at the beginning of a new Congress with a list of laws under that committee's jurisdiction that are due to expire and a list of "subjects and policy areas which the committee might profitably analyze in depth." In addition, this act requires all legislative committees to report at the end of each Congress on their oversight work.

The Congressional Budget and Impoundment Control Act of 1974[4] gave Congress better institutional means for controlling the budget by establishing the Congressional Budget Office, budget committees in both houses, and related processes. Further, it provided a new dimension to oversight by authorizing committees to require agencies under their jurisdiction to evaluate their programs and report the results to Congress. At the same time the Office of Management and Budget (OMB) and the Treasury Department were instructed to respond affirmatively to requests by the General Accounting Office (GAO) and the Congressional Budget Office for information on federal programs; and GAO was directed to establish an Office of Program Review and Evaluation and to recommend to Congress methods for reviewing and evaluating federally funded programs.

SOURCES OF INFORMATION

Information is crucial to effective oversight. Members of Congress find different sources of information helpful in varying degrees. The survey taken in the 100th Congress yielded relevant data as shown in Table 2. For oversight purposes members considered committee staff and personal staff the best sources of information, closely followed by constituents and interest groups. Other congressmen and senators, state and local officals, and GAO were also fairly good sources of information. The least helpful were whistleblowers and political party officials.

CASEWORK

Service to constituents is vital to reelection, and this reason alone is sufficient for legislators to give it a very high priority. Complaints by citizens to elected representatives or their staffs in city councils, county boards of supervisors, state legislatures, or Congress, alleging that they have not been treated fairly or adequately by administrative agencies, usually bring prompt contact with agency officials. Attention is focused on relevant facts, basis for the decision, and prospects for acting favorably and quickly on complaints.

Members of Congress find casework significant in holding administrators accountable for making laws work as intended. The survey of representatives

Table 2
Helpfulness of Different Sources of Information to Members of Congress in Carrying Out Their Oversight Responsibilities

	Ratings by 24 Representatives and 14 Senators (in percentages)		
Sources	Very Helpful	Moderately Helpful	Rarely Helpful
Constituents	53	31	16
Personal staff	83	17	0
Committee staff	87	13	0
Other congressmen and senators	31	58	11
GAO reports	27	62	11
Interest groups	35	62	3
Whistleblowers (agency employees)	6	51	43
State and local officials	28	50	22
News media	22	56	22
Political party officials	3	31	66

Note: Every representative and senator surveyed had oversight responsibilities as chairman of a committee or subcommittee or as ranking minority member of a committee.

Source: Compiled by the author.

and senators revealed that 37 percent believe casework is very effective, 52 percent rate it moderately so, and 11 percent consider it rarely effective.

When such casework is viewed by the legislator and staff solely as service to an individual constituent, the oversight value, while significant in the instance, is from an overall point of view marginal. On the other hand, when legislators use casework as an oversight tool in evaluating our governmental institutions, it has considerable value in exposing the need for changes in both law and administration.

Special office procedures involving inventory, classification and analysis of cases, and personal participation of the legislator and key staff are usually required if the solutions to individual problems of constituents are to be translated into improvements in agency policies and practices. Such follow-through on constituent problems may even lead to changes in law. When this occurs, however, it is the result of a determined effort on the part of a legislator or staff person, and involves considerable work with the agency concerned, relevant interest groups, and appropriate committee staffs and members.

THE APPROPRIATIONS PROCESS

Constituent problems are unpredictable, and oversight flowing from them is sporadic and unorganized. However, the appropriations process, as a mechanism for oversight, is quite different in terms of both regularity and system. In the national government the subcommittees of the appropriations committees in the House and the Senate examine annually the requests for funds of agencies in the executive branch. For many agencies, this constitutes their only *regularly* scheduled review and supervision by Congress. The situation is essentially no different in state and local governments, although in some jurisdictions the legislature meets biennially rather than annually, and budget, finance, or revenue committees instead of appropriations committees may be involved.

Despite the fact that limited time and the size and complexity of the budgets make it impossible for these committees and subcommittees to give careful consideration to all major programs for which funds are requested, various sources of information help focus their attention on important problem areas. Subcommittee staffs, through occasional contact with agency officials during the year, have opportunities for being informed about major policy and program developments that have implications for current or future expenditures. Legislators and committee staff members receive critical and sometimes complimentary information about operations of the agency from interest groups, individual legislators who deal with the agency on behalf of constituents, news media, and committees with legislative jurisdiction. In addition, interest groups lobby members of the committee and staffs for increases or reductions, presenting data and examples of the agency's good deeds, poor deeds, or no deeds.

In general, the road to legislative oversight is somewhat dimly lighted. Language in authorization and appropriations bills is often too general on the purposes for which the monies are to be spent. Contrariwise, such bills may also contain instructions on purposes for which appropriated funds may not be used. These are very specific.

Prior to the annual appropriations hearings, at the request of the subcommittees, agencies submit extensive data, adding details to what appears in their formal budget requests submitted by the chief executive. Further information may be obtained through a special investigation using the committee staff, sometimes supplemented with professionals from the General Accounting Office, the Federal Bureau of Investigation, and other agencies.

Such an inquiry related to the budget of the Defense Department, for example, could be concerned with determining whether various weapons systems lived up to the cost of performance promises in the contract and, if not, why; or whether weapons systems are being developed that are too difficult to operate in battle conditions or too costly to maintain.

At the hearings, top officials of the agencies state their case and are questioned, in the light of information previously obtained, about funds requested for the next fiscal year and expenditures in the current year. Because time is limited, most of these discussions deal with general direction, broad agency policies, and major issues in program administration. Occasionally individual cases are the center of attention. Even without cases, subcommittee members do not have time to review all major policies, programs, and operations in a systematic manner.

Nevertheless, most congressmen and senators believed that the appropriations process is a very good mechanism for oversight. Sixty-eight percent rated it as very effective, 30 percent moderately, and two percent as rarely effective. Career executives also have a high regard for the appropriations process as an accountability mechanism. Sixty-seven percent rated it as very effective, 19 percent as moderately effective, and 14 percent as rarely effective.

While the concept of oversight through the appropriations process is sound, a number of factors diminish its effectiveness. First, there is the matter of time. In preparing for the hearings, the staffs of the appropriations subcommittees are constrained by time to concentrate on those parts of the budget which involve significant increases over the previous year and other proposed expenditures where subcommittee members and senior staff have previously expressed serious concerns. Consequently, while a comprehensive review of agency operations is theoretically possible, realistically, the coverage is quite limited. Hearing time ranges from less than an hour for a very small agency to several days or a week for a major segment of a large department.

Another practical limitation on comprehensive review of agency operations in the appropriations process is the relationship to other legislative processes. In the national government, House and Senate rules prohibit appropriations committees from acting on any program not authorized by law. The legislative committee, not the appropriations committee, has jurisdiction over the substance of legislation; and it is in this legislating stage— sometimes referred to as the authorization process—that maximums are set on the funds that may be appropriated. At all levels of government, appropriations committees and subcommittees operate within policy and program constraints established during the legislative process.

The appropriations process is also limited as an oversight tool by laws which provide for permanent appropriations. These laws are within the jurisdiction of legislative committees. Almost half the federal budget requires no action by Congress, with automatic appropriations determined by outside factors, such as interest costs on the public debt and mandatory payments into the civil service retirement fund. Most state and local governments are confronted with similar conditions.

Finally, there is one intangible element that has enormous influence on the way the appropriations process is used as an oversight mechanism. This is the degree of confidence that ranking members and key staff of the appropriations subcommittee have in the *leadership* of the agency. It is often the crucial factor in determining the depth and breadth of the appropriations hearing and pre-hearing inquiries.

OVERSIGHT BY STANDING COMMITTEES

When permanent (standing) committees are considering new laws or changes in existing laws, officials from relevant agencies of the executive branch are called on to discuss and answer questions about the particular program or related ones for which they have responsibility. This can be a useful part of oversight. If the proposed legislation authorizes new programs, responses from agency officials about how the programs would be administered and the results expected become part of the base for future oversight.

In addition, most continuing programs require annual authorization: that is, legislative authority to fund the program up to a certain amount. This means that legislative committees have the opportunity for reviewing programs, as part of the legislative process to renew authorizations, before any decisions are made in the appropriations process.

The oversight functions of Congress and the special role of its standing committees were first formally established by the Legislative Reorganization Act of 1946:

> To assist the Congress in appraising the administration of the laws and in developing such amendments or related legislation as it may deem necessary, each standing committee of the Senate and the House shall exercise continuous watchfulness of the execution by the administrative agencies concerned of any laws, the subject matter of which is within the jurisdiction of such committee; and, for that purpose, shall study all pertinent reports and data submitted to the Congress by the agencies in the executive branch of the Government.[5]

To clarify the intent, the Legislative Reorganization Act of 1970 substituted "review and study" of administrative actions on a continuing basis for "continuous watchfulness." Some state and local governments have adopted a similar statutory basis for oversight by standing committees, while others see oversight as an implicit responsibility of legislative committees requiring no further authority. Regardless, most legislative committees behave as if oversight is a secondary, not primary, responsibility.

The standing committees have a number of useful tools for achieving effective oversight. They may conduct investigations to determine the competence with which programs are being administered. Hearings may be held to look into specific allegations, to review a nominee's qualifications, or to examine more broadly the adequacy and effectiveness of programs. Provisions may be written into law establishing systematic reporting and evaluation requirements to be fulfilled by the agency in order to facilitate program review by the standing committee.

The chairman and other ranking members of standing committees frequently request the General Accounting Office to obtain and analyze information concerning the operation of a specific agency or program.

As one example, responding to a request from the Chairman and ranking minority member of the Subcommittee on Aviation, House Committee on Public Works and Transportation, the GAO evaluated the Federal Aviation Administration's (FAA) staffing for the nation's air traffic control system. GAO reported that "current technician shortages are beginning to negatively affect equipment performance and other operational areas, such as completion of routine maintenance. . . . the airline industry is experiencing an increase in flight delays caused by equipment failure."[6]

In another instance, responding to a request from the Chairman of the Subcommittee on Readiness, House Committees on the Armed Service, the GAO reviewed the effectiveness of the Naval Audit Services. GAO reported that "serious deficiencies in planning, conducting, and reporting on audits have resulted in few significant findings and recommendations. . . . The Navy, through the Department of Defense concurred with each of our findings and recommendations."[7]

Reports such as these may be used then as part of a committee investigation, hearing, or other means to cause the agency to deal effectively with the problem(s) identified by GAO.

Investigations

Standing committees conduct investigations to determine the need for changes in laws, to find out how well laws are being executed, and to expose improper conduct or ineffective performance by administrators. Investigations are made to develop public opinion about new policies. Sometimes they are initiated simply to obtain publicity for committee members.

Investigations may be undertaken by the full committee, by subcommittees of a standing committee or by a specially established investigating subcommittee. Investigation subcommittees may be either permanent or temporary. In the national government, permanent investigating subcommittees have been created by nine of the 22 standing committees in the House and by one of the 16 standing committees in the Senate. Each investigating subcommittee is expected to conduct investigations for the standing committee and all its subcommittees.

Investigations of agencies are most often initiated by a subcommittee or committee as a result of serious problems, complaints, or improprieties brought to the attention of members of the staff by constituents, interest groups, or the news media. Current concerns of the chairman and members have much to do with whether an investigation will be launched. Investigations have been undertaken by committees or subcommittees of the House and Senate on a broad range of issues affecting a large number of agencies. There are many examples.

A subcommittee of the Senate Governmental Affairs Committee investigated fraud in military procurement and the Defense Department's efforts to combat it.[8] Investigations dealing with energy and the performance of the Federal Power Commission were conducted by a subcommittee of the House Committee on Energy and Foreign Commerce.[9] A subcommittee of the House Post Office and Civil Service Committee investigated the operations of the civil service system and the role of the central personnel agency.[10] A subcommittee of the Senate Finance Committee investigated fraud in Medicaid and what the Department of Health and Human Services (HHS) was doing to prevent it;[11] and a subcommittee of the Senate Committee on Environment and Public Works investigated safety in nuclear-powered electric generating plants and the role of the Nuclear Regulatory Commission.[12]

Once it is decided to undertake an investigation, a variety of techniques and methods are available to secure facts and opinions. The agency may be asked to submit information in writing; an investigator may visit the agency to question employees and review records; leads may be pursued that take the investigators outside the government; and public investigative hearings may be conducted in various parts of the jurisdiction so that interested parties have an opportunity to present their views. (Generally, before witnesses testify in public, they are questioned in private by subcommittee/committee staff to assure that their testimony is relevant and reliable.)

Members of Congress have a high regard for investigations as a tool for oversight. In the survey of representatives and senators, 57 percent rated committee and subcommittee investigations as a very effective mechanism for holding agencies accountable, 41 percent rated it moderately so, and only two percent rated it as rarely effective.

Hearings

The Legislative Reorganization Act of 1970 not only places a responsibility on standing committees of Congress to review the execution of laws within their jurisdiction, but also requires them to report biennially on results of these reviews. Hearings conducted on a regular basis by committees or subcommittees to evaluate administration of laws can be a remarkably effective oversight mechanism. Such hearings may explore in considerable detail specific parts of a program and certain administrative practices; or they may be devoted to a more general review of the entire program. In either event, the effectiveness and efficiency of administration can come under searching review, particularly if policies are controversial, or if criticisms have been leveled at the operation of the program.

Most committee and subcommittee hearings are not conducted on a regularly scheduled basis as part of a plan for comprehensive and systematic oversight. Instead, they are held in response to public criticism of a law or its administration, unexpected problems, alleged improprieties, or even failure to conclude informal discussions with the agency administrator to the satisfaction of the subcommittee chairman. Hearings are useful for oversight in many situations. In fact, the Spring 1988 survey of members of Congress showed that 51 percent saw hearings as a very effective means for holding agencies accountable and 49 percent as moderately effective. It is worth noting that not *one* survey respondent rated hearings as "rarely effective."

Hearings may also be held on policies and plans developed to implement a law, thereby keeping the agency on a short rein with regard to legislative intent. However, as a rule, standing committees and their subcommittees do not exercise such close oversight of executive agencies because most legislators do not consider this function as important as constituent service and legislating. That situation is justified on the grounds that unless there is specific evidence indicating the need for oversight, it does not warrant as high a priority.

Oversight hearings often provide high drama, and legislative or executive action may quickly follow. Hearings on the Federal Bureau of Investigation (FBI) by House and Senate committees in the 1970s[13] revealed some highly questionable actions during the long tenure of J. Edgar Hoover. Changes followed in FBI policies and practices, in the degree of attention given them by the attorney general, and in the quality of congressional oversight.

Hearings by a subcommittee of the Senate Committee on Finance displayed shocking evidence of fraud and abuse in the operation of the Medicaid program.[14] The findings resulted in the establishment of a much more effective investigative and inspection capability in HHS to ferret out fraud, and it stimulated major improvements in control and monitoring by state and local governments charged with administering the program. Investigations and hearings on dozens of other subjects have resulted in headlines and news stories that educated the public, brought changes in laws and administrative practices, and started processes that ultimately put some offenders in jail.

During the second term of the Reagan administration, joint hearings by the Senate Foreign Relations Committee and the Judiciary Committee marked the beginning of a momentous struggle between the president and the Senate over a novel doctrine advanced by the administration. In brief, the administration announced a broad interpretation of the 1972 Antiballistic Missiles (ABM) treaty between the United States and the Soviet Union. This provided the basis for its position that work on the Strategic Defense Initiative (SDI), popularly known as "Star Wars," could go beyond research to development and testing without violating the ABM treaty.

However, when the treaty was being considered by the Senate, witnesses of the administration which had negotiated the treaty gave unequivocal testimony to the contrary. Reagan administration witnesses claimed that "testimony during Senate treaty ratification proceedings 'has absolutely no standing' in terms of establishing other parties' obligations under these treaties. In effect . . . the executive branch is free to ignore the meaning of the treaty as originally described to the Senate of the United States . . . other nations who are party to such treaties can disregard what the executive branch told the Senate at the time of ratification."[15]

Six former secretaries of defense, three in Republican administrations and three in Democratic administrations, entered the controversy with a joint statement which concluded that "the United States and the Soviet Union should continue to adhere to the traditional interpretation of Article V of the Treaty as it was presented to the Senate for advice and consent. . . ."[16] Despite the strong desire of a popular president to proceed with SDI under the so-called broad interpretation of the ABM Treaty, he and the secretaries of defense and state were being held accountable through the legislative oversight procedures.

Legislative bodies generally lay down specific procedural requirements for hearings held by committees and subcommittees to insure fairness as well as to facilitate a productive process. These include coordination with other committees, advance announcement of dates and purpose, submission of statements by witnesses before appearance, questioning of witnesses, voting, and reporting. Standing committees are usually authorized to adopt additional rules of procedure. These may be concerned with such matters as securing competent witnesses, preparing questions, and distributing summaries of testimony to members, and any other considerations that can affect the fairness and value of the hearing.

Accountability is not enhanced when subcommittees and committees abuse their power of investigation in pre-hearing or hearing stages. Mc-Carthyism became a household word as a consequence of abuse of power by Senator Joseph McCarthy in his role as chairman of a Senate investigating committee in the 1950s. Some of the more flagrant abuses involved intimidating witnesses and ruining the reputation of citizens, organizations, and agencies of government by making and publicizing unsupported allegations of wrongdoing. This type of oversight generates fear, produces indecisiveness, and causes many outstanding people to leave public service or decide against entering public service.

Reporting Requirements

Many laws require agencies to make specific reports to standing committees on the administration of policies and programs. These reports offer committees and their subcommittees additional opportunities to oversee operations. Examination of reports may identify areas that committee members or staff wish to explore further on an informal or formal basis to assure that the agency is administering the law as the committee believes it should. Problems that surface may raise questions about the statute as well as the effectiveness of its administration. Unfortunately, legislative requirements for these reports rarely provide sufficient direction to move agencies to prepare comprehensive, well-balanced presentations on progress and problems.

It is not surprising, therefore, that Congress has found the results of reporting requirements only moderately helpful in oversight. The 1988 survey of members revealed that 27 percent rated reporting requirements very effective as a mechanism for holding agencies accountable; 68 percent rated it moderately effective, and five percent saw it as rarely effective.

SPECIAL OVERSIGHT ROLES OF THE HOUSE COMMITTEE ON GOVERNMENT OPERATIONS AND THE SENATE COMMITTEE ON GOVERNMENTAL AFFAIRS

Two committees in the Congress, one in the House and one in the Senate, have unique and important governmentwide oversight responsibilities that cut across agency and policy lines. The House Committee on Government Operations and the Senate Committee on Governmental Affairs have essentially similar jurisdiction over the following areas:

overall economy and efficiency of government operations;

budgeting and accounting, other than appropriations;

reorganizations in the executive branch;

intergovernmental relationships;

legislative oversight procedures and practices; and

reports of the General Accounting Office.

These two committees can investigate, hold hearings, make recommendations to other committees, and initiate resolutions and legislation in these areas, all of which have the potential for influencing significantly the effectiveness of congressional oversight.

In the course of a single Congress during the 1970's and 1980's, each committee received for consideration several hundred bills and resolutions, of which ten percent were enacted into law. In every Congress each committee and its subcommittees held 50 to 75 hearings and prepared about an equal number of reports. Also, in every Congress these two committees received hundreds of reports of investigations or studies of operations of executive agencies made by the principal audit agency of the legislative branch—the General Accounting Office.

The committees are expected to study the reports and make recommendations to the House or Senate as appropriate. This has not been done with any great consistency—nor have the opportunities for further oversight pointed up by GAO reports been exploited fully by these and other committees of Congress. Regrettably, such additional oversight occurs in only the most serious situations or when a member of Congress or a committee was responsible for initiating the particular GAO audit or investigation.

For example, the federal government, as the owner of one-third of the nation's land area, "is responsible for cleaning up perhaps thousands of sites where uncontained hazardous wastes are contaminating soil and groundwater." A 1980 law requires federal agencies to determine whether their facilities and land contain abandoned or uncontrolled hazardous wastes and to take any necessary corrective actions. Concerned about progress in meeting these requirements, the Chairman, Subcommittee on Environment, Energy, and Natural Resources, House Committee on Government Operations, requested GAO to examine the action taken by the 11 agencies that account for nearly all such hazardous waste sites. GAO found that these "agencies have been slow to identify, assess, and clean up their hazardous waste sites." Specifically, from 1980 to 1987, they "identified 1,882 potential sites, assessd about half of them to determine whether they required cleanup, and cleaned up 78 of the 511 sites found to need it." By far, most of this was accomplished after 1984, when Congress intensified its oversight through GAO reviews and subcommittee hearings.[17]

By Rule X of the House of Representatives, its Committee on Government Operations has an additional unique responsibility with regard to oversight of executive agencies. The Legislative Reorganization Act of 1946 requires all standing committees of the Senate and House to oversee the execution of laws within their jurisdiction. Rule X calls on the Committee on Government Operations to have a representative meet, at the beginning of each Congress, "with appropriate representatives of each of the other committees of the House to discuss the oversight plans of such committees and to assist in coordinating all of the oversight activities of the House during such Congress." The Rule requires the Government Operations Committee, within 60 days after a Congress convenes, to report to the House results of these meetings and to make recommendations for improving legislative oversight.

The House Committee on Government Operations has held these meetings and submitted reports at the beginning of each Congress since the Rule was adopted in 1974. Since these reports reflect the plans of committees to the extent that they may have been made in the first 30 to 60 days of a Congress, they are of necessity tentative and incomplete, and inevitably performance has varied considerably. Also, the Government Operations Committee interprets very narrowly its responsibility for assisting in the coordination of "all of the oversight activities of the House." It does not see its responsibility as including any supervision or evaluation of oversight work by other committees; rather, it sees its role as simply compiling the report and furnishing copies to committees so they can "note any areas where there may be a potential duplication of effort."[18] Many committees do not find this report useful.

ADVICE AND CONSENT

The process of "advice and consent" for nominees of the chief executive involves, as a minimum, hearings and recommendations by appropriate committees of the legislative body. Hearings held by committees of the United States Senate in carrying out this constitutional function have often been perfunctory. Only a few legislative committees of the Senate have rules requiring (1) a detailed questionnaire completed by the nominee, before the hearing, designed to shed light on the nominee's background, experience, relevant views on policy issues, and potential conflicts of interest, (2) a hearing with the nominee testifying under oath, and (3) a written committee report that recommends giving or refusing the "consent" of the Senate.

Once the president submits a nomination, the normal practice is for the nominee to visit personally, prior to a formal hearing, with each member of the committee that will be considering the nomination. During these personal visits and at formal hearings there is usually very little penetrating and comprehensive probing of the nominee's policy views and previous activities that could establish a firm base for deciding on qualifications and specific future oversight by the committee. "Advice and consent" processes in state and local governments are no more effective in these respects than in the national government. While the cost in citizen confidence of failing to apply properly these constitutional checks and balances is not quantifiable, it is also not insignificant.

Two appointees of the Carter administration who later became subjects of major controversy sailed through a routine confirmation process. In a voice vote the Senate confirmed Bert Lance for what many consider the second most powerful position in the executive branch—director of the Office of Management and Budget—based on a limited hearing record developed by the Committee on Governmental Affairs. Eight months later, following more thorough hearings by the same committee on his business practices as a banker prior to his appointment, Lance resigned. Although he was subsequently acquitted in federal court of charges brought against him by the U.S. Attorney, the episode adversely affected public support for the Carter administration.

Similarly, the Senate quickly gave its consent to the appointment of David Gartner as a member of the Commodity Futures Trading Commission despite his acknowledgment that he had accepted a large block of stock for his children from a big grain dealer. After confirmation, the president and vice president as well as some members of the Senate became sufficiently concerned to call for Gartner's resignation. He refused on the ground that information about the stock was made known to both the Senate Agriculture Committee and the White House Counsel. Gartner continued to serve despite clear indication that the president would not have submitted the nomination had he focused on the facts, or he would have withdrawn the nomination if the confirmation process had highlighted these facts.

Senate committees generally do not see the Senate's "advice and consent" responsibility as requiring a definitive judgment that the nominee for a position in the executive branch has the necessary qualifications to do the job well. Generally, they rubber-stamp the president's nominees, even those whose qualifications are marginal or nonexistent for the posts to which nominated.

The confirmation process on President Ronald Reagan's nomination of Edward Day as secretary of energy was not designed to reveal how little evidence existed that he would be able to provide effective leadership in this highly complex and vital area. He was confirmed because it is traditional for the Senate to go along with the president's nominations unless serious derogatory information arises that the nominee is unable to refute. When that does occur, or the role of the nominee in a highly questionable activity is unclear, Senate committees do probe quite thoroughly.

This was demonstrated in the extensive hearings of the Senate Foreign Relations Committee on the nomination of Alexander Haig for secretary of state.[19] His role as White House chief of staff during President Richard Nixon's final days caused some doubt. The Senate Committee on Agriculture probed deeply into John B. Crowell, Jr., who had been nominated for assistant secretary of Agriculture in charge of the Forest Service.[20] The committee was interested in determining his role in a company found guilty of conspiracy to rig bids on purchases of public timber. The appointments of both Haig and Crowell were confirmed.

On those occasions when members of the Senate choose to use the confirmation process to establish certain performance expectations, the exchanges have been very revealing and useful as an accountability instrument. They show that the interests of senators range from narrow constituent concerns to broad national policy issues.

In hearings before the Senate Commerce Committee,[21] Senator John Danforth (Republican, Missouri) asked for and got assurance from Drew Lewis, President Reagan's nominee for secretary of transportation, that he would not reverse former Secretary Brock Adams' decision to keep the St. Louis airport in Missouri instead of moving it across the Mississippi River into Illinois. The secretary-designate's view was stated with clarity and candor: "I see no need to change a decision made by Brock Adams. It was not only a sound economic decision, but with you on this committee, it's a sound political decision."

In sharp contrast with this local concern were issues discussed at the hearings held by the Senate Energy and Natural Resources Committee on Reagan's nominee for secretary of interior, James Watt.[22] His most recent employment, as president and chief legal officer of the Mountain States Legal Foundation in Denver, had brought him into frequent public conflict with the Department of Interior over opening more lands to uses beyond recreation and wilderness conservation. To dampen the criticism of the environmentalists he promised that he would not seek any major change in the environmental and land-use laws, but would work within them to achieve higher production of energy and strategic minerals from public lands.

Filling a position a second or third time in the same administration provides opportunities during the confirmation process to seek changes in the administration's policies and practices. When William D. Ruckelshaus appeared before the Senate Environment and Public Works Committee on his nomination to succeed Anne Gorsuch Burford as administrator of the Environmental Protection Agency, he differed with his predecessor on a number of issues to the satisfaction of committee members. For example, he promised to move "expeditiously" to clean up hazardous waste dumps using the "superfund" without waiting to identify those who caused the problem and negotiating contracts on who will pay the costs. All the processes would proceed simultaneously instead of seriatim, thereby achieving some cleanups years sooner.[23]

The long-stalled confirmation process for Roland R. Vautour as President Reagan's third Department of Agriculture under secretary for Small Community and Rural Development was completed affirmatively once he satisfied the committee on a change in administration attitude. Most members of the Senate Committee on Agriculture had been disappointed that previous under secretaries did not "fully implement discretionary programs such as the FmHA (Farmers Home Administration) interest buy-down and rural industrialization loan program. . . ."[24]

Nominees avoid answering questions on controversial issues by saying they have not studied the matter. Former Senator Thomas Eagleton said that most nominees for top position "have no views on anything."[25] However, nominees have not been able to turn aside the question of possible conflict of interest arising from recent employment and current investments when the committee chose to pursue it. For example, on the opening day of his confirmation hearing, James Watt attempted to reserve the option of participating in decisions of the department on cases brought in the future by his former employer—the Mountain States Legal Foundation. When the hearings resumed two days later the committee's chairman and ranking minority member announced jointly that Watt had agreed he would not participate in such cases.

At other times, where current investments could be affected by decisions of the nominee if confirmed, committees have insisted on divestiture to eliminate both the reality and the appearance of conflict of interest. This does lead some outstanding people to refuse nomination to high posts in government because timely divestiture would cause them to suffer substantial financial loss. More often nominees propose and committees accept resolution of potential conflict through creation of blind trusts. Unfortunately, in some instances blind trusts are managed by individuals who are very close to the nominee and to that extent the "appearance" of possible conflict of interest is not completely erased.

For a relatively brief period the confirmation process for nominees to independent regulatory agencies in the federal government was strengthened. These agencies have a quasi-legislative and quasi-judicial role. Early in President Nixon's second term, the intense strain between him and the Democrats who controlled the Senate was manifested in the confirmation process of nominees for these agencies. The Senate Commerce Committee, which acts on nominations for many regulatory agencies, decided to scrap the "clear disqualification test": that is, give consent if the nominee meets the few statutory requirements, remedies any potential conflicts of interest, and has no problem as to honesty.

In floor debate on a nominee in 1973 Senator Gary Hart advanced the argument that the same latitude allowed the White House in choosing cabinet members is not appropriate for members of regulatory commissions. He said, "The makeup of such commissions should reflect to some degree the various views represented in Congress. To argue that for too long Congress has ignored this fact does not persuade me we should continue to forfeit this responsibility."[26] In the same debate Senator Ernest Hollings moved the argument from representativeness to philosophy of the nominee: "Regulatory commissions derive their power and authority directly from Congress. Hence, as members of Congress, we would be remiss in our duties if we did not oversee regulatory activities to insure that they continue to meet the objectives we have set. The philosophy and background of the nominees confirmed by the Senate as commissioners is of overriding importance in effectuating or in frustrating these objectives."[27]

Over the next three years, the Senate asserted its power and advised it would not consent to some appointments because it had doubts about various qualifications of the nominees including the policy direction that they would give to the agencies. In 1976 Senator Frank Moss summed up the new attitude developing in the Senate: "In my view, when considering nominations to independent regulatory agencies the Senate has a special responsibility. . . .

It is incumbent upon the Senate . . . to exercise independent judgment with respect to each nominee. The Senate's consideration of these nominees should go beyond an examination of the nominee's potential qualifications. We must be particularly satisfied that each nominee has the intellectual qualifications and philosophical commitment to enforce Congress' mandate."[28]

Now presidents were beginning to receive advice on qualifications nominees should possess if the Senate's consent was to be obtained; but this was short-lived. In 1977 a Democratic Senate returned to the traditional approach in acting on the nominations of a new Democratic president, and with few exceptions a similarly accommodating approach was taken by the new Republican Senate in 1981 in dealing with the nominations of a new Republican president.

LEGISLATIVE AUDIT AGENCIES

A primary function of independent nonpolitical audit agencies of the legislative branch is to assist the legislative body, its committees, and its members in carrying out their oversight responsibilities. The national government, many states, and some local governments have such agencies.

The United States General Accounting Office

By law, the General Accounting Office is directed to determine whether public funds are being administered efficiently, economically, and effectively. Since 1921 the GAO has assisted Congress in the oversight role through its audit operations. It has subpoena power and is authorized to examine all papers and records of executive-branch agencies, interview officials and employees, and investigate all aspects of the receipt and expenditure of federal funds. Evaluations may be undertaken on its own initiative or at the request of a committee, subcommittee, or member of the House or Senate.

GAO's audit work includes operations of federal agencies, state and local governments and nongovernment organizations that receive or administer federal grants and loans. These evaluations generally result in reports to Congress with copies to organizations investigated. The reports, 700 to 800 a year, present not only results of audits but also recommendations for improving the economy and efficiency of operations and the effectiveness of programs.

Except when a member of Congress requesting the report asks that it *not* be done, agencies audited are given the opportunity of reviewing the draft report in order to identify any factual inaccuracies and to comment on the conclusions and recommendations. Pertinent excerpts of agency comments are appended to the report. Recommendations may call for changes in law as well as agency policies, programs, priorities, and administrative practices. By law, within 60 days of the issuance of the report, agencies are required to submit a written statement to the House Government Operations Committee and the Senate Governmental Affairs Committee specifying action taken or proposed on each recommendation. In addition, any appropriation request submitted by the agency more than 60 days after the date of the report must include a written statement of the agency's action on each recommendation.[29]

With about 5,000 employees, mostly professionals in a wide range of disciplines, GAO is headed by a comptroller general appointed for a 15-year, nonrenewable term. A bipartisan commission of congressional leaders presents three names for consideration. While the president is not bound to make the nomination from these, going outside the list would probably forfeit Senate confirmation. GAO currently enjoys great respect, particularly in Congress, though critics of the agency on Capitol Hill have complained about the length of time it takes to complete audits and reports.[30] Those audited and found wanting frequently allege that reports are more critical than the facts justify. In recent years, GAO has given concentrated attention to both the timeliness and quality of reports and there is some evidence of improvement.

The action of agencies on GAO recommendations is mixed. Some recommendations are implemented even before the report is completed, others are accepted but not acted on, and still others are opposed. Not infrequently, another audit by GAO six months or even years later will reveal that the problems identified earlier remain. In such cases unless a congressional committee demonstrates an interest through the oversight or appropriations process, there is little likelihood of action. However, for the most part, there *is* action. A GAO audit or the imminence of one generally causes agency management to address problems that require attention.

Agencies often claim that the problem was identified and on the way to solution before the GAO audit. This may be so in some instances, but GAO is the catalyst if not always the complete cause of action. The plain fact is that agency managers do not relish being pilloried. GAO reports are not only sent to the agencies, they are made public. The national media find them a great source of news, and reporters do not evidence any reluctance to question managers sharply about waste and other indications of "misdeeds" and "no deeds."

GAO has another important oversight role. The Congressional Budget and Impoundment Control Act of 1974 specifically charged GAO with assisting congressional committees in developing legislative objectives and the methods for evaluating and reporting program performance. The 1974 act also calls on GAO to help committees of Congress analyze and assess program reviews and evaluation studies made by federal agencies. Taken together, these and related requirements placed on GAO to help develop data and information systems for the Congress indicate a growing interest by the Congress in improving its oversight performance. Chapter 8 includes proposals made by GAO to help Congress do a better job of holding agencies accountable.

State Legislative Audit Agencies

Only eight states had legislative auditors or audit agencies in 1951. Now most states have them. The increase reflects a growing concern that review of performance of administrative agencies is not done adequately in normal legislative and appropriations processes.

Generally, legislative audit agencies serve the whole legislature, not just one house. They have professional staffs, largely with accounting backgrounds, since most such agencies started out by concentrating on financial audits. Some have added staff with diversified backgrounds to give increased emphasis to the review of policy and program effectiveness, and to the use of more sophisticated tools in doing so.[31]

A few states have established agencies whose primary focus is the evaluation of program effectiveness. They are governed by joint nonpartisan legislative commissions. Their staffs are multidisciplinary. They use complex analytical techniques and their products are formal reports sent to the legislature and released to the public. New York's Legislative Expenditure Review Commission, created in 1969, was the first such organization. Another is the Illinois Economic and Fiscal Commission. Similar organizations have been established in several other states.

NONSTATUTORY INFORMAL OVERSIGHT

Administrative agencies are held accountable and influenced by legislative bodies and their individual members and staff through a variety of nonstatutory methods. These include informal understandings, personal contacts, statements and questions during hearings and on the floor, and committee reports.

Informal Understandings

When influential legislative members are so inclined, committees and agencies reach informal understandings on such matters as how laws will be interpreted, how soon they will be implemented, agency reorganizations, changes in agency priorities and procedures, how much preparatory work can and should be done by the agency in anticipation of laws being enacted, the extent to which the agency may reprogram funds, and the launching of experimental or pilot programs. These understandings may be achieved through discussions or correspondence between agency officials and the subcommittee or committee chairman or key committee staff. While such agreements are not legally binding, agency executives consider themselves accountable for their execution in letter and spirit. To do otherwise would destroy the trust and confidence needed for an effective legislative-executive relationship.

Personal Contacts

It is quite common for members of legislative or appropriations committees or their principal staff to hold agencies accountable by questioning their policies and performance and advocating changes. Nonofficial personal discussions frequently clarify and resolve differences, create compromises, and otherwise assure the legislative body that the laws are being executed in a manner acceptable to the legislators.

Exchanges on the floor between the sponsors of legislation and other members, as well as questions during committee hearings, are often used to resolve or create ambiguities in the law, to establish legislative intent, and to criticize or praise the policies and practices followed by an agency in executing the laws. In these and related ways individual members of the legislative body are involved in the process of holding agencies accountable for carrying out the law as they intend.

Committee Reports

Committees frequently exercise control over agencies by including instructions and expectations in the reports accompanying bills they recommend. Such direction and guidance may appear in reports by House, Senate, and conference committees. While these are not statutory requirements, they provide a record of legislative intent that is quite clear. Here are some excerpts that are considered typical.

(a) The committee clearly intends that the matter be reconsidered after some experience has been gained under the new program.

(b) It is intended that the Secretary administer these requirements in a manner which gives * * * a reasonable benefit of the doubt in marginal cases.

(c) With respect to the meaning of the term * * * the conferees intend the results reached in * * *. The term is not to be interpeted as including * * *.

(d) By "an agency" the conferees intend to include criminal law enforcement authorities as well as other agencies.

(e) The committee welcomes and encourages this approach * * *.

(f) The committee wishes to make clear that the Special Commission shall only consider the valuation placed on these claims as the value of the property at the time of its loss or destruction.

(g) It is contemplated that the area limits would be regularly updated * * *.

(h) * * * the committee does urge * * * to move forward with accelerated programs under existing authority.

(i) The committee expects these agencies to function as * * *.

(j) The committee would approve and encourage these sales * * *.

(k) The committee would view with strong disfavor regulations abrogating the local decision-making power.

(l) The committee intends for the Secretary to promote * * *.

(m) The committee believes strongly that two-year controls * * *.

(n) The committee clearly expects that when the Secretary has substantial reason to believe that a requirement of the bill will not be fulfilled, he will disapprove the pending application, at least partially, until the problem is solved.

(o) The Conferees wish to clarify the interpretation of the language contained in subsection (b) * * *. Accordingly, * * * the Secretary should distinguish and exclude those * * *.

(p) Your committee expects the * * * rules to establish reasonable time limits within which decisions must be reached.

(q) * * * it is the committee's intent that the * * * should not intrude.

(r) While the committee is generally pleased with the performance of * * * in its conduct of programs relating to * * *, it feels that many * * * have not received sufficient evaluation and technical expertise from * * * in order to ensure that their operations are responsive * * *.[32]

Administrators are inclined to view such "advisories" as *requirements*, knowing full well that they can be very important in future oversight by the legislature and the judiciary. To illustrate, an Air Force General who appeared to have disregarded a direction in a committee report suffered the full fury and wrath of the committee chairman at a subsequent hearing where he sought to justify his position. "Your motive was to deceive Congress. . . . Do you think we should sit here and give one ounce of credibility to the garbage you have given to the committee?"[33] thundered the chairman. The fact that certain guidance in a committee report represents the means for gaining support for a bill from only one additional member of the committee in no way diminishes its significance.

THE IRAN-CONTRA AFFAIR

The investigation of the Iran-Contra affair was one of the most important and widest conducted by Congress in recent decades. It reached into many parts of the executive branch (Executive Office of the President, Departments of State and Defense, Central Intelligence Agency [CIA], etc.), commercial activities in the United States, events in foreign nations, and activities of foreign governments. As an oversight investigation by the Congress, it was unique in many respects. It was the first joint investigation conducted by two separate committees, one of the House (Select Committee to Investigate Covert Arms Transactions with Iran) and one of the Senate (Select Committee on Secret Military Assistance to Iran and the Nicaraguan Opposition). It was the first time joint hearings were held by two such committees; and "the first time that committees of the House and Senate had ever submitted a combined report to their respective Chambers—including the names and views of members of both Chambers."[34]

There was a remarkable bipartisan and bichamber cooperation in organizing and conducting the investigation. The chairmen, Senate committee vice chairman, House committee ranking minority member, and members of the committees were deeply involved in determining the lines of inquiry, directing staff in obtaining documents and developing evidence, choosing witnesses for deposition or public testimony, and preparing questions for witnesses. Investigative teams consisted of both committee staff members. The two committees divided primary responsibility for potential witnesses. Thus, Vice Admiral John H. Poindexter, National Security Advisor, was designated a "Senate witness," which meant that Senate committee members and staff had the primary (but not exclusive) role for preliminary preparations and that Senate counsel took the lead in examining him at the public hearings. The House committee had primary responsibility for Lt. Col. Oliver L. North, a member of the National Security Council (NSC) staff.[35]

The investigation began in January 1987, and continued through October. Over 300,000 documents were examined and more than 500 interviews were conducted and depositions taken. Public participation in this accountability process was achieved through open hearings where facts that had been withheld and concealed for over two years were revealed. The joint public hearings were conducted between May 5 and August 3, 1987. For 40 days, testimony was heard in public from 28 witnesses. Four witnesses testified in four days of closed hearings. During the public hearings, 1,092 exhibits were presented.[36]

The remainder of this section dealing with the facts and accountability aspects of the Iran-Contra affair are based entirely on the *Report of the Congressional Committees Investigating the Iran-Contra Affair.*[37]

The investigation had its origins in a November 3, 1986 issue of *Al-Shiran*, a weekly newspaper published in Lebanon, that reported the United States had sold arms secretly to Iran. Later reports asserted that the sales were made to win the release of American hostages in Lebanon. (Just as many Americans remained hostage after Iran received the arms; three were freed and three more were taken.) Initial denials by the Reagan administration were reversed on November 25 when Attorney General Edwin Meese also announced at a White House briefing that proceeds from the Iran arms sales had been "diverted" to the Nicaraguan resistance *at a time when U.S. military aid to the Contras was prohibited.* This raised serious questions about the adherence of the administration to the constitutional processes of government and the rule of law.

In cutting off all funds, after vigorous debate, for the Contras' military and paramilitary operations Congress was exercising its constitutional power over appropriations. The bill, with this restriction, commonly referred to as the Boland amendment, was signed into law by the president on October 12, 1984. At the same time, the president told his National Security Advisor to find a way to keep the Contras' "body and soul together." Based on this charge, staff of the National Security Council (a White House advisory body) became an operational entity that secretly ran the Contra assistance effort and later the Iran initiative. Lt. Col. Oliver L. North was placed in charge of both operations.

To support the Contras, funds totaling over $35 million were raised secretly in 1984 and 1985 by the president, the NSC advisor, and other NSC staff from foreign governments and private sources. North's Contra support operation was given logistical and tactical support by Central Intelligence Agency, State, and Defense personnel. With the help of former CIA Director William Casey, a private "Enterprise" was created by North to deliver specific military and related support to the Contras. At the same time, administration officials were telling congressional oversight committees in public and secret testimony that the administration was not "soliciting and/or encouraging" other countries to give funds to the Contras, nor was it coordinating military support to the Contras, because the Boland amendment prohibited such activities.

"These covert actions directed by North were not approved by the President in writing as required. Congress was not notified about it as required. And the funds to support it were never accounted for. The operations functioned without any of the accountability required of government activities. It was an evasion of the Constitution's most basic check on executive action—the power of the Congress to grant or deny funding for Government programs."[38]

In the summer of 1985, over the repeated opposition of the secretaries of State and Defense, the president approved a proposal for the sale of arms to Iran to improve relations with Iran and gain release of the American hostages. The secretaries had called the proposal a straight arms-for-hostage deal with a government officially designated by the United States as a supporter of international terrorism. They argued that it would violate the Arms Export Control Act and the U.S. arms embargo against Iran that was imposed in 1979 when U.S. embassy employees in Tehran were taken hostage. In fact, written presidential approval for some arms shipments did justify the sales solely on the basis of obtaining return of the American hostages.

North saw in these sales to Iran the opportunity to generate funds that could be diverted for the Contras. "According to North, CIA Director Casey saw the 'diversion' as part of a more grandiose plan to use the Enterprise as a 'stand alone,' 'off-the-shelf,' covert capacity that would act throughout the world while evading Congressional review. To Casey, Poindexter, and North, the diversion was an integral part of selling arms to Iran and just one of the intended uses of the proceeds."[39]

In the weeks that followed the first disclosure on November 3, 1986, of the Iran arms sales, the president, Poindexter, Casey, and Robert McFarlane (Poindexter's predecessor as National Security Advisor) all told false stories; North rewrote NSC staff chronologies with McFarlane's help; Poindexter and North separately shredded and altered many documents; North's secretary, with North's knowledge, removed classified documents from the White House. The fact-finding inquiry conducted by Attorney General Meese at the direction of the president that provided the basis for the attorney general's White House briefing on November 25, 1986, departed from standard investigative techniques. Fundamental processes of governance had been disregarded; the rule of law was subverted; and a cover-up was in process.

"The common ingredients of the Iran and Contra policies were secrecy, deception, and disdain for the law. . . . The United States Constitution specifies the process by which laws and policy are to be made and executed. Constitutional process is the essence of our democracy and our democratic form of government is the basis of our strength. Time and again we have learned that a flawed process leads to bad results, and that a lawless process leads to worse."[40]

This unprecedented joint investigation in the first session of the 100th Congress demonstrated the enormous capacity and power of Congress to hold the chief executive and his appointees accountable. As this is written, during the second session of the 100th Congress, various legislative proposals are being considered to reduce the possibility of a similar breakdown in our constitutional processes in the future.

OTHER CONSIDERATIONS

Despite its obvious importance, oversight does not enjoy a high priority among legislators. Unless it reveals a scandalous situation, the work is generally considered dull, with the potential to be troublesome politically. Oversight can lead to changes that powerful interests oppose, or even raise questions about the legislator's own previous work on the committee. For elected officials the incentives favor looking ahead, not back. Response to current concerns of individual constituents and work on legislation desired by influential groups have more direct bearing on future elections—and political survival is paramount.

Coupled with this marginal motivation for personal involvement in oversight is the growing difficulty in enacting legislation. Consensus has been harder to achieve as single-issue partisans have been unwilling to compromise, and differences have been fought over with greater tenacity. The higher demands on time of members operating in this legislative jungle, plus an enormous increase in constituent service, have resulted since World War II in a fivefold growth in number of employees in the House and Senate.

Consequently, it is increasingly common that professional staff members under the aegis of a committee or subcommittee fill some of the gap created by more requirements for oversight and members' own lack of time for personal participation. Often young, almost always well-educated, bright, and highly motivated, many professional staff members have been heavily involved in overseeing the bureaucracy. While their activities overall are in accord with the members' general views, there is some uneasiness in Congress and the agencies about the extent to which their personal values and priorities, rather than those of the members, influence program administrators on many specific questions that arise in the course of oversight.

The range of means available for legislative oversight is formidable. The very fact that means exist and can be brought to bear on the bureaucracy is in itself a powerful deterrent to wrongdoing. Many instances can be cited where this enormous capacity has been used effectively. For positive results over a sustained period, the work of the Senate Committee to Investigate the National Defense Program during World War II, chaired by then Senator Harry Truman, is considered a classic. The Committee's motto was "There is no substitute for a fact."[41] In seeking an effective execution of laws, the Committee was instrumental in prodding the military departments and other wartime agencies to make changes that improved our fighting capacity, reduced delays in production of war materiel, and saved billions of dollars.

Numerous proposals have been made for improving legislative oversight. Former Comptroller General Elmer Staats, on the occasion of completing his 15-year term, expressed the view that Congress could improve its oversight by being "more specific and realistic when establishing goals and expectations for policies, programs, and administrative reforms," and by focusing "more of its analysis, debate, and actions on broad policy areas ... with a much longer time horizon in mind."[42] This idea and others are described in Chapter 8.

NOTES

1. 60 Stat. 132 Sec. 136 (1946).
2. 82 Stat. 1098 (1968).
3. 84 Stat. 1140 (1970).
4. 88 Stat. 297 (1974).
5. 60 Stat. 832 Sect. 136. In addition, Rule X, Clause 2 and Clause 4, of the House of Representatives provides more specific instructions.
6. Report of the U.S. General Accounting Office, RCED–87–137, September 25, 1987, p. 2.

7. Report of the U.S. General Accounting Office, AFMD–88–12, February 24, 1988, p. 1.

8. The Washington *Post*, October 16, 1987, p. A–21.

9. U.S., Congress, House, Subcommittee on Oversight of the House Committee on Energy and Foreign Commerce, *Report on Adverse Actions Against Professional Members at the Federal Power Commission*, 95th Cong., 1st sess., 1977.

10. U.S., Congress, House, Subcommittee on Manpower and Civil Service of the Committee on Post Office and Civil Service, *Final Report on Violations and Abuse of Merit Principles in Federal Employment*, 94th Cong., 2d sess., 1976.

11. U.S., Congress, Senate, Committee on Finance, *Report on Medicare-Medicaid Anti Fraud and Abuse*, 95th Cong., 1st sess., 1977.

12. U.S., Congress, Senate, Subcommittee on Nuclear Regulation of the Committee on Environment and Public Works, *Staff Study on Nuclear Accident and Recovery at Three Mile Island*, 96th Cong., 2d sess., 1980.

13. U.S., Congress, House, Hearing Before the Subcommittee on Civil and Constitutional Rights of the Committee on the Judiciary, *FBI Counter Intelligence Programs*, November 20, 1970, 91st Cong., 2d sess.; U.S., Congress, House, Hearings Before the Subcommittee on Courts, Civil Liberties, and the Administration of Justice of the Committee on the Judiciary, *Wiretapping and Electronic Surveillance*, April 24, 26, 29, 1974, 93rd Cong., 2d sess.; U.S., Congress, House, Hearings Before the Subcommittee on Civil and Constitutional Rights of the Committee on the Judiciary, *FBI Oversight*, February 27, 1975, 94th Cong., 1st sess.; U.S., Congress, Senate, Hearings Before the Select Committee to Study Governmental Operations on U.S. Intelligence Agencies and Activities, *Federal Bureau of Investigation*, November 18, 19, December 2, 3, 9–11, 1975, 94th Cong., 1st sess.

14. U.S., Congress, Senate, Committee on Finance, *Report on Medicare-Medicaid Anti Fraud and Abuse*, 95th Cong., 1st sess., 1977.

15. "Interpretation of the ABM Treaty," statement by Senator Sam Nunn, *Congressional Record*, March 11, 1987, pp. S–2967–68.

16. "Statement by Former Secretaries of Defense on the ABM Treaty," *Congressional Record*, March 13, 1987, p. S–3173.

17. Report of the U.S. General Accounting Office, RCED–87–153, July 24, 1987, pp. 2–3.

18. U.S., Congress, House, *Oversight Plans of the Committees of the United States House of Representatives*, 95th Cong., 1st sess., 1977, H. Rept. 95–43, p. 4.

19. U.S., Congress, Senate, Hearings Before the Committee on Foreign Relations on the nomination of Alexander Haig, January 9, 10, 12, 13, 14, 1981, 97th Cong., 1st sess.

20. U.S., Congress, Senate, Hearings Before the Committee on Agriculture, Nutrition, and Forestry on the nomination of John B. Crowell, March 31, 1981, 97th Cong., 1st sess.

21. U.S., Congress, Senate, Hearings Before the Committee on Commerce, Science, and Transportation on the nomination of Andrew Lewis, January 7, 1981, 97th Cong., 1st sess.

22. U.S., Congress, Senate, Hearings Before the Committee on Energy and Natural Resources on the nomination of James Watt, January 7–8, 1981, 97th Cong., 1st sess.

23. The Washington *Post*, May 6, 1983, p. A–3.

24. News Release, Senate Committee on Agriculture, Nutrition, and Forestry, November 19, 1987.

25. U.S., Congress, Senate, Hearings Before the Committee on Governmental Affairs on the nomination of David Stockman, January 8, 1981, 97th Cong., 1st sess.

26. U.S., Congress, Senate, *Congressional Record*, June 13, 1973, p. S–19497, 93rd Cong., 1st sess.

27. Ibid., p. S–19505.

28. U.S., Congress, Senate, *Congressional Record*, May 24, 1976, p. S–7851, 94th Cong., 2d sess.

29. U.S., Congress, Legislative Reorganization Act of 1970, Sect. 236, 91st Cong., 2d sess.

30. Frederick C. Mosher, *The GAO* (Boulder: Westview Press, 1979), pp. 281–85.

31. Edgar G. Crane, *Legislative Review of Government Programs* (New York: Praeger, 1977), pp. 24–37.

32. U.S., Congress, Senate, Committee on Government Operations, *Congressional Oversight*, 94th Cong., 2d sess., July 1976, Committee Print, prepared by Congressional Research Service, U.S. Library of Congress, pp. 62–63.

33. U.S., Congress, Senate, Defense Appropriations Subcommittee, *Hearings on Advanced Logistics Systems*, Part VIII, 95th Cong., 1st sess., 1977.

34. *Report of the Congressional Committees Investigating the Iran-Contra Affair*, 100th Cong., S. Rept. No. 100–216, H. Rept. No. 100–433, November 1987, p. 884.

35. Ibid., pp. 684–85.

36. Ibid., pp. 685–86.

37. Ibid., pp. xv, xvi, 3–22.

38. Ibid., pp. 4–5.

39. Ibid., p. 8.

40. Ibid., p. 11.

41. Harry S. Truman, *Memoirs by Harry S. Truman* (Garden City: Doubleday, 1955), pp. 167–86.

42. Presentation by Elmer B. Staats at The Brookings Institution Seminar on Improving the Accountability and Performance of Government, Washington, D.C., May 6, 1981.

5

Citizen Participation

in the Accountability

Processes

Large numbers of individual citizens and many interest groups throughout the United States are, justifiably or not, at the very least uncertain about the performance of government bureaucracies, and more often they view them as unresponsive, ineffective, and to some extent unnecessary. Dissatisfaction with the cost and performance of governments has led to a variety of approaches for citizen participation in the work of government bureaucracies. Some types of participation have been initiated by citizens; others have been the result of deliberate action by the legislative or executive branch. The former evidences grass-roots vitality in this constitutional democracy; the latter underscores a concern for hearing from those whose presence might otherwise not be felt.

Citizen involvement in administrative processes serves three purposes that relate directly to accountability: first, it lets public administrators know how citizens perceive the performance of an organization; second, it provides participating citizens with information that can help them make judgments as to what that part of government can and should do; and third, it leads to better government and increased confidence in it.

Citizen participation may be a short-term special activity or more continuing and permanent. Organizing a single effort and obtaining useful results are commonplace. The goal is clear. Busy and able citizens interested in the subject are often willing to serve temporarily on special committees or similar bodies; and public administrators find it quite easy to provide essential information and staff support for an effort that will be completed in a week, a month, or even six months. It is far more difficult to institutionalize citizen participation as an effective permanent mechanism concerned with the continuing operations of government and, consequently, few such permanent mechanisms exist.

Establishing permanent citizen-participation mechanisms requires some reconciliation of natural points of conflict between agency responsibilities and interests of citizens. In implementing laws, public administrators try to satisfy the broad public interest with an eye to long-term needs. Individual citizens often bring a narrower view of the problem and an interpretation of the public interest in a shorter time frame. On the other hand, the cumulative insights of a citizen group can add significant depth and breadth to an understanding of the needs of the citizenry and to the consideration of alternatives.

An operational problem of no minor importance has to do with time: the great majority of citizens are not available during the regular working hours of government. This problem has become more acute in recent years as women who used to serve as volunteers on numerous citizen committees have accepted full-time employment outside the home. Achieving citizen participation in a permanent mechanism therefore requires sensitive accommodations in scheduling meetings, arranging for continuing staff support, and providing necessary information to the citizens involved.

For both ad hoc and permanent citizen participation, the choice is between using an existing mechanism and creating a special one. There are many existing mechanisms for obtaining citizen participation: these include public hearings, opinion polls, and citizen groups established for a variety of purposes. Periodic public hearings can be conducted by administrators on difficult or controversial policies and problems; polls on relevant public issues can be taken by professional public-opinion surveyors; and many citizen groups already organized to serve different needs can often be used to obtain citizen input on a particular subject. A brief look at each of these follows.

PUBLIC HEARINGS

Valuable advice on existing and proposed policies and priorities is obtained from citizens by some agencies through public hearings. Former Judge Harold Leventhal of the U.S. Court of Appeals, District of Columbia, testified that citizen groups have "identified issues and caused agencies and courts to look squarely at problems that would otherwise have been swept aside and passed unnoticed."[1] Public hearings provide a practical means for letting citizens know that administrators are listening, for enabling citizens to express their views directly to decision makers, and for promoting citizen involvement in the administrative process that can result in increased accountability.

To be reasonably effective, public hearings must be announced sufficiently in advance not only to make it possible for citizens to formulate their own ideas and to plan for attendance, but also to allow time for citizens to discuss the issues among themselves and for those with common points of view to make joint and complementary presentations. Statements by unorganized and organized citizens can be more sharply focused when the announcements of public hearings define the purposes of the hearings as precisely as possible. Public hearings are apt to be better attended if the locations, dates, and times of the hearings are most convenient for those whose views are sought.

The cost of participating has effectively prevented concerned citizens from involvement in hearings before regulatory agencies, or in informal pre-hearing proceedings, thereby depriving decision makers of significant competing views and a wider range of considerations. During the 1970s a number of federal agencies including the Federal Trade Commission (FTC), Environmental Protection Agency (EPA), National Highway Transportation Safety Administration (NHSTA), and the Department of Energy (DOE) began "intervenor funding"—direct payment to needy citizen groups to meet the expenses of participating and thus to permit them to redress somewhat the advocacy and information imbalance in public hearings previously dominated by regulated industries.

Specific statutory authorizations to use appropriated funds for this purpose have been given to a few regulatory agencies.[2] In addition, the U.S. comptroller general has ruled that many other regulatory agencies have inherent authority to use appropriated funds to pay reasonable fees of attorneys and expert witnesses and other costs of needy intervenors in the absence of specific statutory prohibitions and provided their participation could "reasonably be expected to contribute substantially to a full and fair determination."[3]

Accountability through the hearing process becomes more apparent when there are reports to the public as a whole, or at least to those citizens who participated, on decisions made after the hearing. Citizens are inclined to participate again and to encourage others to do so if there is evidence that hearings were held in good faith, not merely for the sake of appearances.

POLLS

Public attitudes are important in all governments, but particularly in democratic societies. They reflect expectations stemming from promises included in public policy and perceptions of performance in fulfilling those promises—the citizens' baseline for accountability.

Opinion collectors from large and small organizations are constantly sampling public views on a wide range of subjects. Information obtained can be helpful to administrators as they make policies and decide on priorities. Administrators who watch and use polls are more concerned with trends in attitudes than with percentages at one point in time. Changes in attitudes about a government organization can be influenced by public administrators—by their decisions, their performance, their openness, and in the final analysis by their responsiveness to what is generally accepted as the public interest.

Conducting opinion surveys and using the data require considerable expertise. The phrasing of questions and the contexts in which they are asked can affect the answers. Survey data can confuse and deceive. Therefore, administrators who use opinion polls, whether the data were prepared for other purposes or specially designed for them, must consider carefully the relevance of the questions, the survey sample, and any other forces that could affect the results. Polls can be useful but they are not a substitute for the reasoned judgment of the public administrator. Executing laws calls for all sorts of difficult management decisions in environments where opinions may change.

ADVISORY COMMITTEES

Ideally, advisory committees serve in a completely objective and professional manner: clarifying the problems, identifying and evaluating relevant facts, considering alternatives, recommending action in the public interest, and then remaining available for further advice as the recommendations are considered by the administrator. However, advisory committees are not always established to offer objective advice. They may be created to help resolve conflicts between different groups. They may serve as a sounding board for new ideas. They may provide prestigious appointments for political supporters. Sometimes they simply provide a convenient means for rejecting or modifying a course of action that has powerful support. At other times they are used to build support for a policy initiative to which the executive is already committed.

A number of cities and counties have established citizen groups that advise the legislative body on policy issues *and* serve in an oversight role on the effective execution of policy. A unique type of citizen participation in the form of advisory committees was authorized for District of Columbia residents as part of its home rule legislation. Elected advisory neighborhood councils have been established in each neighborhood area where five percent or more of the registered voters petitioned that this be done. These councils advise the District of Columbia government on policy issues including plans for city services (streets, recreation, health, safety), zoning changes, and licenses of importance to their own neighborhoods. In doing so they provide judgments on how the government is performing in their neighborhoods.

Another unique approach to advisory committees is that followed in San Diego County, California. Each of the six major agencies in the government of this large metropolitan county has an advisory committee to clarify the relevant needs and views of the citizens. To assure in-depth impact, each agency advisory committee has established a family of advisory subcommittees that work with different parts of the agency. In all, about 700 citizens serve on various advisory committees, providing almost continuous organized citizen participation in the governing policies and processes of the county.

Whatever the purpose in establishing an advisory committee, the selection of its membership is critical to the final outcome. The administrator who is genuinely interested in obtaining expert advice from knowledgeable and responsible persons will strive for an advisory body whose combined membership has both expertise and balance on all major aspects of the issue. Representativeness may also be an important consideration. If the advisory committee can be seriously challenged on any of these grounds, the impact of its conclusions and recommendations will be greatly diminished; that, in turn, will diminish its credibility in subsequent accountability processes.

The *President's Private Sector Survey on Cost Control*, better known as the Grace Commission, achieved fewer cost-reducing changes than it might have because its reports appeared to have a strong antigovernment bias and lacked credibility in other respects. President Reagan established the Commission by Executive Order 12369 on June 30, 1982. It was charged with identifying opportunities for making the federal government more efficient and less costly. The chairman, J. Peter Grace, head of W. R. Grace and Company, recruited a 161-member executive committee from the top ranks of the nation's largest corporations; they, in turn, helped recruit another 2,000 volunteers from the private sector. These volunteers, organized in 36 task forces, studied 22 federal agencies and a number of crosscutting issues such as personnel, procurement, and data processing.

After 18 months' work, the Commission produced 47 reports containing 2,478 recommendations. The work of the Task Force on Personnel Management provides a classic example of how not to achieve change. While the federal personnel system needs to be improved, and some of the Commission's recommendations would have enjoyed wide support, the Task Force Report was subjected to devastating criticism.

"Critics charged that the estimates of cost saving were exaggerated and misleading; that the research, analysis, and recommendations were of mixed quality and in some cases inconsistent; and that a 'business bias' dominated the results (because a 'conflict of interest' occurred when members of some of the task forces had financial interests relating to the study's conclusions, for example, the privatization of Veterans' Administration hospitals). Critics have also charged that the commission's advice favoring more use of practices in the private sector (including contracting and user fees) indicated that the commission misunderstood the structure and purposes of the federal government. Furthermore, the commission's methodology has been questioned; critics have alleged that the process that the commission followed was overly secretive and hidden from congressional involvement. Finally, it has been argued that the commission greatly underestimated the costs, salaries, and benefits prevailing in the private sector and that by choosing to treat the entire federal establishment as one organization similar to large private firms rather than a cluster of many different types of departments and agencies, the commission made unfair and unreasonable comparisons between the federal government and the private sector."[4]

The Task Force ignored the overriding political reality that a political process created the civil service system, and therefore significant reforms of the system can be achieved only through that process. Unfortunately, the members and key staff of the authorization committee, in this case the House Post Office and Civil Service Committee, were kept in the dark by the Grace Commission about the issues being explored even though the Commission's work probably would result in proposals requiring legislative action. Chairman William Ford expressed unhappiness with this state of affairs in his opening statement at a hearing he conducted on May 24, 1983:

From the very outset of its inquiry, this subcommittee has encountered difficulty in prying even the most routine information from the survey's executives. The work of these people has been shrouded in secrecy, perhaps to the detriment of the many civic-minded corporate officials who served on the various task forces. For the record, I feel compelled to say that never in more than 18 years in Congress have I encountered such mystery concerning a presidential blue ribbon panel ostensibly pursuing legitimate objectives.[5]

Chairman Ford's news release on the Grace Commission report on personnel management also made secrecy an issue. "This report is a deceitful attempt to heap more discredit on federal workers by blatantly exaggerating their pay and benefits and by recklessly bending fact as far as proposed savings are concerned—statistical chicanery—in order to produce a document this distorted and biased, the need for secrecy was paramount."[6] The action about which Chairman Ford complained was not simply an oversight. Keeping the agenda and approach secret and locking out the committee and staff were deliberate.

Other organizations whose members have an important stake in the issues considered were treated in the same way. With one limited exception, those organizations too were locked out of the process. There was no consultation on the retirement issue with the National Association of Retired Federal Employees, which has 500,000 members, or the various unions that represent over 1.5 million federal employees. Federal employee unions also have a strong interest in other personnel management subjects explored by the Grace Commission, such as pay, health insurance, and contracting out; but they were not consulted on any of these topics. Only in the study of reduction-in-force did the task force on personnel management seek limited input from unions.

The Grace Commission may have doubted that organizations representing employees and retirees possessed any facts and insights in a wide-ranging study of the federal civil service; but there is no doubt that the leaders of these organizations disagreed. They intended to influence the action taken on the recommendations. They represent more than two million employees and retirees and possess effective means for communicating with their members. Excluding them during the process of finding facts and developing proposals invited suspicion and hostility. At best, it indicated a gross insensitivity to political realities; at worst, it projected an image of arrogance and disrespect for democratic decision making.

Achieving change through the political process depends greatly on the credibility of the reformers as well as the process. A central issue is whether the overall effort to bring about legislative changes is perceived by decision makers and those who may be affected by the recommendations as being in the public interest and conducted responsibly. Credibility depends heavily on positive answers to at least these questions: Are the objectives of the undertaking clear and in harmony with fundamental needs and values of society? Are those conducting the study professionally competent? Is the publicity initiated or stimulated by those in charge of the reform effort in keeping with the facts?

It seems to me that the credibility of the Grace Commission suffered in all three areas: there was confusion over objectives; there was a lack of first-rate performance in developing relevant data; and there was significant misinformation generated in promoting the recommendations. I discussed the basis for these conclusions in an essay published in 1985.[7]

Advisory committees perform best when they have clear charters that specify what is expected and by when. The chances of fulfilling their purposes are increased when those appointing them demonstrate continuing interest through periodic contacts to check on progress and problems. As for advisory committees that do not perform according to their charter and in the public interest, the cause of good government is served by abolishing them as soon as practicable. In other words, while advisory committees can help administrators and help hold them accountable, they too need to be held accountable.

"MAXIMUM FEASIBLE PARTICIPATION"

The Economic Opportunity Act of 1964,[8] centerpiece of President Lyndon Johnson's War on Poverty, advanced a revolutionary concept. The residents served by federally funded Community Action Programs, the poor and the uneducated, were to be given a significant voice in planning and operating these programs. Leaders of the administering agency, the Office of Economic Opportunity (OEO), interpreted the statute's requirement for "maximum feasible participation" as a mandate to train the powerless to use power. For many of these programs citizen participation turned into citizen governance—New England town-meeting style.

The Demonstration Cities and Metropolitan Development Act of 1966[9] administered by the Department of Housing and Urban Development (HUD) also adopted the concept of wide participation and expanded it to include "maximum opportunities for work and training" for those affected by the programs. The secretary of HUD characterized the concern for citizen participation thus: "in too many cities the customary institutions and processes of representative government seem sometimes unable to identify the serious problems of many citizens—as the citizens define them—and accordingly fail to enlist them in problem solving. In too many cities, citizens appear cut off from providing information and opinions to their representatives. In turn the people do not understand what government is doing to and for them . . . we have learned that if the poor are to become contributing citizens they must have the chance to work as well as to march, to speak, or to vote. They must be involved as laborers and contractors as we build and rebuild their homes. . . ."[10]

Not everyone was happy with these new developments in public policy and administration. Taxpayers saw money being wasted in some widely publicized failures caused by a lack of managerial experience and training in the governing community-action groups. Many local officials in general-purpose governments saw in the type of citizen participation fostered by OEO and HUD new centers of political power that would inevitably threaten the established governmental system and its leaders. After Johnson left office the opposition coalesced, OEO was abolished, and "maximum feasible participation" gave way to the more traditional methods of citizen involvement.

The Federal Water Pollution Control Act of 1972[11] illustrates the change in direction. Section 101e makes clear that public participation in the implementation of the law is desirable. The Environmental Protection Agency issued rules that strongly encouraged state and local governments to invite and facilitate citizen participation as *plans were developed* for federally financed projects. Specifically, they were urged to consult with interested persons through workshops and advisory groups, provide them with current relevant information, and notify them of public hearings—a far cry from having representatives of affected citizens serving as a governing body.

THE OMBUDSMAN

In almost every form of citizen participation that leads to holding bureaucracies accountable, citizen initiative is a vital factor. Some governments make it easy for citizens to get information about what is being done on a particular problem. In others, the behavior of the bureaucracy practically convinces citizens that there is a conspiracy to prevent the right official from learning about the problem. Citizens complain that it's almost impossible to find out whom to contact on a problem: of interminable delays in getting through on the telephones, the need for endless repetition of the reason for calling, and infinite transfers to other offices where the lines are invariably busy. Personal visits are often equally unproductive and distressing, as the citizen is shunted from one office to another, and all the while having to restate the problem.

To help deal with this situation, a number of jurisdictions have created centralized points of contact for citizens. These offices, whose principal role is to respond correctly and quickly to citizen inquiries about the office or official to contact on a problem, have been established by the national government in major cities throughout the country, and by some state and local governments. A relatively small number of central complaint offices go further by helping citizens solve their problems.

One good example is Denver's Office of Citizen Response (OCR), a unit of the Agency for Human Rights and Community Relations. It was established by the city council and mayor in 1974 to serve the city's residents, who number about 500,000, a third of them minority-group members. Citizens of Denver bring to OCR's attention each month an average of 150 requests for information and 75 complaints. With a comprehensive directory of city units and functions, and a person capable of asking sufficiently pointed questions to be reasonably certain that the referral will be made to the proper place, OCR gives the citizen the telephone number and, in many cases, the name of the person who should be contacted. If it appears that the citizen may have difficulty in communicating because of a language problem, OCR contacts the official about the problem and advises the citizen of the result.

As for complaints, the Denver office deals with many simple and some difficult situations, all of which have frustrated the citizen by the time the issue comes to OCR. The citizen may have complained to the wrong agency and failed to receive a reply, or may have contacted the proper agency, only to be turned down or left suspended without action. OCR follows up and encourages the agency concerned to explore the problem further to try to find some means to assist the citizen. By causing the agency official to look at the problem more intensely, OCR's efforts frequently bring some positive action, even though the citizen may not receive everything requested. Through OCR, citizens with complaints learn about the processes within the agencies and who to contact directly if they have similar problems in the future.

OCR is not authorized to investigate any agency of government, nor may it issue subpoenas or direct that specific action be taken. If, however, the director of OCR believes that an agency is not treating a citizen the way it should, as a last resort the problem may be referred to the mayor. The fact that this can be done and has occurred is in itself a good incentive for serious and early consideration of citizen complaints. Monthly and quarterly reports help. They keep the mayor and city council informed about OCR's activities and the kinds and numbers of complaints for each department.

OCR is an effective operation because of the continuing interest of elected officials, determined efforts to make and keep the public aware of its role, and constructive liaison established with city agencies. In addition, OCR has initiated useful working relations with Colorado's Citizens' Advocate Office, the federal government's information center in Denver, and numerous nongovernmental service agencies so that citizens in that metropolitan area can be guided to any of these organizations when they might be helpful in resolving problems.

INVESTIGATIVE REPORTING

Good investigative reporting is the result of long and tedious work to obtain all the facts necessary to reveal an unacceptable situation. Quite unlike a reporter who relates what is readily observable and available, an investigative reporter does an in-depth study to find the obscure and sometimes hidden information that tells the real story of what happened and why.

Governments—national, state, and local—are prime targets for investigative reporters. With millions of employees and billions of dollars in expenditures, the temptations and opportunities for all manner of corruption and mismanagement are very great. The reporter may be stimulated to pursue a subject by a word here, an article there, a series of seemingly unconnected events—almost anything can trigger a suspicion in the mind of an investigative reporter (or the editor). Then the basic underlying question—Why?— is asked, and a reporter starts down a trail that might lead to the exposure of wrongdoing and ultimately to corrective action. Occasionally, a reporter's incompetence or unbridled ambition leads to false charges.

Excellent investigative reporters are imaginative, tenacious, and systematic. They are highly motivated and usually have strong feelings about government officials acting in the public interest. They keep voluminous files of information and sources of information. Their research is carefully documented, checked, and cross-checked. Inaccurate statements and libelous comments are not tolerated by responsible news organizations.

Today's investigative reporters have the advantage of the computer, both as a source of information and as a means of verification. Even today, though, all the background facts and figures have not been classified and computerized, and investigative reporters still spend long hours poring over individual transactions recorded in the archives of federal and state agencies, city halls, and courthouses. Despite freedom-of-information laws, some relevant records are hidden, unintentionally or otherwise, and somehow they must be found. No lead is ignored. Interviews are crucial, but rarely can notebooks or tape recorders be used—they inhibit the source. A good memory is essential, as is the self-discipline to make an accurate record immediately after the interview.

Investigative reporters are somewhat like detectives. They must ferret out every clue, assemble a mass of information into a logical order, reach a conclusion, and be able to prove their thesis beyond a reasonable doubt. Although the bottom line of the investigative reporters' work might be the same as the results of an FBI investigation or an agency's own internal-audit team, their methods of operation are not quite the same. Reporters have no official standing. No one is *required* to talk to them, to answer their questions, to produce documents for their perusal. In truth, their only credential, the press pass, more often intimidates people—few want to risk seeing in a newspaper their own names linked to some important deficiency in government. Thus the art of persuasion comes into play as reporters search for a chance to look at some evidence, get a copy of a document, or discover the name of a possible informant.

Investigative reporters also work for radio and television, and their work is important and has produced results. The number of programs produced are small but increasing. Cost is a serious limiting factor. Whereas one newspaper reporter can work alone, a television reporter needs the backup of camera crews, technicians, lighting—and hopes for a photogenic subject.

Watergate is probably the most famous example of investigative reporting. Almost equally famous were the reports of the MyLai massacre and illegal actions of the Central Intelligence Agency. There have been many other stories that were more or less sensational in their time. Not every story results in immediate action but each fulfills one of the most important functions of the news media: to keep the public informed, thereby increasing the possibilities that necessary action will be taken.

The Des Moines *Register and Tribune* published a series of articles on corruption in the administration of the Packers and Stockyard Act and the inspection of grain for export. Shortly thereafter, Congress passed corrective legislation creating a new federal grain-inspection service, tightening procedures for weighing, and establishing a more restrictive conflict-of-interest standard.[12]

William Sherman of the New York *Daily News* investigated fraud and abuse in New York's medical assistance program. The articles led to government investigations that in turn led to several indictments and the recovery of $1 million in fraudulent billings.[13]

A reporter in Detroit uncovered the story of a police inspector who was part owner of a towing firm that profited from the sale of falsely designated abandoned cars. The abandoned-auto section of the police department has now been reorganized and there are fewer official car thefts in Detroit.[14]

Clark Mollenhoff, considered by many as the finest investigative reporter in the latter half of the twentieth century, was deeply concerned about increasing public disillusionment with the press. He said, "It is this continuing and growing danger of government action encroaching upon the free press that makes it essential for the press to establish sound investigative techniques and standards of fair play that are consistently applied without political partisanship or bias." While continuing to advocate "aggressive policing of the action of government agencies" by the press, he also urged that investigative reporters follow "Seven Basic Rules."

Rule One: Avoid political partisanship.

Rule Two: In seeking facts and answers make a conscientious and determined effort to be equally aggressive whether the public officials are men you admire or distrust.

Rule Three: Know your subject, whether it is a problem of city, county, state or federal government, or whether it involves big labor or big business.

Rule Four: Don't exaggerate or distort the facts or the law.

Rule Five: Deal straight across the board with your sources and investigation subjects alike.

Rule Six: Do not violate the law unless you are prepared to take the consequences.

Rule Seven: Use direct evidence when writing a story that reflects adversely upon anyone and give that person an opportunity for a full response to the question raised.[15]

Investigative reporters have been instrumental in holding public officials accountable. "The press can't save society, but it can provoke others to take action."[16] The impact on accountability is even greater. It goes beyond the individual case; it does so by helping to keep citizens continually interested in how well the bureaucracy is serving the public interest.

SPECIAL INTEREST GROUPS

Special interest groups are of two basic types. "Economic" groups are organized to represent and further the economic interests of individuals and organizations engaged in agriculture, labor, business, and the professions. "Cause" groups are organized to represent individuals and groups who are committed to single issues such as environmental protection, civil rights, consumer protection, right to bear arms, and abortion rights (or opposition to them). For our purposes, they are all considered special interest groups, and as such they seek to influence the content of public policy and its execution.

These groups can be, and often are, viewed in diametrically opposite ways. Since they do not seek to achieve political legitimacy and accountability by capturing public office, as does a political party, their efforts to persuade public officials and candidates to adopt their ideas are seen by some as sinister and evil attempts to impose a minority position on the majority. On the other hand, the actions of interest groups provide evidence of the diversity in our society and the vitality in our democracy: majorities are merely temporary coalitions of minorities, and the public interest is often found in the compromises achieved among contesting special interests.

Alexis de Tocqueville observed in the early years of the Republic that we are a nation of "joiners"[17]—a nation of interest groups. That is no less true today. More than three million farmers are members of the American Farm Bureau Federation, and another half million divide their memberships between the National Farmers Union and the National Grange.

The American Federation of Labor-Congress of Industrial Organizations (AFL-CIO) is a 15-million member conglomerate of numerous affiliated unions which represent retail clerks, factory and construction workers, government employees, and many others. Separate labor organizations represent five million additional workers.

The Chamber of Commerce of the United States, the largest of the interest groups representing business, has more than five million individuals and forty thousand companies as members. Member corporations of the National Association of Manufacturers number 16,000. Other smaller but very influential business interest groups include the Business Roundtable and the Conference Board, whose memberships provide a roster of the biggest and most successful corporations in the country.

Associations of professionals engage in considerable career-development activities; but very often they are strong advocates on issues that affect their economic well-being. The largest include the National Education Association, with a membership of almost one million teachers and education administrators, the American Federation of Teachers (AFL-CIO) with 400,000 members, and the American Medical Association with 200,000 members. There are hundreds of other organizations with memberships in the thousands.

The giants of the "cause" groups are the American Association of Retired Persons, with more than 25 million members, the National Rifle Association, with two million members, the National Association for the Advancement of Colored People, with almost 500,000 members, the Sierra Club, with 150,000 supporters, and the American Civil Liberties Union, with over 100,000 members.

Among special interest groups with the same central concerns there are often sharp differences, particularly as concerns priorities and approach. Workers may organize an independent union rather than affiliate with the AFL-CIO; teachers may believe their interests are more compatible with the priorities of the American Federation of Teachers than with those of the National Education Association; business people may decide that the approach of the Textile Association of America is more in keeping with their views than that of the National Association of Manufacturers; and activist lawyers may find the attitudes in the National Lawyers Guild more hospitable to their interests than the American Bar Association. This fragmentation among organizations (and even within each organization) on specific issues further demonstrates the great diversity in our society.

For interest groups to be effective, they must lobby government officials. Lobbying is an effort to influence government action. Lobbyists must communicate with those who make the laws and those who execute them. To do so is to exercise a constitutional right guaranteed by the First Amendment: the right "to petition the government for a redress of grievances." Although lobbying is an inherent part of the democratic process, it has acquired a bad image because of the questionable practices of some lobbyists—for example, sophisticated and blatant bribery and intense pressure in favor of narrow special interests to the detriment of the larger public interest.

Laws determine what administrative agencies will do and, with few exceptions, agencies decide how, when, and where they will do it. During the lawmaking process, interest groups lobby to have their positions adopted on matters of substance, method, priorities, and timing. To the extent that they succeed through specific provisions in law or legislative background (or both), they have established a framework for holding accountable the administering agency. Expectations unfulfilled in the legislative process become the focus of lobbying attention at the implementation stage, with interest groups trying to persuade the agency to administer the law in ways that best meet their objectives.

The process of lobbying ranges from exerting raw pressure to simply furnishing relevant information. For elected officials, the former includes actions that can affect the future of the official, such as advertisements in the news media, grass-roots letter-writing drives on specific policies or programs, and substantial campaign assistance in the form of money and/or workers for the incumbent or a challenger. For agency officials, raw pressure by interest groups can take the form of withdrawing support for certain policies and programs for which support was avidly sought by the administration or the agency, and actively opposing rather than supporting the appropriations requests of the agency.

However, most successful lobbying is of a different nature. Providing technical expertise and factual information in an atmosphere of general helpfulness to resolve conflicting positions is often the most effective form of lobbying in both the legislative and executive branches.

A survey of 175 Washington, D.C. based interest groups—corporations, trade associations, unions, and other citizen organizations—revealed that all or almost all of them or their associated political action committees (PAC) used a wide range of techniques to influence both the Congress and executive-branch agencies. All but one or two testified at congressional committee hearings and contacted officials directly and informally. Better than 90 percent entered into coalitions with other groups in trying to achieve their policy objectives through legislation and executive action. Over 80 percent mounted grass-roots lobbying to influence policy-making in Congress or the agencies through such means as advertisements, "canned" editorials and news items, media events, press conferences, and letters from members to policymakers.

Unions, much more so than corporations, trade associations, and other citizen groups, sought to advance their policy objectives by engaging in public protests (90 percent), endorsing candidates for Congress and the presidency (95 percent), contributing work or personnel to political campaigns (70 percent), and publicizing voting records (90 percent).[18] Through these and related means, special interest groups sought not only to affect the content of laws but also to hold agencies accountable for administering laws as they would prefer.

Effective lobbying of executive bureaucracies begins with recognition of one overriding fact—agencies have a *clientele orientation*. That is, many agencies in national and state governments were established primarily to service specific groups. Farmers and farm problems are the concern of the United States Department of Agriculture and similar departments in the states; promoting and assisting business is the major reason for having the United States Department of Commerce; and all states have departments with similar responsibilities; to provide a focus on the problems of those who work for others, and those who *want* to work but cannot find jobs, is the responsibility of the United States Department of Labor and similar agencies at the state level.

Some agencies have a varied clientele, and none more so than the Department of Health and Human Services: millions of older citizens on social security, millions of low-income people receiving Medicaid, millions of aged and disabled benefiting from Medicare, millions of families helped by Aid to Families with Dependent Children, millions of blind persons receiving supplemental income, and millions more receiving other benefits, including grants for thousands of researchers in the biological and behavioral sciences.

When administrators want to change policies and programs, or develop new ones, they consult with the organizations that represent their clients, as well as with other organizations whose members would be affected by the proposals. This consultation takes place because agency administrators need to know with reasonable certainty how these groups will be affected, and how they will react. Agencies consult because they may need the groups' support within the executive branch or within the legislative body; if they cannot get their support, perhaps they can at least reduce the degree of opposition. Agencies consult because they often need the groups' expertise during planning and their cooperation during implementation.

Of course, should an agency be so politically insensitive as to *fail* to consult, lobbyists would not hesitate to offer their unsolicited advice, unless, as a matter of strategy, it was decided that the very failure to consult would itself be a valuable asset later in defeating or significantly modifying the agency's proposal.

Normally, special interest groups influence administrative agencies in a continuous process carried on at several levels. The top leadership of major interest groups and the head or deputy head of the agency meet from time to time to exchange perceptions on progress and problems of common concern. Key staff members of the interest groups and the agency have frequent contact, mainly to check facts and judgments on the effect of proposed or existing policies and practices. Subsequently, the groups and the agency consider individual problem cases and share selected reports and information on the actual workings of policies and program; the interest groups may express pleasure or dissatisfaction with the administration of the program and encourage changes and, ultimately, may take the unresolved issues to the chief executive or principal aides, the legislative body, the news media, or all of these. As a last resort, there are the courts.

"BETTER GOVERNMENT" INTEREST GROUPS

Citizen organizations dedicated broadly to "better government" have been labelled public interest groups. Two objectives are held in common by almost all of these organizations: broader citizen representation in the decision-making processes of government and more accountable government. On these grounds they can be characterized as "better government" interest groups, although they do not always agree on specific issues.

The growing importance of organizations seeking to counterbalance the influence that special interest groups have with government agencies is a phenomenon of the past three decades. They have assumed a public advocacy role, seeking and achieving participation in legislative and agency decision-making processes on a variety of issues where the interests of large numbers of citizens have not previously been expressed. Their efforts have resulted in federal courts redefining "legal standing" to permit intervention by such public advocacy organizations in certain agency proceedings from which they were previously excluded. In addition, as will be discussed later, the courts have overturned administrative decisions as a result of suits brought by these organizations.

Simultaneously, better government interest groups have pressed hard to have government agencies facilitate and institutionalize wider citizen participation in policy-making and administrative processes. As noted earlier, the cost of intervention is prohibitive for many citizens and groups; better government interest groups have, therefore, urged (with some success) that funds be appropriated for regulatory agencies to pay the expenses of needy intervenors. A few agencies have decided on their own to fund participation and also to provide in-house advocacy assistance.

A larger undertaking, to establish a national agency for consumer advocacy, was not successful, but it continues to be considered important. The proposed agency, without any regulatory responsibility, would represent consumer interests in the administrative proceedings of other agencies and in seeking judicial review of agency decisions. Better government interest groups argue that administrators will make better decisions when they have a broader range of relevant facts and views.

Wider public representation in agency decision-making processes is a new and still evolving means of increasing administrative accountability. Three organizations—Common Cause, Ralph Nader's Public Citizen groups, and the League of Women Voters—have been in the vanguard of campaigns to increase citizen participation in government decision making and to take other actions to make government more accountable.

Common Cause

Common Cause was founded in 1970 by John Gardner. Its concern from the beginning has been to make government more accessible, more responsive, and more accountable. As an independent, nonpartisan organization, it is oriented to issues rather than parties or candidates. Common Cause is not trying to reduce the power of any unit or level of government; rather, it seeks to make the power accountable. It holds that the greatest obstacles to accountable government are money and secrecy: the capacity of money to buy political outcomes, and the habit of doing the public's business behind closed doors. It has had remarkable success in securing legislation in both national and state governments in areas of campaign-financing reform, lobbying disclosure, conflict of interest, and open government. Its focus is more on the process than on the substance of government.

Common Cause is financed solely by modest dues and contributions from more than 275,000 members. While there is a small, full-time, paid staff of competent professionals—researchers, lawyers, and lobbyists—and a few office assistants, an enormous amount of work is done by part-time volunteers: college students serving as interns, homemakers, lawyers, doctors, and people in many other occupations. The Washington *Post*'s David Broder has characterized the members as an elite group of upper-income, highly educated, liberal suburbanites.

The policies and priorities of Common Cause are set by a 60-member governing board, one-third of whom are elected each year by mailed ballots from the membership. In addition, the organization's agenda and priorities are determined in very broad terms by an annual referendum. At quarterly meetings of the governing board the professional staff in Washington has an influential voice in determining the specific bills and amendments that Common Cause will support, and then it develops and carries out a lobbying strategy. On state issues, priorities and strategies are determined in much the same way by Common Cause members in the particular state.

Lobbying by Common Cause is carried on as both an inside and outside effort. Professional lobbyists in Washington, supported by researchers and lawyers, and one or several lobbyists in each of many state capitals do the inside job of contacting legislators, administrators, and their key staff personnel and explaining to them the Common Cause positions. At the same time, through monthly newsletters and supplemental issuances, the grassroots organization is kept informed and mobilized to do the outside job on selected issues: to let legislators, other public officials, and the news media know how Common Cause members view the issues.

To facilitate sharply focused communication, the membership rolls are broken down by state, congressional district and, often, by state legislative district. Volunteer telephone chains are set up in each unit so that a "lobbying alert" sounded in Washington or a state capital brings prompt citizen participation. An effective local Common Cause unit will have coordinators for the telephone chains, while other members will be responsible for developing issues, getting publicity, recruiting members, and serving as a speakers' bureau—all this done by volunteers.

Common Cause does not segregate itself from other citizen groups. It will participate whenever practical with citizen organizations that have similar views on a particular issue in a joint effort to bring about change. That effort may include lobbying the decision makers, holding news conferences, and even pursuing an objective through the courts. Cooperative efforts helped give eighteen-year-olds the right to vote, pass the Clean Air Act, open up the Highway Trust Fund to mass-transit funding, create a more responsible congressional budget process, and deregulate the airline and trucking industries.

Common Cause has become one of the leading citizen organizations on accountability by focusing attention in a constructive way on the failures of government. Common Cause's president put it this way: "By accountability, we mean making our political system competitive, letting citizens know what's going on, correcting political abuses of power, guarding against lapses of integrity, and building institutional competence."[19]

A good indication of Common Cause's effectiveness is the comments of its critics and admirers:

Common Curse . . . You're just a bunch of lobbyists . . . John Gardner is a "common crook." (Former Representative Wayne Hays, [D-Ohio] who resigned from Congress after the Elizabeth Ray scandal)

It is an amazing organization . . . it is no accident that Congress changed enormously in the . . . years of Common Cause's life. (Senator William Proxmire [D-Wisconsin])

I shall consider it a compliment if I continue to enjoy a very low rating by Common Cause. (Former Representative Robert Sikes [D-Florida], reprimanded by the House of Representatives following a Common Cause complaint)

I think you perform a service for the country, and I want to commend you . . . I just hope everybody appreciates what they are getting. (Former Senator Charles Percy [R-Illinois])

It seems very strange to me that the greatest body in the world, the U.S. Senate, has bowed for two weeks before the altar of Common Cause. (Senator Orrin Hatch [R-Utah], during debate on a code of conduct for the Senate)

Common Cause has been an extraordinary guardian of the integrity of our election process . . . they have helped create the climate of reform. (Former Vice President Walter Mondale)

They have conducted one of the most vicious and reprehensible campaigns I have ever seen in my life. (Former Representative Edward Hebert [D-Louisiana] after he was ousted as Chairman of the Armed Services Committee)

Common Cause established a reputation as a strong supporter of the budget process and has long had a keen interest in the promotion of workable and effective legislative procedures. (Former Senator Edmund Muskie [D-Maine])

I have never had great respect for your organization, but I have even less respect now. You are a dishonorable group of people, who are doing a disservice to the people of America. (Representative Charles Wilson [D-California], censured by the House for financial misconduct)[20]

During the formative years, Common Cause gave most of its attention to achieving public financing of presidential campaigns, reforming the congressional seniority system, and strengthening the congressional codes of ethics and their application to corrupt practices. Its efforts were not limited to these areas, though; it also worked for legislation relevant to holding administrative agencies accountable through freedom-of-information, sunshine, and sunset laws. In the latter part of the 1970s, Common Cause began to shift even more of its attention to the executive branch, that is, to making the agencies more accountable to the citizens.

While the full range of its program is still developing, clearly these subjects are receiving considerably more attention: vigorous Senate confirmation processes, abuse of executive/administrative power, misuse of secrecy to mislead both Congress and the public, retain limits on federal employee participation in partisan politics, and strengthen the Ethics in Government Act and its administration.[21]

New issues are added to the agenda from time to time. At its February 1988 meeting, the National Governing Board of Common Cause initiated an effort to watchdog the "Pentagon's so-called black budget, or funding for secret development and production of weapons systems." In focusing on the tension between the public's right to know and the government's need for secrecy on sensitive weapons projects, Board members expressed concerns about inadequate oversight creating "a potential for the cover-up of waste, mismanagement and fraud."

Four months later, disclosure of a wide-ranging investigation of bribery and fraud in military procurement involving many Defense Department contracts totaling tens of billions of dollars gave added credibility and urgency to this issue on Common Cause's agenda. At the same meeting, board members discussed covert operations, including how to define such operations and where appropriate covert operations end and inappropriate ones begin.[22] In a democratic society, such clarification and establishing reliable means for accountability weigh heavily on policymakers and other concerned citizens.

Public Citizen

In 1968, Ralph Nader, with help from a few underpaid lawyers and law students, published a report on his investigation of the Federal Trade Commission (FTC).[23] It was a strong condemnation of the operations of a federal agency where the processes that were supposed to produce decisions in the "public interest" were heavily influenced by information furnished by the private interests regulated by the agency. There were few opportunities for citizens who could be affected adversely by FTC decisions to challenge the presentations of these powerful groups. Ex parte contacts with the decision makers by the same private interests were common, and secrecy was the order of the day.

The highly publicized report on FTC's decision-making processes was followed by investigations and reports on other government agencies. Nader's Raiders became a familiar sight. Their critical conclusions were reported extensively by the news media; they stimulated congressional hearings. Nader was often a star witness. Some legislation resulted and many administrative practices were changed to make government both more open and more accountable.

Funds for Nader's operations came largely from a few foundations and the fees from his speeches and writings. The nature of his work and his personal commitment to the cause of responsible government captured the imagination of talented young people who were newly graduated or still in college and professional schools. They were eager to work with him for little or no pay. It was only a matter of a few years before new Nader-type organizations were created, frequently involving one or two people who had worked with Nader and would continue to have close ties with him.

Some of the better known of these organizations are the Center for Law and Social Policy, the Washington Research Project, the Center for Science in the Public Interest, and Nader's own Public Citizen. Each has a small professional staff and a citizen policy board that meets periodically to decide on objectives and overall strategy for achieving change and securing financial support. The prime target of these organizations is unconcerned, incompetent, or corrupt government—government that is too responsive to special interests, and ignores the broader public interest. The organizations deal with shortcomings in all three branches of government, using methods ranging from investigations and highly publicized exposés to class-action law suits designed to provide remedies as well as useful precedents.

The League of Women Voters

One of the oldest and most respected and productive better government interest groups is the nonpartisan League of Women Voters of the United States. With over 125,000 members in 1,400 units spread over all 50 states, the League is a potent force in education about the processes of government and the importance of citizen participation. Through its publications the League provides a continuous flow of new tools for improving accountability.

Know Your Community, the League's 46-page guide for citizens on how to "take a good look at the structure and functions of their local government," makes the League's case for citizen involvement at the very beginning:

Wherever you live, the services that affect you most directly are those that the city, county, township, school district provide. Yet most people don't know who does what, where to go to complain, who's in charge.

How does a citizen's local government or a department of it work now? Who is to blame when it seems not to work? What are the long-range problems? Which are short-term? Is the lack of money and capable people the trouble? Conflicting or overlapping responsibilities? Is the problem one that can't be handled by the city but needs to be treated regionally? Or by the neighborhood? Is the system itself set up wrong or is why it doesn't work because of the kinds of people in charge? Not enough people? Poor management?

The average citizen—if he can't get help with a problem—may in his frustration want to change the system. But he can't make much of a start unless he knows something about "the system," or at least about the part he wants changed. And a little digging may show that it isn't the system but the people in charge that are at fault. Or he may find out that his local government wants to do the things he would like it to do, but can't—because the state constitution or the state legislature won't let it raise the money or provide the services.

If a citizen wants to bring about change in the government of his community, he ought first to know how the existing apparatus is meant to work, what limits there are on the department that concerns him, and who imposes them, how a part fits into the rest of the system.

And beyond the correction of particular problems, citizens and citizen organizations have a tremendous stake in finding workable solutions to the ever-increasing demands on governments. Future problems, as well as ones that exist now, need to be taken into account. If citizens are to make intelligent proposals for change, they will want first to know as much as they can about their present government, its structure, its functions, what it can do now and what it is unable to do. They will also want to know about neighboring governments and about the more comprehensive systems of which their local government is a part, whose actions affect them.[24]

Know Your Community provides the members of the League and others with well organized and clearly stated questions (over 300) on the structure and functions of local government, financing, services provided, and exercise of control by citizens. Members of local units of the League find these questions enormously helpful as they study all or part of their local governments with a view to making them more responsive to the interests of the citizens. Similar publications on county and state government, and the public school systems, are also used extensively.

Aside from how-to-do-it pamphlets, including guidance for actions, such as testifying at public hearings, the League prepares for its members and other citizens factual publications on a wide range of public policy issues: energy conservation and production, land use, environmental quality, urban decline and redevelopment, and human resources. In addition, the League provides information designed to improve the election process—the very foundation of a representative democracy. The League's guidance on how to generate more issue-oriented campaigns, and how to cause candidates to speak to the major concerns of the voters has been very effective in establishing a base for future accountability. The League's local and state organizations issue a variety of publications designed to inform citizens and involve them in the problems and processes of government.

SUMMING UP

In the competition for attention of decision makers in legislative bodies and executive agencies, more so than most special interest groups, the better government groups have at least two of three very valuable assets: dedicated and talented members, large constituencies, and great appeal for the news media. In the long run, these may provide a suitable counterweight to those interest groups that have vast economic power and the will to use it to influence government decision makers.

Citizen participation in holding bureaucracies accountable is most effective when administrators recognize that such initiative is firmly grounded in two principles of constitutional democracy—political equality and liberty—and when that recognition leads to creation of an environment that encourages citizen involvement with the work of the agency. Fulfillment of these conditions can lead to more realistic expectations on the part of citizens, better responsiveness of administrators to the needs of citizens and, ultimately, to greater confidence in the administrative institutions of government.

NOTES

1. U.S., Congress, Senate, Committee on the Judiciary, Hearing on S. 2715, Public Participation in Federal Agency Proceedings, 94th Cong., 2d sess., 1976, p. 86.

2. 94 Stat. 376 (1975); 90 Stat. 2023 (1976); 94 Stat. 1681 (1980).

3. Comptroller General of the United States, B–139703, December 3, 1976.

4. Charles H. Levine, ed. *The Unfinished Agenda for Civil Service Reform, Implications of the Grace Commission Report* (Washington: The Brookings Institution, 1985), pp. 3–4.

5. *Report of the Task Force on Personnel Management of the President's Private Sector Survey on Cost Control,* Hearing Before the Subcommittee on Investigations of the House Committee on Post Office and Civil Service, 98th Cong., 1st sess., 1983, p. 57.

6. News Release, House Post Office and Civil Service Committee, April 14, 1983.

7. Bernard Rosen, "Civil Service Reform: Are the Constraints Impenetrable?" *The Unfinished Agenda for Civil Service Reform,* ed. Charles H. Levine (Washington: The Brookings Institution, 1985), pp. 12–15.

8. 78 Stat. 508 (1964).

9. 80 Stat. 1255 (1966).

10. Robert C. Wood, "A Call for Return to Community," *Public Management,* International City Management Association (July 1969), pp. 2–3.

11. 86 Stat. 816 (1972).

12. Paul N. Williams, *Investigative Reporting and Editing* (Englewood Cliffs, N.J.: Prentice Hall, 1978), pp. 248–50.

13. James H. Dygert, *The Investigative Journalist* (Englewood Cliffs, N.J.: 1976), pp. 23–27.

14. David Anderson and Peter Benjaminson, *Investigative Reporting* (Bloomington: Indiana University Press, 1976), pp. 37–38.

15. Clark R. Mollenhoff, *Investigative Reporting, from the Courthouse to the White House* (New York: Macmillan, 1981), pp. 356–60.

16. Dygert, *The Investigative Journalist,* p. 16.

17. Alexis de Tocqueville, *Democracy in America* (New York: Harper and Row, 1966).

18. K. L. Scholozman and John R. Tierney, *Organized Interests and American Democracy* (New York: Harper and Row, 1986), pp. 197, 412, 431.

19. Common Cause, *Frontline,* editorial, Washington, D.C., May-June 1978.

20. Common Cause, *1970–1980, A Decade of Citizen Action in Common Cause,* Washington, D.C., 1981.

21. *Common Cause Magazine,* Jan/Feb 1988, pp. 42–43.

22. *Common Cause Magazine,* March/April 1988, p. 39.

23. Edward Cox, Robert Felmeth, John Schulz, *Nader Report on the FTC* (Washington, D.C.: Center for Study of Responsive Law, 1969.

24. League of Women Voters of the United States, *Know Your Community* (Washington, D.C., 1972), p. 3.

6

Judicial Review of

Administrative Actions

The judicial power shall extend to all cases, in law and equity, arising under this Constitution, the laws of the United States, and . . . to controversies to which the United States shall be a party. . . . [1]

The right of the people to be secure in their persons, houses, papers, and effects, against unreasonable searches and seizures, shall not be violated. . . . [2]

No person shall be deprived of life, liberty, or property without due process of law. . . . [3]

No state shall . . . deprive any person of life, liberty, or property without due process of law. . . . [4]

These principles provide the constitutional authority for courts to review actions of administrative officials. In addition, the Federal Tort Claims Act of 1946[5] allows the federal government to be sued in the same manner and to the same extent as a private individual, with a few specified exceptions, thus establishing both judicial review and the possibility of financial compensation for those injured by acts of administrative agencies.

A HIERARCHY OF COURTS

At the state and national levels, the systems of checks and balances between the three branches of government make administrators judicially accountable to a hierarchy of trial and appellate courts. In the federal government trial courts for most cases are the 94 district courts. Citizens may file suits in these courts against the United States government seeking to compel an administrator to act the way they desire. Agency officials may also enlist the courts. When agencies are unable to secure compliance with their decisions, they may seek an order from a federal judge. A United States attorney employed by the Department of Justice represents the administrator in such proceedings.

Whatever the decision of a district court, the losing side may appeal to the appropriate one of 12 United States courts of appeals, often referred to as circuit courts. Some statutes, as those governing the Securities and Exchange Commission and the National Labor Relations Board, provide that appeals from actions of the agency shall be taken directly to a circuit court (rather than a district court). Here almost all cases are decided by a panel of three judges. If the circuit court rules *against* the administrator, the case will be appealed to the Supreme Court only if the solicitor general of the United States, the third-ranking presidential appointee in the Department of Justice, determines such action is warranted. If the ruling of the circuit court is against the citizen, the latter may appeal to the Supreme Court.

Whether the appeal is by the government or by a citizen, the Supreme Court will take the case for decision only if at least four justices agree to do so. Otherwise, the decision of the court of appeals stands. Of course, if a similar case should arise in another circuit, and that court's ruling is contrary to the first, there is increased likelihood that the Supreme Court will accept an appeal in order to resolve the legal uncertainties created by conflicting decisions from courts of equal rank.

A number of special courts provide citizens with an avenue of judicial review for certain types of administrative decisions. For example, in the national government, the United States Tax Court deals with disputes between taxpayers and the Internal Revenue Service, and the United States Customs Court decides disputes between citizens and the Customs Service. The decisions of these courts are subject to review by a court of appeals.

The high cost of challenging the government's administrative actions in the courts has discouraged many citizens from using the judicial system—even when they believed their cause was very good. Congress took remedial action at the federal level by passing the Equal Access to Justice Act.[6] This requires federal agencies to pay the legal expenses of those who successfully litigate against administrative actions. To avoid payment, agencies must show that decisions in question were "substantially justified." Individuals with a net worth of over $1 million and businesses with a net worth of over $5 million are not eligible for reimbursement. Labor unions and nonprofit organizations are eligible regardless of their financial status. The extent to which this law has been applied since it became effective in 1981 is shown in Table 3.

The Department of Health and Human Services was the agency named in 85 percent of all equal access applications. Twenty-seven other agencies

Table 3
Decisions on Equal Access to Justice Act Applications, 1982 through 1987

Year	Total Applications	Applications Denied	Applications Granted	Total Awarded
1982*	33	23	10	$264,339
1983	141	93	48	$778,502
1984	296	130	166	$1,417,211
1985	577	157	420	$1,912,768
1986	672	108	564	$2,567,910
1987	482	95	387	$3,844,431

* Effective October 1, 1981 through June 30, 1982

were involved in at least one equal access decision. For 1987, as in prior years, almost all (97 percent) of the amount awarded was for attorney fees. The remainder was for other expenses, such as travel and photocopying.[7]

POWER OF JUDICIAL REVIEW

For public administrators the reach of the courts is broad and deep. When administrators are challenged by parties affected by their decisions, courts can decide whether the administrator interpreted the law correctly, whether the administrator was required to act and failed to do so, whether the administrator acted within or beyond the authorized power, whether the administrator acted capriciously, whether the evidence was adequate to support the administrator's decision, and whether the administrator violated the individual's rights to "due process" and equal protection of the law.

For the most part, trial courts respond to complaints by taking one of three actions: they grant relief to the plaintiffs by ordering all or part of what they seek, dismiss the claims, or suspend any decisions, pending further consideration by the administrators of designated issues. An administrator's decision will be voided if the court finds that the decision was unconstitutional, beyond the authority of the agency, or based on substantial factual error, or that the action was arbitrary or otherwise contrary to law. Appellate courts affirm or reverse the action of the trial court or remand the case to the trial court with instruction for further consideration of specific issues.

In thus holding public administrators accountable, courts of necessity make policies that affect administrative behavior. Decisions of the United States Supreme Court and lower courts give direction to public administrators from the lowest to the highest levels. The behavior and decisions of part-time police chiefs in small villages, law-enforcement administrators in our largest cities, and the Director of the Federal Bureau of Investigations were affected by the Court's decision in *Miranda* v. *State of Arizona*[8] which held that confessions would be admissable only if persons arrested had been advised of their rights before the confessions and had been specifically told that whatever they said could be used against them.

School superintendents and government administrators at city, county, state, and federal levels were affected by *Brown* v. *Board of Education*[9] in which the Supreme Court reversed its earlier decision by declaring that "separate" cannot be "equal." These and many other cases have had an enormous effect on the discretion and decisions of public administrators throughout the country.

Even the chief executive's decisions are subject to judicial review. In the Watergate decision,[10] a unanimous Supreme Court, with four of President Nixon's own appointees, including the chief justice, denied to the president the right he claimed under the separation of powers to decide for himself whether to surrender tapes of conversations held in the White House that had been subpoenaed by the special prosecutor. The Court rejected the notion of unlimited executive privilege and once again affirmed the power of judicial review. In doing so it quoted from an earlier decision: "Deciding whether a matter has in any measure been committed by the Constitution to another branch of government, or whether the action of that branch exceeds whatever authority has been committed, is itself a delicate exercise in constitutional interpretation, and is a responsibility of this Court as ultimate interpreter of the Constitution."[11] Nixon complied with the Court's decision and the consequences are historic. Once the contents of the tapes became public the first resignation of a U.S. president quickly followed.

As instruments for holding public administrators accountable for making laws work as intended and for exercising lawful discretion, the courts differ from legislative and executive institutions in one major respect. The judicial branch is relatively passive: courts do not take the initiative in reviewing the work of the public administrator; instead they act only when a case is brought to them by a party of interest. A decision resulting from such a case may be very narrow in its application, deciding the controversy for only a single situation; or it may be much broader in scope and govern many administrative actions under similar or related conditions. Traditionally, courts have tended toward the former.

Differences between decisions of administrators and those of courts often result from the fact that administrators establish policies and procedures for *future* applications without having detailed information on all conceivable cases that may arise. Courts, on the other hand, generally decide individual cases where most or all of the relevant information is available and the consequences of a favorable or unfavorable decision are quite evident. At least, this was the situation until the last half of the twentieth century when courts began moving into more social policy cases involving more unknowns.

Roger Cramton, Dean of the Law School at Cornell University and former Chairman of the Administrative Conference of the United States, sees two types of judicial review of administrative action. One he characterizes as traditional, providing a "sober second look at what government has done that adversely affects a citizen. . . . The issues are narrow and well-defined; and the relief is limited and obvious. Has a welfare recipient been denied a benefit to which he is entitled by statute? Was fair procedure employed by the agency? Were constitutional rights violated?" The second type of judicial review he characterizes as "more of general problem-solving than of dispute resolution." Issues put before the courts call for answers to such questions as "What is life? When does death begin? . . . Shall the Concorde fly to our shores?"[12]

It is plain that the first type of judicial review is useful in the specific situation; but, in addition, the process adds to citizens' overall confidence in the fairness of government—no minor matter in a society where government is based on consent of the governed. However, the second type is far more complex because it projects the courts into areas of social policy that are ill defined and lacking in consensus. It is this type of judicial review, much of which deals with administrative decisions, that has embroiled the courts in serious public controversy and raised questions about an imperial judiciary.

In deciding what the law means in particular cases, and what administrators are permitted or required to do under law, courts are in effect making *policy* that often controls, and, at a minimum, influences administrative action. Because this is policy made by case law, it is rarely comprehensive, even though a succession of cases on a particular issue may incrementally produce a fairly broad policy. Traditionally the courts have recognized that making policies and plans that are comprehensive is the business of the legislative and executive branches, and courts are inclined to defer to these bodies on such matters. However, in recent decades when the legislative and executive branches failed to act to protect constitutional and statutory rights of citizens, some courts have increasingly shown a willingness to render decisions that cover a broad area, and in the process earned the title of activist courts.

ACTIVIST COURTS

The United States District Judge in Alabama during much of the 1960s and 1970s, Frank Johnson (since a member of the Fifth Circuit Court of

Appeals) is often cited as a leading activist judge. His decisions required Alabama's administrators to take specific and comprehensive actions in the operations of the mental health and penal institutions. In the latter case,[13] he facilitated the efforts of prisoners to file a class action suit which alleged that placing people in Alabama's prisons constituted cruel and unusual punishment in violation of the Eighth Amendment to the Constitution. The state subsequently agreed with the charge and then Judge Johnson directed substantial changes in the state prison system, changes requiring expenditures in the tens of millions of dollars.

His decision in another case[14] also required action by the state's legislative and executive branches. Judge Johnson ruled that a lack of staff or facilities is not an acceptable basis for failing to provide suitable and adequate treatment for the mentally ill. He laid down detailed program-management instructions. For example, with the help of expert testimony, the Judge specified that for dishwashing and laundry use there should be adequate hot water with a temperature of 180 degrees Fahrenheit at the equipment.

Judge Johnson explained his so-called activist record as a response to the "Alabama punting syndrome." He said that "the history of Alabama is replete with instances of state officials who could have chosen one of any number of courses to alleviate unconstitutional conditions but who chose instead to do nothing but punt the problem to the courts."[15] This situation is not unique to Alabama. Other judges, federal and state, have also picked up the ball and run with it, as did Judge Johnson. Best known are the cases involving busing and equal employment opportunity. The resulting court decrees influenced crucial management decisions.

Such judicial involvement in policy and administration has drawn mixed reviews from legal scholars. Some fear, as does Archibald Cox, professor of law at Harvard, that that involvement will encourage unique reliance on the courts and thereby weaken self-government through democratic processes.[16] On the other hand, legal scholars like Cox's colleague at Harvard, Abram Chayes, argue that this is a natural and *desirable* development because increasingly we are living in a "regulatory state," that agency regulations stimulate lawsuits, which in turn produce more judicial interventions. While advocating a cautious approach by judges in deciding whether to make managerial decisions, Professor Chayes cites these reasons for being confident of judges' ability to order very specific remedies:

1. The judge's profession insulates him from narrow political pressures. . . .

2. The solutions can be tailored to the needs of the particular situation and flexibly administered or modified as experience develops. . . .

3. The procedure permits a relatively high degree of participation by representatives of those who will be affected by the decision. . . .

4. The court, although traditionally thought less competent than legislatures or administrative agencies in gathering and assessing information, may have unsuspected advantages in this regard. Even the diffused adversarial structure of public law litigation furnishes strong incentives for the parties to produce information. . . . The judge can engage his own experts to assist in evaluating evidence. Moreover, the information that is produced will not be filtered through the rigid structures and preconceptions of bureaucracies.

5. The judicial process is an effective mechanism for registering and responding to grievances generated by the operation of public programs in a regulatory state.[17]

Many legislators and public administrators are particularly troubled by this judicial activism because little or no consideration is given by judges to the financial obligations imposed by their decisions. Budget strategies painstakingly crafted through the political process have been wrecked. Compliance with court decrees has required state and local governments to raise taxes in the face of taxpayer revolts and to shift funds from other equally important needs. Advocates of programs that were adversely affected by these reductions were not heard by the courts. Opponents of judicial activism find the impact of the courts on fiscal priorities an affront to representative democracy.[18]

Two developments are worth noting. The idea is being advanced in and outside Congress of restraining activist judges by prohibiting the courts from considering cases that deal with certain social issues, such as busing and school prayer. Some "court watchers" believe the serious attention given this proposal is already having an effect. They point out that in the 1980s, the Supreme Court issued a number of decisions that appeared to show more deference than usual to the elected representatives of the people. The Court upheld the right of Congress to exclude women from draft registration despite arguments of women's rights groups that such exclusion violated constitutional guarantees of equal rights; the Court ruled that Congress has preeminent powers in national security matters.[19] In other cases, dealing with the rights of mental patients[20] and prisoners,[21] the Court overruled lower courts to permit legislative bodies to prevail.

THE ADMINISTRATIVE PROCEDURE ACT

To minimize the need for courts to intervene in the administrative process, particularly on issues involving regulation by the national government, Congress passed the Administrative Procedure Act (APA)[22] in 1946. In formalizing administrative procedures for making decisions in federal agencies, APA compromised between those who favored unlimited administrative discretion and those who wanted administrators to follow rigid procedures, like those used by courts, and subject to complete judicial review. The act requires regulatory agencies, those with quasi-legislative and quasi-judicial authority, to follow designated procedures in establishing rules (policies) that administrators will apply, and in making determinations under those rules in individual cases.

Federal agencies make most of their rules in accordance with an informal procedure specified in the law: the proposed rules and supporting data must be published in the Federal Register with notice that comments will be received by the agency during a designated period; the agency *may* hold a hearing; the agency decides on the rules after considering the comments; and the agency publishes adopted rules in the Federal Register stating the reasons for their adoption and including responses to all comments filed during the period established for comments.[23]

Citizens appealing actions of administrators to the courts often challenge not only the procedures and substance of the actions but also the rules for decision making adopted by the agency under the APA. In 1971, the Supreme Court held that, in determining whether the secretary of transportation acted arbitrarily and capriciously in making a rule under the APA that was applied in a particular case, the reviewing court must conduct "a thorough, probing, in-depth review . . . " of the "full administrative record that was before the Secretary at the time he made his decision."[24] This means that courts will review the procedures followed by an agency in making a rule, the reasons given for proposing the rule initially, and the justification for approving it finally.

Under the APA, when decisions of agencies are challenged, they are first appealed *within* the agency to an administrative law judge who is an employee of the agency but completely independent of the officials making administrative decisions, and then to a federal court if the appellant finds that decision unacceptable and wishes to contest it further. A court will uphold the challenge to the agency's action only if it determines that such action was "arbitrary, capricious, an abuse of discretion, or otherwise not in accordance with law" or was "unsupported by substantial evidence."[25]

The APA has had the intended effect of limiting judicial involvement in the administrative process, particularly with regard to the procedures followed in deciding individual cases. Courts have also evidenced considerable respect for expertise in administrative agencies by practicing restraint in examining the substance of *policy* decisions.

However, individual and class action suits alleging that administrators have failed to act, or acted unsatisfactorily to protect the public interest, have been filed with increasingly greater frequency and many of the resultant court decisions reveal some scrutiny of the substance of administrators' decisions as well as the law and procedure followed in making them. Often it is difficult if not impossible to separate policy from procedure as the courts determine whether there has been administrative due process and fundamental fairness in interpreting and applying the law. Picking up where the compromises left off in enacting the Administrative Procedure Act, the district and circuit courts, guided by the Supreme Court, have tried to strike a balance between substantive fairness and procedural efficiency in reviewing the decisions of administrators.

Goldberg v. *Kelly*[26] presented this classic dilemma to the Court. Welfare administrators in New York State and its local governments were cutting off assistance under the federally funded program of Aid to Families with Dependent Children without a hearing because hearings are expensive and frequently result in costly delays. Hearings were granted on request only *after* removal from the welfare rolls. Here the government's interest in conserving its financial and administrative resources clashed sharply with humanitarian concerns. Stopping payments as soon as welfare officials had reason to believe a recipient was ineligible clearly contributed to the governmental need for efficiency and economy.

However, writing for the Court's majority, Justice William Brennan balanced this need against "the interest of the eligible recipient in uninterrupted receipt of public assistance, coupled with the State's interest that his payments not be erroneously terminated." The Court held that the fundamental principles of due process "require that a recipient have timely and adequate notice detailing the reasons for a proposed termination and an effective opportunity to defend by confronting any adverse witnesses and by presenting his own evidence and arguments orally."

Where lower courts have imposed procedures on administrators' decision making that go beyond the requirements of APA, the Supreme Court has objected strongly. In *Vermont Yankee Nuclear Power Corp.* v. *Natural Resources Defense Council*,[27] Justice William Rehnquist, writing for a unanimous Court (seven justices participating), took exception to reviewing courts' "engrafting their own notions of proper procedures upon agencies entrusted with substantive functions by Congress." While not completely foreclosing the possibility that there might be circumstances that would "justify a court in overturning agency action because of a failure to employ procedures beyond those required by statute . . . " he concluded that "such circumstances if they exist, are extremely rare."

CASES EXCEED CAPACITY

The effectiveness of the judiciary in holding administrators accountable is adversely affected by increasing backlogs and resulting long delays before cases are decided. From 1970 to 1980, the number of civil cases pending at the end of the year in U.S. district courts doubled to 186,113. This included 20,592 cases pending three years or more, an increase of 1,500 over the previous year. The higher backlog was directly related to a marked rise in the number filed—from 87,321 in 1970 to 168,789 in 1980. Almost half of these involved federal agencies as plaintiffs or defendants.[28]

To speed the process, Congress increased the number of judgeships for federal district courts in 1978 from 399 to 516 and again in 1985 to 575. Unfortunately, this increase in judges was essentially nullified by a steady increase in cases filed in subsequent years. Thus, by 1987, the number of civil cases filed that year was 238,982; the number completed was 200,850; and at the end of the year, there were 243,159 pending. The number of cases pending in district courts over three years stood at 19,782, very close to the number seven years earlier. More recently, approximately one-third of the cases involved federal agencies.[29]

The number of appeals filed in circuit courts in 1987 was 35,176, a 50 percent increase over the number filed in 1980. (Federal agencies were plaintiffs or defendants in 6,292 of the cases filed in 1987.) During the same seven-year period, the number of appeals pending at the end of the year increased by 25 percent, from 20,252 in 1980 to 26,008 in 1987. A 27 percent increase in the number of circuit court judges in this period for a total of 156 was simply too few to reverse the upward trend.[30]

Increases in the number of pending cases lengthen elapsed time before decisions are made. Delays between the time cases are taken to court and the decisions, to say nothing of longer delays when there are further appeals, and the attendant cost, discourage citizens from challenging administrative actions. This takes on added significance when one considers that the nationwide reversal rate in 1987 by the courts of appeals for all types of cases was 13.5 percent. The reversal rate among the 12 circuits for all civil cases showed a high of 22.1 percent in one circuit court and a low of 7.6 percent in another. The importance of judicial review of administrative decisions is reflected in the fact that in 1987, the reversal rate by all circuit courts in appeals from decisions of administrative agencies was 9.6 percent, with a high among the 12 circuits of 19.9 and a low of 4.5.[31]

Backlogs and long delays in rendering decisions also limit the effectiveness of judicial review in almost all states. Furthermore, it appears that state courts upset administrative agency decisions even more frequently than do the federal courts. A study of 521 cases decided by the highest appellate courts in California, Michigan, New York, and Pennsylvania revealed that state and local administrative agencies were reversed 44 percent of the time.[32]

A further limitation on judicial review as an accountability mechanism is unique to the Supreme Court. The Court takes no more cases than it can hear and decide, which is about 140 to 150 a year. The number of cases appealed to the Court annually has increased from 1,500 to almost 5,000 since the mid–1950s. Therefore, the Court has been compelled to choose a constantly decreasing proportion of the cases presented to it. While the volume of cases involving agency administrative decisions submitted to the Court has not grown in quite the same proportion as the total number of cases submitted, it has increased substantially. Yet the Court finds it necessary to refuse to review all but some 15 to 20 out of more than 100 such cases that are appealed from the circuit courts.

Justice Byron White has characterized the Supreme Court's power to "pick and choose its cases and the fact that the Court is able to review only a constantly decreasing proportion of the cases presented to it" as the most important factor in assessing the Court's work where administrative action is at issue.[33] Generally, the Court will not accept for review a decision of a court of appeals that found an agency decision rationally based in fact and law. That does not mean a different decision would be unacceptable; but it does demonstrate strong judicial preference for the agency's decision if there is reasonable justification for it.

Similarly, the traditional judicial respect for agency long-standing interpretations of its controlling statutes provides an additional basis for refusing to review cases decided by circuit courts. Of course, when four or more members of the Court think that the agency interpretation was wrong, even if it is long-standing and supported by a circuit court, the case is accepted for review.[34]

ACCOUNTABILITY TO THE JUSTICE DEPARTMENT

There is another dimension to accountability through judicial review. In the national government, it relates to the unique role of the Department of Justice in most litigation where the United States government is a party. While almost every federal agency has lawyers that provide legal counsel to officials of the agency, with few exceptions these lawyers are not authorized to represent their agencies in court. Instead, the authority to litigate is placed with the Department of Justice.

By executive order, President Franklin Roosevelt centralized the litigation function in the Department of Justice, and this includes the power to decide whether and how to prosecute and defend.[35] Subsequently it was made clear in statute that unless otherwise provided by law, only officers of the Justice Department under the direction of the attorney general may conduct or supervise "litigation in which the United States, an agency or officer thereof is a party, or is interested."[36]

Over the years, a few agencies, notably independent regulatory commissions, have been given authority in statute to litigate their own cases, and a few other agencies are permitted by the Justice Department to participate actively or to conduct the litigation subject to the direction of the Justice Department.

Locating the litigation function in the Department of Justice provides an additional means for holding administrators accountable. As a first step, agency lawyers must present their side of the case to lawyers in Justice's Civil Division. In deciding whether to litigate, and how, the action of the administrator is for all practical purposes being reviewed. Conflicts frequently arise between agency and Justice lawyers over interpretation of laws and pertinent court decisions. While agency lawyers have a strong commitment to achieving agency goals, Justice lawyers tend to look at the issues not only on their merits but also in terms of continuing relationships with the courts on many cases involving many agencies.

Nevertheless, it has been a long-standing practice in Justice to accede if at all possible to an agency request at the trial court level. Justice commonly defends agency administrators in district court by avoiding the substance of the complaint and instead arguing that the plaintiff lacked standing to sue, or had not used all administrative remedies to deal with the complaint, or that the court had no jurisdiction over the matter. If it becomes necessary to deal with the substance, Justice lawyers most often argue that courts should not judge the merits of the case and the correctness of agency action if there was substantial evidence to support it, even though the judge might have come to a different conclusion if she or he were making the initial decision.

Beginning in the late 1960s, the district courts have been more inclined to put aside or leapfrog the procedural arguments and turn to the substance. This may be a reaction to the growing power of administrators, some evidence of their abuse of this power through action or inaction, strong legal challenges by public interest groups often accompanied by campaigns to generate public support, and growing concern that the government was using procedural arguments excessively to prevent examination of the merits. With this tendency of district courts to reach for the merits of a case, the lawyers at Justice are giving more attention to substance as well as procedure in the first place.

The decision to take a case to district court also reflects a consideration of possible court-ordered remedial actions if the case is decided against the agency on the merits. All in all, while agencies can still reasonably expect that their request to be represented in the district court by Justice will be granted, there is a somewhat more searching examination of the legal basis for the administrator's actions than in earlier years.

When a district court rules *in favor* of the agency and the other party appeals, the Justice Department routinely defends the appeal. However, this accommodating attitude by Justice changes significantly when consideration is being given to appealing to the circuit court a decision of the district court that is *adverse* to the administrator. The review is much more searching in deciding whether to appeal an adverse decision of a circuit court to the Supreme Court. Appellate courts examine very thoroughly the agency's action, and therefore Justice Department lawyers concerned with deciding whether to appeal will do likewise.

At the appellate level, the Justice Department is greatly concerned with its credibility in court; advocating a position that is unacceptable to the courts weakens the department's role in other cases. Even if the Justice Department has no fault to find with the administrator's action, it has one other major consideration in deciding whether to appeal. Does the case involve a rule of law that is very important to the government generally, not only in the case at hand; and, if so, are the facts in the case sufficiently favorable to risk a decision that could have wide application? Similarly, if an important rule of law is at stake, the department may consider whether the circuit court which would decide the particular case on appeal has evidenced in related cases a disposition contrary to the agency's position.

In answering these questions, the administrator's action is not in question; although if the adverse decision of the district court is not appealed, the public view may be that the administrator was found wanting. Within the Justice Department, the initial judgment on whether to appeal a decision of a district court unfavorable to an agency is made by the Appellate Section of the Civil Division. The final decision is made in the Office of the Solicitor General.

As indicated above, the administrator's actions are weighed in a process that goes beyond accountability for carrying out a specific law as intended and exercising reasonable discretion. For all these reasons, and also because agency officials may consider a case unimportant or may conclude on further reflection that the agency's position is not justifiable, the majority of district court decisions adverse to agencies are not appealed.

The restraint on appealing is evident in a study made of 374 administrative agency cases lost by the government in federal district courts. The agencies recommended appeal in only 131 cases (35 percent). Of this number, Justice's Civil Division recommended appealing 97 (26 percent of the original 374). The solicitor general "is inclined to appeal fewer cases than the Justice lawyers who make their recommendations to him . . . and he is at odds with the agencies even more often . . . he differs with the agencies not so much on the legal merits of their cases as on the wisdom and expediency of pursuing them to their outermost limit."[37]

PERSONAL LIABILITY

The doctrine of immunity for public officials based on the traditional immunity of government goes back to early English law—sovereign immunity. "The king can do no wrong," and since he could claim the acts of his ministers as his own, they shared in his immunity. Until recent years, courts interpreted this "common law" by granting absolute immunity from suit to officials who must exercise independent personal judgment in performing their duties.[38]

Now this wall of immunity has been broken, although not demolished; and at all levels of government, more and more officials are being sued by citizens adversely affected by their actions. For federal officials this flows largely from a 1971 decision of the Supreme Court[39] that ruled that federal narcotics agents could be sued personally and were liable for damages when they made searches that violated citizens' constitutional rights. Subsequent

Supreme Court decisions made clear that such personal liability is not limited to those engaged in law enforcement.

In *Scheuer* v. *Rhodes*[40] the Court held that

... in varying scope, a qualified immunity is available to officers of the executive branch of government, the variation being dependent upon the scope of discretion and responsibilities of the office and all the circumstances as they reasonably appeared at the time of the action on which liability is sought to be based. It is the existence of reasonable grounds for the belief formed at the time and in light of all the circumstances, coupled with good-faith belief, that affords a basis for qualified immunity of executive officers for acts performed in the course of official conduct.

In *Wood* v. *Strickland*[41] the Court further developed the doctrine of limited immunity by holding that

... a school board member is not immune from liability for damages ... *if he knew or reasonably should have known* that the action he took within his sphere of official responsibility would violate the constitutional right of the students affected, or if he took the action with the malicious intention to cause a deprivation of constitutional rights or other injury to the student.

Later, in *Butz* v. *Economou*[42] the Court underscored the liability of federal and state officials when they are sued for deprivation of a constitutionally protected right, but at the same time it established an absolute immunity for agency officials acting in an adjudicatory or prosecutorial capacity. The Court reasoned that immunity for these officials is appropriate since their duties are quite comparable with those of judges and public prosecutors, for whom immunity is essential to assure proper performance.

The common law immunity of state and local officials was first limited by the Civil Rights Act of 1871.[43] It provides that "every person who, under color of any statute, ordinance, regulation, custom or usage of any state or territory, subjects or causes to be subjected any citizen of the United States or other person within the jurisdiction thereof to the deprivation of any rights, privileges or immunities procured by the Constitution and laws shall be liable to the party injured in an action of law, suit in equity, or other proper proceeding for redress." Courts have interpreted this section as meaning that an individual official can be sued separately from the state or local government for violation of constitutional and related civil rights.

In 1980 the Supreme Court by a six-to-three vote interpreted Section 1983 of the Civil Rights Act of 1871 in a manner that greatly expands the liability of state and local officials. The Court ruled in *Maine* v. *Thiboutot*[44] that state officials could be held liable for violations of any federal statute. In effect, the Court said that Section 1983 was not limited to violations of the Constitution and related "equal rights" statutes.

Writing for the minority, Justice Lewis Powell dissented strongly with the majority's interpretation of Section 1983 as contrary to "history, logic, and policy." Pointing to the consequences of the Court's ruling on which the majority was silent, Justice Powell wrote: "In practical effect, today's decision means that state and local governments, officers, and employees now may face liability whenever a person believes he has been injured by the administrator of any federal-state cooperative program, whether or not that program is related to equal or civil right." Scholars in administrative law have characterized the implications of *Maine* v. *Thiboutot* as "startling."[45]

In a 1988 decision, *Westfall* v. *Erwin*[46] the Supreme Court "significantly decreased the protection available to federal employees against liability for common law torts such as negligence, assault, battery, defamation, etc. Prior to *Westfall*, absolute immunity generally was available if the employee acted within the 'outer perimeter' of federal employment. In *Westfall*, the Court unanimously ruled that 'absolute immunity from state-law tort actions should be available only when the conduct of federal officials is within the scope of their official duties and the conduct is discretionary in nature.' Noting only that more than 'minimal discretion' is required the Court refused to specify the quantum of discretion necessary for immunity. Moreover, the case does not end once the federal defendant convinces a court that he was acting within the scope of employment and exercising more than a minimal amount of discretion. The Supreme Court held that an additional step is required: the court must balance the benefits to the government of immunity against the benefit to the plaintiff of financial recovery. The sole guidance given to the lower courts was to consider in each case 'whether the contribution to effective government in particular contexts outweighs the potential harm to individual citizens'."[47]

This mandatory balancing test added greatly to the uncertainty about whether federal employees are protected when they act. Employees of state and local governments are similarly affected since this and related Supreme Court decisions weigh heavily with courts in those governments.

Making public administrators personally liable for their official actions is an accountability sword with two sharp edges. One side cuts deep in the interest of acting responsibly—keeping high on the administrator's agenda the need for executing law as intended. The other side cuts deep by encouraging timidity, vacillation, and unimaginative administration of the law.

The Department of Justice does represent federal employees who are sued for acts performed or not performed in their official capacity. (Such representation is not made available to federal employees in federal criminal or agency disciplinary proceedings.) Two criteria must be met for the Department of Justice to represent a federal employee/defendant. "The employee's actions giving rise to the suit must reasonably appear to have been performed within the scope of his federal employment. . . . It must be determined that providing representation is in the interest of the United States.

It is generally in the interest of the United States to represent employees in order to establish the legality of the way they perform their duties and to promote vigorous performance of duty by relieving employees of the burden of defending suits."[48] While some state and local governments have adopted similar policies, others provide for neither defense nor indemnification when a plaintiff files suit against a government employee.

Bills had been introduced in every Congress beginning with the 95th to make the federal government the exclusive defendant in all tort suits involving federal employees acting within the scope of their employment. The Court's decision in *Westfall* v. *Erwin* injected a new sense of urgency as to the need for such litigation.

Legislation approved in the 100th Congress is intended to relieve employees of apprehension about making on-the-job decisions that could result in a financially crippling personal liability lawsuit. It will benefit plaintiffs by *assuring* them compensation if a court makes an award since the government would be liable. The public would benefit, because employees would be less likely to shrink from making difficult decisions out of fear that if they are later judged to have been wrong, they will have to pay damages out of their own pockets.[49]

THE CHANGING NATURE OF JUDICIAL REVIEW

When laws are being written, administrators normally seek maximum discretion for carrying them out. In recent years it has become very clear that wide administrative discretion provided in statutes is an invitation to greater control by the judiciary. This is particularly evident when laws give direction to agencies in such broad terms as eliminating "unfair or deceptive acts or practices in commerce"[50] and establishing "consumer product safety standards that are reasonably necessary to prevent or reduce an unreasonable risk of injury."[51]

Where is the line between "unfair" and fair practices in commerce? Where is the line between an "unreasonable" risk of injury and a risk that is acceptable? Whatever the decisions made by agencies in administering such laws, they are likely to be challenged in court as either falling short or exceeding the intent of the law.

Courts hold administrators accountable primarily by reviewing their actions in two areas: the *procedures* used in making decisions and the *substance* of the decisions. The basis for federal court review of procedures used by administrators are constitutional requirements for "due process" and procedural requirements in individual statutes.

As noted earlier, the Administrative Procedure Act of 1946 reduced substantially the intervention of the courts in the *process* of decision making in individual cases. This was achieved by defining and spelling out in the law the procedural requirements for formal agency adjudication, including such steps as a hearing by an administrative law judge, an opportunity for cross-examination of witnesses, an initial decision by the judge and, on request, a further review within the agency.

Simultaneously, APA opened a whole new area for judicial intervention by establishing in less well-defined terms the procedures to be followed by agencies in adopting rules (policies). Since most agency rules are created through an APA process called informal rule making, the courts have been called upon again and again to interpret relevant provisions of the act in different situations. For example, the provision that a "statement of basis and purpose" be included when a rule is published in the Federal Register has now been interpreted as requiring a response to opposing arguments formally submitted upon the agency's initial request for comments.

As for holding administrators accountable for the *substance* of their decisions, most courts have focused on the question of the adequacy of evidence in support of the decisions. Administrators are constantly challenged on whether there is "substantial evidence" to support their decisions, or whether they acted with "arbitrariness." This has made it necessary for administrators to explain fully the reasons for their decisions in both individual cases and rule making. Since the record used by an administrator in making a rule serves as *the* record for the reviewing court, the need for a fully documented basis for adopting a rule has strengthened accountability back to the beginning of the administrator's decision-making process.

At the same time, in reviewing decisions of administrative agencies, federal courts proceed on the assumption that the agency's *interpretation* of the governing statute should be upheld, so long as that construction is not unreasonable. As the Supreme Court enunciated the principle: "When faced with a problem of statutory construction, this court shows great deference to the interpretation given the statute by the officers or agency charged with its administration."[52]

However, there is considerable sentiment for amending the Administrative Procedure Act to eliminate this presumption in favor of agency action in order to reduce the opportunity for abuse of administrative power.[53] The Bumpers Amendment would require the courts to decide *independently* all relevant questions of law. In addition, it would impose the burden on the agency, where its jurisdiction is in question, to demonstrate that its actions are based on "language of the statute or, in the event of ambiguity, other evidence of ascertainable legislative intent."[54] Opponents believe that some presumption of legality should attach to the actions of administrative bodies, and that otherwise confidence in the governmental process is undermined.[55]

In the latter half of this century, making agency policy has shifted significantly—from setting precedents through decisions on individual cases to using the APA informal rule-making process. At the same time, the Supreme Court softened its position on "standing," and began permitting agency rules to be challenged in trial courts without waiting for their application to specific situations. Traditionally, the Supreme Court had held that to challenge an agency action in court, the plaintiff must have suffered an injury in fact. The new approach to "standing" is based on a reinterpretation of this provision of the APA: "a person suffering legal wrong because of an agency action, or adversely affected or aggrieved by such actions within the meaning of any relevant statute, shall be entitled to judicial review thereof."[56]

Now challenges are accepted from parties who *may become* adversely affected as part of a class. This redefinition of "standing" is beginning to appear in legislation. The Magnuson-Moss Act of 1975[57] specifically permits "any interest person (including consumer or consumer organization)" to file a petition for judicial review of the agency rule. Wide application of this new "doctrine of standing" may well make the courts the supervisors in fact of the administrators.

Not to be forgotten is the plain fact that judicial review of administrative decisions is also affected by who is sitting in judgment. When Justice Hugo Black was asked by news commentator Eric Severeid to explain what had changed to cause the Supreme Court in 1954[58] to reverse its 1985 decision in *Plessy* v. *Ferguson*[59] and rule that "separate" could not be "equal," he answered "the judges."

THE VALUE OF JUDICIAL REVIEW

The great value of judicial review in holding bureaucracies accountable is evident in cases where courts reversed administrative decisions; the determination not to appeal most of these reversals; and the impact of the reversals on future agency actions. Despite the fact that administrative decisions subjected to the judicial process are only a small fraction of all decisions made by federal agencies, and notwithstanding the fact that this process is exceedingly slow, there is little doubt that judicial review has a profound effect on administrators.

Knowing that the courts are there, knowing that an increasingly litigious citizenry—individuals and organizations—is prepared to go to court, knowing that citizens may be reimbursed for their legal expenses if they do go to court; knowing that the Justice Department will examine the agency's action as to both procedure and substance, knowing that agency officials are not free of personal liability: all this strongly encourages administrators to be mindful of the intent of the law and the rights of individuals as they make policy and manage programs.

NOTES

1. U.S., Constitution, Art. 3, Sect. 2.
2. Ibid., Amend. 4.
3. Ibid., Amend. 5.
4. Ibid., Amend. 14.

5. 60 Stat. 812 (1946).

6. P.L. 96–481, October 1980.

7. Annual Report, Director, Administrative Office of United States Courts, 1987, pp. 96–101.

8. 87 S. Ct. 11 (1968).

9. 347 U.S. 483 (1954).

10. *U.S.* v. *Nixon*, 418 U.S. 683 (1974).

11. *Baker* v. *Carr*, 82 S. Ct. 691 (1962).

12. Roger Cramton, "Judicial Law Making and Administration," *Public Administration Review* (September/October 1976): 551–55.

13. *Newman* v. *State of Alabama*, 349 Fed. Supp. 278 (1972); *Pugh* v. *Locke*, 406 Fed. Supp. 318 (1976).

14. *Wyatt* v. *Stickney*, 325 Fed. Supp. 781 (1971); *Wyatt* v. *Stickney*, 344 Fed. Supp. 373 (1972); *Wyatt* v. *Stickney*, 344 Fed. Supp. 387 (1972).

15. Washington *Post*, July 18, 1976.

16. Archibald Cox, *The Role of the Supreme Court in American Government* (New York: Oxford University Press, 1976).

17. Abram Chayes, *Harvard Law Review* 89, no. 7 (May 1976): 1307–8.

18. Harry L. Miller, "The Right to Treatment; Can the Courts Rehabilitate and Cure?" *The Public Interest*, no. 46 (Winter 1977): 107–8; Nathan Glazer, "Should Judges Administer Social Services?" *The Public Interest*, no. 50 (Winter 1978): 65.

19. *Rostker* v. *Goldberg*, 101 S.Ct. 2646 (1981).

20. *Schweiker* v. *Wilson*, 101 S.Ct. 1074 (1981).

21. *Rhodes* v. *Chapman*, S.Ct. Docket #80–332 (1981).

22. Public Law 404, 79th Cong., 2d sess., 1946.

23. 5 U.S.C., sect. 553 (1976).

24. *Citizens to Protect Overton Park, Inc.* v. *Volpe*, 401 U.S. 416 (1971).

25. Public Law 404, Sect. 10, 79th Cong., 2d sess., 1946.

26. 397 U.S., 254 (1970).

27. 435 U.S. 519 (1978).

28. Annual Report, Director, Administrative Office of United States Courts, 1980, pp. 2, 83.

29. Annual Report, Director, Administrative Office of United States Courts, 1987, pp. 7, 8, 117, 169, 213–6.

30. Ibid., pp. 3, 51, 138.

31. Ibid., pp. 155–8.

32. American Bar Association, *Administrative Law Review* (Summer 1980): 493.

33. American Bar Association, *Administrative Law Review* (Winter 1974): 107–8.

34. *H.K. Porter Company, Inc.* v. *National Labor Relations Board*, 397 U.S. 99 (1970).

35. Executive Order 6166, June 10, 1933.

36. 28 U.S.C. 516; 28 U.S.C. 519.

37. Donald L. Horowitz, *The Jurocracy* (Lexington: Lexington Books, 1977), pp. 51–57.

38. *Spalding* v. *Vilas*, 161 U.S. 483 (1896); *Barr* v. *Matteo*, 360 U.S. 564 (1954).

39. *Biven* v. *Six Unknown Named Agents of Federal Bureau of Narcotics*, 403 U.S. 388 (1971).

40. 416 U.S. 232 (1974).

41. 420 U.S. 308 (1975).

42. 98 S.Ct. 2894 (1978).

43. Ch. 22, 17 Stat. 13, Title 42, Sect. 1983 (1871).

44. 100 S.Ct. 2502 (1980).

45. Gary C. Marfin and Herome J. Hanus, "Supreme Court Restraints on State and Local Officials," *National Civil Review* (February 1981), pp. 83–89.

46. 56 U.S.L.W. 4087.

47. John J. Farley, *The Representation and Defense of the Federal Employee by the Department of Justice*, Torts Branch, Civil Division, U.S. Department of Justice, February 1988, pp. 9–10.

48. Ibid., p. 3.

49. P.L. 100–694, November 18, 1988.

50. 38 Stat. 730 (1914).

51. 86 Stat. 1207 (1972).

52. *Environmental Protection Agency* v. *National Crushed Stone Association*, 101 S. Ct. 295 (1981).

53. U.S., Congress, House, Judiciary Committee, Subcommittee on Administrative Law and Governmental Relations, *Statement of Senator Dale Bumpers in Support of H.R. 746*, 97th Cong., 1st sess., March 24, 1981.

54. S. 67, 97th Cong., Sect. 706 (c).

55. U.S., Congress, House, Judiciary Committee, Subcommittee on Administrative Law and Governmental Relations, *Statement of Representative John Mockley*, 97th Cong., 1st sess., March 24, 1981.

56. Public Law 404, 79th Cong., 2d sess., 1946.

57. P.L. 93–637, 1975.

58. 347 U.S. 483 (1954).

59. 163 U.S. 537 (1895).

7

Other Instruments for

Accountability

In the 1960s and 1970s, growing public concern about the responsiveness of national, state, and local governments provided a favorable environment for creating additional instruments to help hold bureaucracies accountable. Laws were enacted and organizations established to shed more light on the gap between governments' promises and performance.

FREEDOM OF INFORMATION ACT

It is the nature of bureaucracies, and particularly government bureaucracies, to make records, to collect records, and to keep them secret. Access to these records often provides different bases for evaluating the performance of agencies and new opportunities for holding their administrators accountable.

On July 4, 1966, President Johnson signed the Freedom of Information Act (FOIA)[1] with a ringing declaration about the importance of openness in government for our freedom and independence. The Justice Department was given responsibility for administering the law. The department's guidelines to agencies made clear that disclosure of government documents was to be the general rule, not the exception. The law identified specific exemptions from disclosure which relate primarily to personal data on individuals, business and trade secrets, classified information affecting the national security and foreign policy, and certain inter- and intra-agency memoranda.

In announcing the Justice Department's guidelines, the attorney general said, "If government is to be truly of, by, and for the people, the people must know in detail the activities of government. Nothing so diminishes democracy as secrecy."[2]

This represented nothing short of a revolution in government information policy. Less than ten years earlier, hearings held by a Special Subcommittee on Government Information of the House Government Operations Committee revealed a "none-of-your-damned-business" attitude on the part of federal agencies. For example, such routine information as names and salaries of federal employees would not be released except when a responsible reporter wanted the information for a reasonable purpose; and the government would decide who was "responsible" and what was "reasonable." The names of cattle companies which had been given permits to graze their stock on government-owned land were held secret. Similar secrecy surrounded the amount paid by the government to rent an office building in a major city inside the United States.[3]

By the early 1970s it was apparent that the high expectations of the 1966 law were not being fulfilled. Many agencies engaged in stalling tactics in response to requests for information, since there were no deadlines for compliance and no penalties for violations. Some agencies charged excessive fees for copying and document searches to discourage inquiries. Numerous exemptions concerning investigatory files and internal memoranda were interpreted so broadly as to defeat the purpose of the legislation; and the courts were not authorized to review such cases de novo and examine records in camera to decide whether all or any part of the records could be withheld under the exemptions.

To address these weaknesses, Congress passed a bill in 1974 to amend the law.[4] President Ford vetoed the bill for constitutional (encroached on executive authority) and operational (too burdensome) reasons. The veto was overridden largely because of Watergate abuses and other government misdeeds that were kept secret, and partly because there was a widely held belief in Congress that executive agencies did not try hard enough to achieve the intent of the 1966 law.

In 1986, on the recommendation of the Reagan administration, the FOIA was again amended to deal with two persistent problems: (1) the need to adequately protect law enforcement records, and (2) the need to reduce the cost of administering the program. To meet the first need, the amendments increase significantly the authority of federal agencies to refuse to release law enforcement records. Prior to the amendments, only "investigatory" records could be withheld. Now potentially *all* "records or information compiled for law enforcement purposes" can be withheld.[5]

With regard to costs, it is undeniable that FOIA has added to the cost of government. A 1980 bulletin from the Department of Justice stated that in 1978 alone, federal agencies spent a total of $47 million to administer that law.[6] To lower the cost, the 1986 amendments authorize agencies to charge the full costs of reviewing documents and otherwise processing requests for information under FOIA when those requests are made for commercial purposes: for example, requests by organizations that resell government records or information. There are special fee limitations applicable to non-commercial requesters. The amendments also tighten the standards for waiving charges. Only if disclosure is in the "public interest" because it is likely to "contribute significantly to public understanding of the operations or activities of the government" may the charges be waived.[7]

The Freedom of Information Act as amended gives any person the right to ask for any government record that she or he "reasonably describes" in writing. The agency must furnish the record unless there is a specific exemption in the law that permits the agency to refuse. In the latter circumstance, there is a right to appeal within the agency and a further right to appeal to a federal district court. District courts may enjoin agencies from withholding information, punish employees who fail to carry out the orders of the court, award attorneys' fees and costs to successful litigants, and call on the U.S. Office of Personnel Management to consider disciplining agency employees who deliberately and improperly withheld information requested. At all stages, including action by the court, the law specifies short time limits for action.

To help individuals and organizations make use of the law, each agency is required to publish in the Federal Register:

a description of the agency organization and where to submit requests for information;

statements about how the agency conducts its business; and

its rules of procedures, substantive rulings, and general policies.

Agencies must make available for public inspection and copying:

statements of policy not published in the Federal Register;

decisions on cases (to protect privacy of individuals, identifying details may be deleted);

administrative staff manuals and instructions to staff that affect the public; and

any reasonably segregable portion of a record after deleting portions that are exempt.

Early in the Carter administration, the Department of Justice advised agencies that it would not defend them in FOIA suits unless disclosure of the information is demonstrably harmful, even if documents do legally fall within exemptions of the act.[8] In other words, the government would not withhold information unless it is important to the public interest to do so;

agencies should lean to public disclosure when making decisions on access to federal records. Many states have enacted similar laws and have adopted a similar attitude in applying them to specific requests.

In 1981, the Reagan administration presented a different attitude in applying the act. The Department of Justice revoked the "demonstrably harmful" doctrine and advised agencies that "current policy is to defend all suits challenging an agency's decision to deny a request submitted under the FOIA unless it is determined that (a) the agency's denial lacks a substantial legal basis; or (b) defense of the agency's denial presents an unwarranted risk of adverse impact on other agencies' abilities to protect important records.[9]

Apparently responding to this change in attitude, many agencies have shown little concern about complying with some of FOIA's affirmative disclosure requirements. In a review conducted of components of 13 cabinet-level departments and the Veterans Administration in 1986, GAO found numerous instances where agencies did not publish or keep current and available to the public required information about the organizations and their record systems. This diminishes the ability of the public to deal effectively with those agencies on FOIA matters.[10]

While the benefits are not quantifiable, there is no doubt that the Freedom of Information Act has had a significant qualitative impact on the accountability of government agencies. Tens of thousands of individuals and hundreds of issue-oriented organizations have made use of the FOIA to find out what the bureaucracies are doing and why. In many cases, agencies have changed their policies and practices as a result of these disclosures. All large agencies now employ full-time people whose professional commitment is to carry out the law properly. The federal experience has encouraged over 40 states and several foreign countries to adopt the freedom-of-information concept. Opening up the processes of government and reducing secrecy are making governments behave more often in ways that are acceptable to the citizens. This is no small achievement in democratic societies.

RIGHT TO PRIVACY LAWS

Privacy is a constitutionally protected right. The Fourth Amendment provides that "The right of the people to be secure in their persons, houses, papers, and effects, against unreasonable searches and seizures, shall not be violated. . . . " Supreme Court Justice Brandeis and others have noted that the right to be let alone is highly prized. It was inevitable that the era of the computer and electronic data banks would bring legislation adding a new dimension to the values inherent in the Fourth Amendment by giving individuals some control over information about them maintained by the national government.

The Freedom of Information Act reflects the conflicting values of openness in government and personal privacy. Specific provisions in the act exempt from release personnel, medical, and investigatory records about individuals other than to the one requesting the information. The Right to Privacy Act,[11] passed in 1974, the same year that the Congress amended the Freedom of Information Act, goes beyond these provisions and enhances accountability by

1. permitting people to know what records government has about them;

2. allowing individuals to add information to their own records in order to correct them; and

3. prohibiting agency officials from revealing to others any information about an individual without that individual's permission. (Intentionally releasing such information can subject the official to a $5,000 fine.)

The Right to Privacy Act sharply limits the authority of agencies to maintain information on religious and political activities; such information may be maintained only when specifically authorized by law or the individual or required in law enforcement. The law also restricts the authority of agencies to sell or rent government mailing lists. Federal officials who violate the act are subject to civil and criminal penalties.

Both the FOIA and the Privacy Act limit administrators' discretion: the former by severely restricting the authority to keep government information secret, and the latter by sharply limiting authority to disseminate information about individuals that they themselves furnished to the government. In considering the relationship of these two laws, it is useful to keep in mind that the exemptions on access to information in the FOIA are discretionary, not mandatory. Before passage of the Privacy Act, an agency could, but was not required to withhold information that would, if disclosed, constitute a clearly unwarranted invasion of personal privacy. With passage of the Privacy Act, an agency no longer has that discretion.

This change is quite clear, but problems in administration remain because there are conflicting interpretations about congressional intent regarding the key phrase "clearly unwarranted invasion of personal privacy." The Report of the Senate Governmental Affairs Committee calls on administrators to balance the opposing interests: "protection of an individual's private affairs from unnecessary public scrutiny, and the preservation of the public's right to government information."[12]

Balancing these interests would seem to require the exercise of considerable administrative discretion. The Report of the House Government Operations Committee appears, however, to allow no such administrative discretion: "The limitation of a 'clearly unwarranted invasion of personal privacy' provides a proper balance between the individuals' rights of privacy and the preservation of the public's right to government information by excluding those kinds of files the disclosure of which might harm the individual."[13] When administrators' decisions are challenged, the courts decide.

The Office of Management and Budget (OMB) was given responsibility to administer the Privacy Act—provide guidance and assistance to agencies and oversee their performance. In 1983, the Government Information, Justice, and Agriculture Subcommittee of the House Committee on Government Operations completed an investigation of administration of the law by the Office of Management and Budget. As a result of this investigation, the committee issued a report[14] which concluded that OMB's oversight of agency actions under the act was deficient and that there was a need for better representation of privacy considerations in executive-branch decision making. Believing that there might be real shortcomings in the way agencies deal with statutory requirements, the subcommittee called on the General Accounting Office (GAO) to review Privacy Act operations at major departments and agencies.

After conducting its review, GAO concluded that agencies are administering the law in a highly decentralized manner and "often have not established clear lines of responsibility and accountability for Privacy Act functions. All of the 14 agencies had Privacy Act officers or their equivalent; however, the officers' limited responsibilities and resources indicated that ... improvements were needed in adhering to OMB guidance relating to such activities as computer matching programs, risk assessments, evaluations, and training."[15]

Specifically, GAO found that many agencies had no evidence of having made required risk assessments for newly created or modified record systems to assure security and confidentiality; accurate data on computer matching were not being reported as required to OMB; and the training needs of the hundreds of agency Privacy Act officers responsible for compliance with the law had not been assessed or provided in a systematic manner. A later review revealed that agencies were not complying with the requirement that they publish in the Federal Register in a timely manner notices of record systems that contain personal information on individuals. In examining the adequacy of such public notice with regard to 53 record systems in eight agencies, GAO found that only 24 met the requirements.[16] All these deficiencies adversely affect the government's commitment to protecting individual privacy.

The benefits to the individual and to society generally of the Privacy Act, properly implemented, are obvious. One major problem has developed which is *not* beneficial to society: the Privacy Act denies access to records that would provide information on the results achieved by certain government programs. For example, it has discouraged longitudinal research on the effectiveness of federally funded programs in such areas as drug treatment, work training, and criminal rehabilitation, because they require periodic contacts with those who participated in order to note their progress.

Having such data available would make possible better decisions on the value of certain public policies and on whether programs that flow from them should be changed, enlarged, reduced, or terminated. New ways are being sought to obtain this information without infringing on the privacy rights of individuals concerned.

Another step to protect privacy was taken with enactment of the Right to Financial Privacy Act in 1979.[17] It regulates the ability of federal agencies to gain access to customer account records held by financial institutions. "Customer" is defined as an individual person or a partnership with five or fewer members. It does not apply to corporations, associations, and large partnerships. The act places restrictions on the use of those records that a federal agency does obtain. The restrictions on access and use of records are intended to protect the privacy of the contents of the records, including any oral recounting or summary of information on the record.

Access to financial records is regulated through use of a certification mechanism. The federal agency seeking access certifies to the bank that it has complied with one or more of the five specified means of access: customer authorization, administrative summons or subpoena, search warrant, judicial subpoena, and formal written request in accordance with published regulations. To use any of these access mechanisms, the agency must determine that there is "a reason to believe" that the records sought are relevant to "a legitimate law enforcement inquiry." Furthermore, the act requires that the customer of the proposed access be given advance notice and the opportunity to challenge the access in court. If the customer goes to court, access is prohibited until the case is decided.

The act authorizes several exceptions, the major one being access pursuant to a subpoena from a federal grand jury. No certification or advance notice is required. In addition, in an emergency situation, if a court decides that advance notice would harm an investigation, a federal district court can excuse the advance-notice requirement and issue an order prohibiting the financial institution from notifying the customer that the records will be accessed.

As for restrictions on use of financial records, these pertain to transfer of records obtained under the act from one agency to another. There are no restrictions on transfers within an agency. Interagency transfer of such records is prohibited unless the *transferring* agency certifies that the transfer is in accordance with a legitimate law enforcement inquiry within the jurisdiction of the agency requesting the records. The customer must be notified of the transfer within 14 days, but the customer has no right to submit an advance challenge that would stop the transfer until a court has adjudicated the issue.

The restrictions placed on federal officials in right-to-privacy legislation constitute standards of accountability for federal officials: standards designed to protect a cherished constitutional right.

SUNSHINE LAWS

Freedom-of-information laws open the *processes* of bureaucracies to public view. Sunshine laws also open up government; but the focus is more on how decisions are made in *multiheaded* government agencies. Such laws attempt to establish clearly the public's right to know as an essential first step in holding these agencies accountable for what they are doing.

The independent regulatory commissions such as the Securities and Exchange Commission, Interstate Commerce Commission, Federal Power Commission, Federal Trade Commission, and other multiheaded agencies, totaling about 50, are now governed by the Sunshine Act approved in 1976.[18] It prohibits ex parte communications, that is, private communication between a person having an interest in a decision of the body and a member of the decision-making body. The law requires these agencies or parts of agencies to give notice in advance of their business meetings of top officials, and to hold them open to public observation, unless agency officials vote to close a session for a specific reason permitted by law. Such reasons may include discussions of information dealing with the national security, personnel problems, information that invades the privacy of individuals, and commercial and financial information that could damage a company's competitive position.

When meetings are closed, agencies are required to make and keep a verbatim transcript. The reason for closing a meeting can be challenged. Ultimately a federal district court decides, based on a review of the transcript, whether the agency was justified in closing the meetiing. The burden of proof is on the agency. If the court finds the agency's decision was not justified, in whole or in part, then the transcript or that part that should have been open is made available to the public.

All 50 states and many local jurisdictions have some kind of sunshine laws. In all jurisdictions, open decision making spells less influence for special interest groups—but it also creates problems. It is more difficult to deal rationally with conflict in a public arena. Compromises are harder to work out, particularly where representatives of groups whose positions may need to be modified are themselves under attack by hard-liners from within their own organizations. Some decision makers in multiheaded agencies also complain that sunshine laws prevent useful, informal discussion and speculation with colleagues that could lead to better decisions in formal public sessions. Others disagree.

In the federal government, fewer publicly announced meetings of decision makers appear to be one consequence of the sunshine law. A Congressional Research Service survey of 59 agencies covered by the law revealed that over a five-year period the number of meetings dropped by 31 percent, from a high of 2,297 in 1980 to a low of 1,596 in 1984.[19] Some agencies have substituted nondecisional staff briefings for public meetings to facilitate informal discussion with policy makers. Later, publicly announced meetings are held to take formal action. These agencies may be complying with the letter of the law, but the spirit of the law appears to be suffering.

On the whole, despite shortcomings, it is demonstrable that the Freedom of Information Act, the Privacy Act, and the Sunshine Act are powerful tools for opening administrative agencies to increased accountability. Add to these a variety of new laws relating to disclosure of financial condition and possible conflict of interests, restrictions on revolving-door employment, recording of contacts with all parties of interest, and registration of lobbyists, and it is quite apparent that citizens and organizations interested in holding government bureaucracies accountable are now in a strong position to do so.

SUNSET LAWS

The fundamental idea of sunset laws is to compel government agencies and programs to prove their value or automatically face extinction in a designated number of years. Colorado pioneered in 1976 with a sunset law that gave 40 of its state regulatory agencies a seven-year life cycle. To start a new life cycle requires affirmative legislation.

Common Cause, a strong advocate of sunset laws, has developed ten basic principles to guide states considering such legislation.

1. Programs and agencies should automatically terminate at a certain date unless affirmatively recreated by law.

2. Termination should be periodic (e.g., every seven or nine years) in order to institutionalize the program review process.

3. Like all significant innovations, introduction of the Sunset mechanism will be a learning process and should be phased in gradually.

4. Programs and agencies in the same policy area should be reviewed simultaneously in order to encourage coordination, consolidation, and responsible pruning.

5. Existing entities (e.g., budget and planning offices, legislative auditor) should undertake the preliminary program evaluation work, but their evaluation capacities must be strengthened.

6. In order to facilitate meaningful review, the Sunset proposal should establish general criteria to guide the program evaluation process.

7. Substantive preliminary work must be packaged in manageable decision-making reports for top decision makers to use in exercising their common sense political judgment.

8. Substantial committee reorganization is a prerequisite to meaningful Sunset review.

9. Safeguards must be built into the Sunset mechanism to guard against arbitrary termination and to provide for outstanding obligations and displaced personnel.

10. Public participation in the form of public access to information and public hearings is an essential part of the Sunset process.[20]

More than half the states now have some type of sunset laws. These laws differ from each other mainly in the length of the life cycle and in the agencies covered. All of them force the legislative body to make a clear decision, after an agency or program has been in existence for a specified period, about whether it should be continued. The political reality is that the executive is also compelled to make this evaluation and arrive at a conclusion in order to take a position with the legislature.

This puts the spotlight on the central issue in accountability: what was the *promise* of the original law, and what has been the agency's *performance* in carrying it out? It is up to the agency, its supporters, and its detractors to present the results achieved and convince elected officials that the program is worth continuing; is worth continuing at the same level, a higher level, or a lower level; or should be abolished. Of course, the legislature and the chief executive arrive at their conclusions through the normal political process in which interest groups have a major role, and compromise is the key to a decision.

The national platforms of both the Democratic and Republican parties endorsed the sunset idea for the federal government in 1976. That same year sunset bills were introduced with strong bipartisan support, and reintroduced in the next two Congresses. Hearings were held by the House Government Operations Committee and the Senate Governmental Affairs Committee.[21] While much of the testimony was favorable, some serious questions remained largely unanswered. These arose from the experience of the states:

1. Will administrators concentrate so many resources and so much time on building a case for renewing the agency's or program's life cycle that important but low-visibility issues are left unattended?

2. Will administrators compromise the public interest in order to curry favor with powerful special interests in return for their support to continue the program?

3. Will the legislative body build its capability for continuing oversight and evaluation to facilitate wise sunset decisions?

4. Will sunset laws help the legislative body and the chief executive exercise the necessary political courage to curtail or end programs that are not in the public interest but are strongly supported by powerful special interest groups?

Sunset legislation has not been considered formally by committees in recent Congresses, although it is an issue that remains alive in the minds of some members.

While it is still too soon to evaluate the effectiveness of sunset laws, one conclusion is evident. Covering all agencies by sunset laws has made it impossible for legislative bodies to do high-quality evaluations and make wise judgments. In other words, if there is more to review than can be done well, evaluations will be perfunctory and uneven, and decisions to end or extend the life of programs will not be based, even in part, on a serious consideration of relevant facts.

CIVIL SERVICE REFORM ACT

To improve management in the national government, the Civil Service Reform Act of 1978 (CSRA)[22] places an unprecedented emphasis on performance standards and evaluations—that is, on accountability. Greater individual and organizational accountability are the high promise of this legislation.

The new law makes it possible to hold presidential appointees and other federal executives and managers more accountable for achieving results by giving them increased discretion in personnel matters. In addition, the new law calls for presidential appointees and federal managers to be held accountable for making personnel decisions in accordance with merit principles.

Presidential Appointees and Senior Executives

In creating a Senior Executive Service for top career executives and comparable political appointees, the Civil Service Reform Act requires:

that performance objectives and standards be established in each agency for each job to which these high-level managers are assigned;

that senior executives be regularly and rigorously judged on how well they manage and results achieved by organizations they head;

that senior executives be rewarded or penalized within the agency according to their performance and results they do achieve; and

that presidential appointees (heads of agencies, deputies, assistant secretaries, and their equivalents) fulfill their responsibility for assigning senior executives, career and political, to jobs they can do well, and removing any who are unable to perform in a fully satisfactory manner.

These requirements in law are significant in another respect. In every administration, some presidential appointees and their own appointees, even after a year or two in office, tend to portray themselves as being apart from the "bureaucracy." Any such posture is now completely lacking in credibility. Presidential appointees do not hold office to *observe* the bureaucracy and serve as outside commentators.

Oversight institutions as well as the public can now hold these executives accountable for doing what the law specifically calls for in the way of establishing performance standards, making evaluations, and using appropriate personnel actions to reward good producers and penalize poor ones. All of these measures further the achievement of effective and efficient government operations.

No longer is it acceptable for political executives in the agencies to detach themselves from these fundamental responsibilities for managing. Characterizing poor performance by bureaucracies they head as failures by *others*, rather than their own failures, quickly establishes a major reason for failure. Since presidential appointees are in at least the three highest levels of positions in each agency, the implications of the law for them are clear: those who are unwilling to assume fully the obligation to manage—or are incapable of doing so—should not hold these offices.

Middle Managers and Supervisors

Along with requirements that make it easier to hold presidential appointees and senior executives accountable, there is a major breakthrough for holding accountable those who report to senior executives. Mid-level managers no longer receive automatic salary step increases simply because they have been rated "satisfactory." Instead, specific performance standards are established for each of these managers. They are evaluated annually on effectiveness of their management and results achieved by the units for which they are responsible. The amount of any annual pay increase depends in part on what is happening to salaries for comparable work in the private sector, but the size of the increase depends primarily on performance. To raise a manager's pay based on performance, a written justification must show performance above the basic level of acceptability. In other words, merit pay is the rule.

The act also provides the basis for strengthening accountability beyond performance of mid-level and higher managers. The entire organization is affected because performance criteria for every manager must focus in part on that manager's success in having subordinate supervisors meet their responsibilities for performance appraisal. This involves *establishing suitable performance standards in all units and for every employee*, seeing that subsequent evaluations are fair, and that there is follow-through with appropriate appreciation, encouragement, new assignments, training, and rewards or penalties.

A related accountability feature affects newly appointed supervisors at every level. Recognizing that on-the-job experience generally provides the best information on whether a person will be effective, the new law provides that the first year as a supervisor will be a probationary period. Those who do not perform successfully are to be moved into appropriate nonsupervisory jobs before the probationary period ends, and managers can be held accountable for making these decisions in a timely manner.

Performance Appraisal

The strong emphasis on individual accountability flowing down through the hierarchy as a result of establishing clear organizational objectives and individual performance standards was intended to

open opportunities for thousands of federal employees to apply untapped skills, knowledge, and enthusiasm to the essential work of government;

reduce wasteful and unproductive activities and practices;

eliminate considerable confusion and inaction caused by a lack of clear purpose and expectation; and

infuse in those parts of bureaucracy that behave in a faceless and inflexible manner a new sense of "caring" born of individual accountability.

A crucial element for fulfilling these expectations was the requirement that employees in the executive branch participate with their supervisors in periodic reexamination of their own job requirements and performance through the performance appraisal process.

Performance appraisal is critical to achieving the high promise of the Civil Service Reform Act. In well managed public and private organizations, it is widely recognized that establishing and sustaining good performance appraisal systems is very difficult but essential for effective and efficient operations. Three areas require continuing attention: (1) developing performance standards that are job related, objective as possible, observable, and documentable; (2) applying these standards rigorously, that is, overcoming the natural tendency of many supervisors to evaluate subordinates more favorably than warranted; and (3) following through with appropriate action—recognition/awards for superior performance, training where indicated, and penalties when appropriate.

Disciplining and Dismissing Employees

No doubt it is easier to dismiss poor managers once performance standards are established; and the same is true for nonmanagerial employees when performance standards exist for their jobs. In addition, CSRA reduced modestly the evidence required for removal based on performance. Instead of continuing to require a "preponderance" of evidence to support a dismissal for poor performance, the law calls for "substantial" evidence, which is a lesser standard.

Many in the news media and the public were caught up in the rhetoric of the campaign for civil service reform; and they gave their support in the belief that managers would be able *summarily* to fire an employee for poor performance. The reality is quite different. "Due process" is a basic value, and it lives for federal employees too. Employees must be given reasons for proposed adverse actions, and their responses must be considered. Managers continue to be held accountable for their actions in this area, even though appellate processes have been simplified somewhat and decisions are rendered sooner.

At the same time, it is well to keep in mind that managers in both the public and private sectors have become more cautious about taking adverse personnel actions because of an increasing tendency by those affected to countercharge: women charge discrimination based on sex, blacks and Hispanics allege racial discrimination, and white males charge discrimination in reverse.

Nevertheless, the widely held view that incompetence can now be dealt with expeditiously, along with the requirements for performance standards and evaluation discussed earlier, leave little doubt that it is now possible to hold federal managers accountable for action in this area. Very little sympathy will go to those who fail to initiate necessary disciplinary or removal action because they believe the requirements for "due process" are unreasonable, or because there may be personal risks or unpleasantness arising from countercharge.

Central Personnel Agency

The president's Reorganization Plan,[23] which accompanied CSRA, includes major changes in the organization for central personnel leadership and operations. These have important accountability implications.

The bipartisan Civil Service Commission was split into two agencies. One of these is a new Office of Personnel Management (OPM) designed to serve as a strong management-oriented central personnel agency making policies, carrying out central personnel operating functions, and *ensuring that agency personnel policies, programs, and practices accord with merit principles established in law.* The director of this powerful new office, appointed by the president with the advice and consent of the Senate, has a nominal four-year term, but holds office at the pleasure of the president; therefore, the director is less independent than the former Civil Service Commissioners.

Not only is OPM responsible for enforcing civil service laws, rules, and regulations, but also in those areas where OPM has delegated its authority to agencies, OPM must "establish standards for agency performance and an oversight program to ensure the authority delegated is administered in accordance with merit system principles and OPM standards."[24]

Reports of studies conducted separately by two agencies responsible for overseeing OPM's performance, GAO and the U.S. Merit Systems Protection Board (MSPB), revealed that personnel directors of most federal agencies surveyed saw OPM's evaluation and compliance work as having deteriorated.[25] OPM has not utilized its ample authority to meet the statutory responsibility for holding federal agencies accountable for complying with civil service laws and related requirements, despite strong reminders to successive OPM directors by the chairman of the House Subcommittee on Civil Service.

Merit Systems Protection Board

Because of the unique political context in which personnel policy for the federal service is made and executed, the 1978 civil service reforms created a Merit Systems Protection Board headed by three members appointed by the president with the advice and consent of the Senate. No more than two members can be from the same political party.

The board is the guarantor that federal managers will be held accountable for making decisions affecting employees in accordance with merit principles. In law for the first time is a specific listing of merit principles and prohibited personnel practices. The absence of such provisions in the past often made it impossible to hold managers accountable if they engaged in unfair personnel practices. An Office of Special Counsel, the head of which is appointed by the president with the advice and consent of the Senate, investigates allegations of prohibited personnel practices and, if the evidence supports the allegations, the special counsel prosecutes the case before the members of MSPB. In addition to deciding whether agencies engaged in prohibited personnel practices and, if so, ordering appropriate corrective action, MSPB adjudicates employee appeals from the administrative decisions of agencies.

The CSRA gives the MSPB the role of watchdog for the merit system with some unique responsibilities and powers aside from adjudicating employee appeals and investigating and deciding on alleged prohibited personnel practices.

1. The board is required to analyze activities of the Office of Personnel Management and report annually to Congress on whether actions of the office "are in accord with merit principles and free of prohibited personnel practices."

2. The board is authorized to review policies made by the director of OPM and is required to strike down, in whole or in part, any such policy that violates merit principles or permits prohibited personnel practices. The board is also required to "prohibit future agency compliance with any rule it determines to be invalid."

To preclude pressure and strengthen its independence within the executive branch, the board is authorized to submit its requests for appropriations and its recommendations for legislation directly to Congress rather than through the president's Office of Management and Budget. The members of the board and the special counsel have fixed terms and are removable only for cause, rather than serving at the pleasure of the president.

Most of the board's resources are devoted to adjudicating employee appeals. Initial decisions are made by the board's administrative law judges. Appeals from decisions of administrative law judges are decided by the board. The administrative law judges receive about 6,500 employee appeals each year. As a first step, appellants and agencies are encouraged to resolve their differences informally, and about 20 to 25 percent of the cases are concluded in this manner.

Decisions on the remaining cases reverse or mitigate agency actions in one out of every four cases. About one-third to one-fourth of the cases decided by administrative law judges are appealed to the board. Over 90 percent of the judges' decisions are affirmed by the board.[26] In thus acting on employee appeals, MSPB is holding federal agencies accountable for complying with laws and other government-wide and agency requirements when they take disciplinary or other adverse actions against employees.

As for meeting its statutory oversight responsibility for reporting annually to Congress on whether OPM activities are "in accord with merit principles and are free of prohibited personnel practices," the record of the board is, at best, mixed. In an essay on the first four years under the Civil Service Reform Act, wherein major failings by the Office of Personnel Management with regard to merit were discussed, this paragraph was included on MSPB:

And what does the watchdog say about all these matters which bear heavily on the premier merit principle? [Appointment and advancement based on "relative ability, knowledge, and skills after fair and open competition."] The last report to Congress of the Merit Systems Protection Board, issued in December 1982, states that it has no evidence that actions of OPM during calendar 1981 "contravened the merit principles or involved the commission of prohibited personnel practices." In fact, it is very hard to find anything significant in the report that relates to this vital merit principle. Some observers might therefore charge that the watchdog is suffering from several disabling infirmities: blindness, deafness, and muteness. But in all fairness to the presidentially appointed members of the board and the staff, I believe these disabilities are institutionally genetic and not environmentally induced. The fact is that the board is simply too far removed from the action to serve as an effective watchdog for assuring that the policy decisions of the director of OPM are in harmony with merit principles.[27]

While recent MSPB reports on OPM have identified some OPM failures to act as well as actions which are contrary to the letter and spirit of the merit principles, too often these reports are equivocal and do not move OPM directors to change the targeted policies and practices.

Federal Labor Relations Authority

The Civil Service Act created an independent bipartisan agency to administer that part of the law dealing with labor-management relations within the federal government. Among the responsibilities of the Federal Labor

Relations Authority (FLRA) are the requirements to decide complaints of unfair labor practices filed by employee unions against agency management or vice versa.

In the first eight years of its operations, FLRA received 43,159 unfair labor practice complaints. About 90 percent of these were filed by unions and another five percent by employees—all against agency management. In the most recent years, the median age for such cases from receipt to disposition ranged from 50 to 60 days.

The issues most often raised in these cases were interference, restraint, or coercion of union or union members by agencies for union activity; failure to bargain with unions on changes in personnel policies or practices; bad faith bargaining; or discrimination by agency against union/union members.[28]

In only a small percentage of the cases have the charges of unfair labor practice against the agency been upheld by the FLRA. Nevertheless, by deciding these and other cases, FLRA holds agency managers accountable for dealing with unions in accordance with laws and related requirements established by FLRA as well as those in contracts negotiated between agencies and unions.

WHISTLE-BLOWING

Agency employees are in a unique position to help hold the bureaucracy accountable. Many employees can see for themselves whether their own agency is meeting its responsibilities as it should, or whether it is failing to do so because of incompetence, lack of will, dishonesty, lack of resources, a combination of these, or some other factor.

Some employees start thinking about whistle-blowing when they begin to believe that a public administrator "should and could, but won't." When an employee becomes convinced that corrective action by the responsible official is unlikely, and finds that situation unacceptable, then the ingredients for whistle-blowing exist.

The employee may seek to hold accountable a supervisor who appears to be ignoring the employee's criticism by complaining to a higher-level official within the agency or to a unit specifically designated for receiving such complaints, such as an inspector general's office. This is whistle-blowing inside the agency. Failing to get satisfactory action at this level, the whistle-blower may go outside the agency but remain within the executive branch—turning to a central audit agency, or even the office of the elected chief executive.

The whistle-blower may feel that complaining still has not resulted in acceptable action and may decide to go to the legislative body—to an appropriations or oversight committee, or to an individual legislator. Alternatively, a whistle-blower may go to the news media to air concerns. In any event, whether the whistle-blower proceeds systematically along these lines or goes directly to the news media or legislature, corrective action is likely to begin, *if* the complaint is supportable.

Often the charges of whistle-blowers do not stand up. This may occur because they are misinformed, reason about the facts in a faulty manner, are trying to settle some personal scores, or simply believe their policy and management judgments are better and should prevail. Whether or not the charges are soundly based, and whether or not corrective action is taken, the whistle-blower is rarely viewed as a hero by managers inside the organization. In fact, the whistle-blower may be subjected to reprisals, including formal discipline. Such actions may raise important constitutional issues.

The Supreme Court has denied public agencies the right to remove an employee who is critical of the employer. In *Pickering* v. *Board of Education,*[29] which involved a public school teacher who was discharged because of a letter he wrote to the local newspaper criticizing the fiscal policy of the Board of Education, the Court overturned the discharge and held that the teacher's speech was protected by the First Amendment, even though there was some question as to whether the statements in the letter were correct. The Court went on to say:

It is possible to conceive of some positions in public employment in which the need for confidentiality is so great that even completely correct public statements might furnish permissible grounds for dismissal. Likewise, positions in public employment in which the relationship between superior and subordinate is of such personal and intimate nature that certain forms of public criticism of the superior by the subordinate would seriously undermine the effectiveness of the working relationship between them can also be imagined.

The problem in any case is to arrive at a balance between the interest of the teacher (public employee) as a citizen commenting upon matters of public concern and the interest of the state, as an employer, in promoting the efficiency of the public service through its employees.

The Supreme Court has also upheld the right of public agencies to remove employees who have been critical of their employer. In *Arnett* v. *Kennedy,*[30] the Court held that a statutory provision permitting removal of a federal employee for "such cause as will promote the efficiency of the service" is not unconstitutionally vague, as the plaintiff alleged, when it is applied to the separation of an employee for speech that was critical of his employer. In this decision the Court sought to balance the free speech rights of the individual, and the right of the public to information about how the government was operating, with the need for an agency to operate efficiently. The Court put it this way:

We would be blinking at reality if we did not recognize that a class of foreign military officers at an Air Force installation on invitational orders presents special problems affecting the national interest in harmonious international relations. We are certainly not equipped to second-guess the agency judgment that the instructional goals of the Air Force program would be jeopardized by the teacher's volunteering his views on subjects of potential explosiveness in a multicultural group.

It is plain that the issues are now viewed by the Court as far more complex than when Justice Oliver Wendell Holmes issued his famous dictum in 1892 concerning the dismissal of a policeman: "The petitioner may have a constitutional right to talk politics, but he has no constitutional right to be a policeman."[31] Since this area of protected free speech is not a simple matter, the Court has noted in several cases, including *Arnett* v. *Kennedy*, that having available to employees facilities for consultation, such as a general counsel's office, is an important consideration.

We have seen that there are some constitutional protections for responsible whistle-blowers. The heart of the matter is that government employees have a right to free speech, but that right has to be balanced against the public interest in permitting the government to operate efficiently.

The Civil Service Reform Act specifically encourages employees to expose mismanagement, violations of laws and regulations, gross waste of funds, abuse of authority, and substantial and specific danger to the public health or safety. Recognizing that whistle-blowers do not endear themselves to those adversely affected by their allegations, the law designates reprisals against whistle-blowers as a prohibited personnel practice. Of course, whistle-blowers, like all federal employees, are prohibited from revealing information, the disclosure of which is prohibited by law or executive order except if the disclosure is made to the head of the agency, the agency inspector general, or the Office of the Special Counsel.

The Special Counsel is responsible for investigating those employee appeals alleging reprisals that appear to have merit and, if it finds that there was reprisal action, to prosecute the case before the Merit Systems Protection Board. The board is authorized to provide remedies and punish those who engaged in reprisals.

Unfortunately, many kinds of reprisals can be so subtle that they are virtually impossible to prove. Social ostracism and discretionary management decisions involving training, field trips, one-of-a-kind assignments, and promotions where several candidates are well qualified usually involve so many considerations that there is little chance of establishing a clear cause-effect relationship.

A survey[32] of randomly selected federal employees in 15 major federal agencies showed that only a small proportion of those who claimed to know of mismanagement or fraud did anything about it. Nearly half (45 percent) of the 8,600 survey respondents said they had personally observed or obtained direct evidence of a wasteful or illegal activity within the preceding year. Nearly one employee in ten claimed knowledge of such an activity involving more than $100,000. Of the employees who claimed to know about specific wasteful or illegal activities, less than one-third (30 percent) reported it to any other person or group.

Surprisingly, the major reason cited for not reporting wasteful or illegal activities by those who observed it was not fear of reprisal but the belief that "nothing would be done." This was specified by 53 percent. Another 20 percent gave as their reason that they did not think anything *could* be done to correct the situation. The third most frequently cited reason was "I decided that reporting this matter was too great a risk for me."

Of the employees who observed wasteful or illegal activities and chose to report it, 90 percent did so within their supervisory chain of command (mostly to their immediate supervisor). As for results, about half of these employees stated that "the problem was not resolved at all." Many of the employees said they were not sure whether any action was taken.

Among the employees who reported wasteful or illegal activities, 14 percent claimed to have been the victim of some form of reprisal. The most frequently cited forms of reprisal were poor performance appraisal, assignment of less desirable or important duties, and denial of promotion—and again, in most instances, it was very hard to *prove* that reprisal was the underlying reason for management's decision.

In assessing the results of the survey, the MSPB noted that the responses may reflect "misperception of observed events, incomplete understanding of facts, one-sided viewpoints, and self-serving recollections." Nevertheless, the size of the sample and the clustering of responses, supported by hundreds of narrative statements, led the board to conclude that the survey results can be given substantial weight both on their merits and because the behavior of employees is influenced by what they believe regardless of the facts.

For more employees to choose the route of whistle-blowing to deal with mismanagement, waste, and corruption, not only must whistle-blowers become convinced that something "will be done," but ingrained cultural barriers will have to be overcome. From early childhood tattletales and informers are scorned, and in many organizations employees who go public with their criticism are more likely to be viewed as traitors than saviors. Providing a statutory base has given additional respectability to whistle-blowing. As it is further institutionalized and the problems identified by the survey are dealt with, it can become a powerful new force for holding bureaucracies accountable. Even when no whistles are blown, the very existence of the mechanism can be a strong deterrent to malfeasance, misfeasance, and nonfeasance.

THE INSPECTOR GENERAL ACT

In the same month that the civil service reforms were put into law, another law to strengthen accountability in the federal government was passed. The

Inspector General Act of 1978[33] established inspectors general in 12 federal agencies, later extended to 12 more agencies. The inspector general in each agency has responsibility for auditing, investigating, and reporting to prevent fraud, abuse, and waste in federal programs, and simultaneously to promote economy, efficiency, and effectiveness. To facilitate obtaining facts, the inspector general has been given the power of subpoena.

Prior to the act, internal audits and investigations were conducted in these and other agencies, but usually by separate organizational units. This law brings the two functions together under a single official who is appointed by the president with the advice and consent of the Senate and is directly responsible to the agency head. To prevent any interference with vigorous and comprehensive performance, the agency head is specifically proscribed from taking any action that would prevent the inspector general from initiating, carrying out, or completing any audit or investigation. Thus the internal audit and investigation function has been elevated and given a marked degree of independence.

Further enhancing the independence of the inspector general is the requirement in law for semiannual reports to be sent to Congress. These reports

describe significant problems, abuses, or deficiencies in agency operations and programs and the recommendations for corrective action;

identify important recommendations described in previous semiannual reports on which corrective action has not been completed;

identify matters referred to prosecutive authorities and resulting convictions; and

list each audit report completed by the inspector general during the six-month period.

In addition, the inspector general must prepare a special report when informed of particularly serious problems or abuses, and the head of the agency is required to send copies to appropriate congressional committees no later than seven days after receiving the report. This is the bedrock of the inspector general's independence—that the semiannual and special reports be sent by the agency head *without alteration* to the appropriate committees of Congress. The agency head is free to send comments along with each report.

Institutionalizing the independence of inspectors general was set back early in the Reagan administration when all the incumbents were fired. No specific reasons were given. The president's press secretary merely said that the administration wanted people in those jobs who are "meaner than a junkyard dog" to ferret out waste, fraud, and mismanagement.[34] Of course, just being "mean" enough to terrorize the employees will not bring about the cooperation needed to identify problems and their causes. The firings brought expressions of concern from many quarters that the jobs were being politicized despite a Senate report accompanying the legislation that stated that appointments would be made "without regard to political affiliation and solely on the basis of integrity and ability." The Senate report also noted that the president is not required to have "cause" before removing an inspector general, but "the committee expects that there would be some justification."[35]

Five of the dismissed inspectors general were soon reappointed, most of them in the same agencies in which they previously worked, and the administration selected experienced people for the other vacancies. Whether the wholesale dismissals and subsequent appointments will set a pattern for future transitions that will strengthen or weaken the independence, objectivity, capability, and determination of the inspectors general, and enhance or weaken their reputation for having these qualities, only time will tell.

Clearly, without these attributes and a reputation for having them, the recommendations of inspectors general newly appointed by a president may be viewed as part of a system to identify shortcomings of the previous administration as a prelude to finding evidence of improvement during the current administration. One of the dismissed inspectors general commented: "Everybody wants a strong IG operation until it starts investigating them. The administration may start out thinking they want junkyard dogs, and what they may end up getting is French poodles."[36]

The perception that the Reagan administration is somewhat ambivalent on the issue of independence for inspectors general was reinforced when it permitted the Departments of Defense, Justice, and the Treasury to oppose legislation creating inspectors general in those departments unless each inspector general be subject to the authority, direction, and control of the head of the agency. This would constitute a significant departure from the concept of independence that is a hallmark of the Inspector General Act of 1978. While the administration yielded in the middle of its second term to bipartisan demands in Congress for a statutory inspector general in the Defense Department, it maintained its opposition to similar legislation for the Departments of Justice and the Treasury until the final months when it again yielded.

In opposing establishment of a statutory inspector general, the Department of Justice contended that this would superimpose an inspector general over the present authority of the attorney general, allow an independent inspector general to interfere with or jeopardize current external investigations and prosecutions, and require the inspector general to disclose sensitive or classified information. Similarly, the Treasury Department opposed inclusion under the Inspector General Act on the grounds that this would subject its decisions involving economic, tax, and monetary policy to inspector general review, thus dampening the free exchange of ideas necessary for developing economic policy; and it would also allow the inspector general to interfere with any ongoing investigation being conducted by Treasury's law enforcement bureaus.[37]

The objections raised by Justice and Treasury were addressed when statutory inspectors general were established at other federal agencies. The issue of classified information, for example, was faced when consideration was being given to establishing inspectors general in the Departments of Defense and State. GAO, in its reviews of the actual work of statutory inspectors general, found no basis for the kinds of problems anticipated by Justice and Treasury. On the positive side, GAO concluded that these inspectors general have strengthened federal internal audit and investigative work and improved government operations.[38]

President's Council on Integrity and Efficiency

By executive order, President Reagan established a Council on Integrity and Efficiency[39] to coordinate a governmentwide attack on fraud, waste, and mismanagement. Members include the deputy director of the Office of Management and Budget (as chairman), the deputy attorney general, the director of the Office of Personnel Management, the executive assistant director of investigations of the Federal Bureau of Investigation, and all the inspectors general. The chairman of the council reports to the president.

The council is charged with developing standards for the management and operation of inspector general activities, including audit and investigations programs where problems of fraud and waste exceed the capacity and jurisdiction of a single agency. The council provides a forum for exchanging information on the kinds of investigations that produce the best results. It also summarizes and reports overall on the activities of the inspectors general. For the period 1981 through 1987, the council reported that the combined resources of the inspectors general identified "wasteful and inefficient practices and the improved use of $110.5 billion of Federal resources, including:

The $97.7 billion in questioned costs upheld as a result of Inspector General and Defense Contract Audit Agency audits and management commitments to use funds more efficiently;

The $11.8 billion in agencies' commitments to recover funds; and

The $1.0 billion in investigative recoveries and penalties assessed through civil and criminal actions."[40]

For the same period, the work of inspectors general contributed to 22,965 successful civil and criminal prosecutions and 8,177 debarments and suspensions of persons or firms doing business with the government.[41]

Recognizing that there are many agencies in the executive branch that do not have inspectors general and therefore would not be represented on the council, the executive order also established the Coordinating Conference of the President's Council on Integrity and Efficiency. This interagency committee is composed of the chairman of the council and one representative from each executive branch agency not on the council. These representatives are the officials responsible for coordinating in each agency the efforts to eliminate fraud and waste. The conference meets at least quarterly to learn about the activities of the council and discuss ways of improving their own anti-waste and anti-fraud programs.

WASTE AND FRAUD "HOTLINE"

Waste, fraud, and mismanagement are not limited to the internal operations of government. Hundreds of billions of dollars are spent by government through contracts with thousands of business organizations for a wide variety of services and goods. In recent years, articles in *Harvard Business Review*, the *Wall Street Journal, Business Week,* and the general news media have chronicled numerous very costly examples of inefficiency and fraud in the private sector. Mismanagement and corruption in the operations of these government suppliers are also a major cause of waste of tax dollars.

In 1979, the U.S. General Accounting Office (GAO) established a toll-free, nation-wide "hotline" to help in the fight against fraud, abuse, and waste of federal funds. The hotline permits anyone to call GAO directly with relevant information about suspected criminal activities as well as administrative weaknesses involving federal expenditures. Callers do not have to reveal their names. The number is 1–800–424–5454. Most of the statutory inspectors general also have toll-free hotlines for those callers wishing to report directly to them suspected criminal activities involving the resources or employees of their federal agency.

Complaints to GAO relating to an agency with an inspector general are sent to that office for investigation. On serious allegations, GAO tracks the case and the agency must report the results of the investigation to GAO. If the allegation refers to an agency that does not have an inspector general, GAO investigates the allegation. Cases which produce evidence of criminal violations are referred to the Justice Department for further investigation and possible prosecution. Administrative deficiencies, along with recommendations for change growing out of the investigations, are called to the attention of agency executives for appropriate action.

In the first nine years of operation, the GAO hotline received over 90,000 calls of which 13,992 related to federal agencies and were sufficiently specific to follow up. Of these, 11,246 have been closed, with allegations substantiated in 1,589 cases. In another 580, the reported allegations were not substantiated, but the agencies acted to minimize the possibility of improper activity occurring in the future. Specific allegations were received from all 50 states and were directed against almost every agency and the Congress. Twenty-six percent of the complainants were federal employees. Of all the substantiated cases, the most common involved private use of government property, work-hour abuse by federal employees, fraud by recipients of benefits (welfare, social security, disability, and housing), and general mismanagement by government employees.[42]

There are no solid figures on actual savings resulting from the hotline operation. The cost of investigation is substantial. A strict cost-benefit analysis might very well show no net savings. Yet responsible officials believe the hotline provides useful leads for scheduling future audits and that its mere existence is a valuable deterrent.

PUBLIC INTEGRITY SECTION, U.S. DEPARTMENT OF JUSTICE

In the late 1980s, revelations about the Iran-Contra deceits and the corruption in military procurement contracting dominated the news. While every year, in all parts of the nation, at all levels and in all three branches of government, some public officials violate the law, it is reassuring that there are prosecutions and convictions.

The Public Integrity Section of the U.S. Department of Justice, which was established in 1976, has the responsibility to oversee the federal effort to combat corruption through the prosecution of elected and appointed officials. Its attorneys prosecute selected cases against *federal, state, and local officials*. These attorneys are also a source of assistance to law enforcement officials at all levels of government. This ranges from conducting formal training for investigators and prosecutors to providing specific advice on substantive questions, investigative methods, indictment drafting, and motions.

For the first ten years of its existence, the Public Integrity Section reported federal prosecution of government officials by U.S. attorneys as follows:

	Indictments	Convictions
Federal Officials	2,896*	2,583
State Officials	677	540
Local Officials	2,241	1,908

The officials prosecuted were in the judicial, legislative, and executive branches of government.[43] The executive branch cases prosecuted in the tenth year (1986) included these among others:

A former U.S. Internal Revenue Service (IRS) agent was convicted for "conspiring to defraud the United States of over $8 million in taxes by compromising IRS audits in return for approximately $220,000 in bribes." He was sentenced to ten years' incarceration.[44]

A former Assistant U.S. Attorney and Organized Crime Force Special

---

*Almost all of these cases originated with investigations and referrals by agency inspectors general.

Attorney was convicted for "selling confidential investigative information which compromised a series of important investigations." He was sentenced to 16 years in prison.[45]

Two former officials of the U.S. Department of Housing and Urban Development (HUD) pleaded guilty to "felony offenses of conspiracy to defraud the United States and to obstruct justice. They had approved inflated and fraudulent bills from contractors for repair of houses insured by HUD in return for having those contractors do substantial work on their homes." The sentences included imprisonment and $85,000 in civil settlements.[46]

A former Regional Director of the Office of Oversight, U.S. General Services Administration (GSA), pleaded guilty to a "violation of criminal conflict of interest statute. He supervised an investigation of a target of a GSA Inspector General investigation at a time when he was a business partner of the target." As a result of his plea, he was sentenced to two years' imprisonment with 18 months suspended, five years' probation, and a $7,500 fine.[47]

A former official of the Boston Redevelopment Authority was convicted of perjury. "As a prosecution witness in a federal criminal trial on extortion charges, he testified falsely that he did not remember meeting the defendant before the trial and demanding money to influence his testimony at the trial." He was sentenced to one year in prison for perjury.[48]

The former elected Treasurer of the Commonwealth of Pennsylvania was convicted of "agreeing to accept a $300,000 bribe (to be shared with the State Chairman of the Republican Committee for the Commonwealth, who was also convicted) in order to influence the awarding of a contract by a government agency." He committed suicide the day before his scheduled sentencing.[49]

The Commander of the Cook County (Illinois) Sheriff's Vice Control Unit and the Commander of the Sheriff's Intelligence Unit were convicted of "shaking down gamblers, bookmakers, keepers of houses of prostitution over a seven-year period." They were each sentenced to 15 years' imprisonment.[50]

The record demonstrates that some government officials do commit crimes, but they are not exempt from prosecution, conviction, *and* imprisonment. While even one instance of a government official dishonoring the public trust is one too many, it is useful to bear in mind, when considering the number of indictments and convictions listed earlier and the examples cited above, that there are over 16 million federal, state, and local employees.

CODES OF ETHICS

Scholars and practitioners are divided on the value of codes of ethics in influencing employee behavior. Their judgments range over a wide spectrum—codes of ethics are considered anything from counterproductive to helpful in preventing and controlling unethical conduct. The administration of codes of ethics draws similar mixed reviews, with arguments at one end that they are unenforceable because they must be general, and at the other end that they provide necessary warning and standards when disciplinary action may be appropriate.

Regardless of where the truth may lie, the fact remains that there has been a great increase in the number of codes of ethics adopted in the United States. Before 1970, only six states had codes of ethics. In the next two decades, 31 additional states adopted codes of ethics. These codes deal primarily with financial disclosure and prohibitions on behavior that create or give the appearance of a conflict of interest. Employees are prohibited from accepting gifts or favors intended to affect their official actions, disclosing or using for personal gain confidential information, using government resources for private gain, and contacts with the employing agency after the employee leaves government. Fewer than a fourth of the codes include positive guidance, and that is limited largely to self-development and responsiveness to the public. On the whole, state codes of ethics are symbolic, since they are not communicated well to employees and enforcement is spotty and weak.[51]

Nine years before the establishment of a code of ethics in any state, Congress by joint resolution adopted the following code for all federal employees:

Any person in Government service should:

1. Put loyalty to the highest moral principles and to country above loyalty to persons, party, or Government department.

2. Uphold the Constitution, laws, and legal regulations of the United States and of all governments therein and never be a party to their evasion.

3. Give a full day's labor for a full day's pay; giving to the performance of his duties his earnest effort and best thought.

4. Seek to find and employ more efficient and economical ways of getting tasks accomplished.

5. Never discriminate unfairly by dispensing of special favors or privileges to anyone, whether for remuneration or not; and never accept, for himself or his family, favors or benefits under circumstances which might be construed by reasonable persons as influencing the performance of his governmental duties.

6. Make no private promises of any kind binding upon the duties of office, since a Government employee has no private word which can be binding on public duty.

7. Engage in no business with the Government, either directly or indirectly, which is inconsistent with the conscientious performance of his governmental duties.

8. Never use any information coming to him confidentially in the performance of governmental duties as a means for making private profit.

9. Expose corruption wherever discovered.

10. Uphold these principles, ever conscious that public office is a public trust.[52]

Many federal agencies include provisions of this resolution in their information package for new employees, and some agencies incorporate them in their regulations governing employee conduct.

In 1965, President Johnson issued an executive order that not only gave more detailed policy guidance, but also called on the central personnel agency to issue regulations and to coordinate and monitor the actions of the agencies in implementing the policies. The first section states both the policy and its purpose:

Where government is based on the consent of the governed, every citizen is entitled to have complete confidence in the integrity of his government. Each individual officer, employee, or adviser of government must help to earn and must honor that trust by his own integrity and conduct in all official actions.[53]

Other sections lay down standards that are intended to cause employees to avoid any action "which might result in, or create the appearance of

1. using public office for private gain;
2. giving preferential treatment to any organization or person;
3. impeding government efficiency or economy;
4. losing complete independence or impartiality of action;
5. making a government decision outside official channels; or
6. affecting adversely the confidence of the public in the integrity of the Government.

To these same ends, the order established financial disclosure requirements for heads of agencies, full-time commissioners, and presidential appointees in the Executive Office of the president.

Additional ethics guidance is received by federal, state, and local employees who are members of professional associations that have codes of ethics, sometimes called codes of professional responsibility. Often these codes assert values that go beyond those in government codes. It is not unusual to find in them a commitment to (1) honoring the dignity of the individual being served, (2) a degree of knowledge and skill that evidences competence, and (3) cooperation with others in the profession.

Codes of ethics have been adopted for both symbolic and substantive reasons. They proclaim that certain behaviors are acceptable and others not. Advocates of codes believe that they cause more employees to be sensitive to ethical issues in their daily work, and that in itself helps hold government bureaucracies accountable. Few suggest that codes alone are the answer. Rather, codes of ethics are viewed as one *additional* tool to help government employees reach high standards of ethical conduct; such standards are, of course, essential to establishing and maintaining citizen confidence in government.

ETHICS IN GOVERNMENT ACT

For 13 years, President Johnson's executive order was the central ethics policy for the executive branch of the federal government. In 1977, following GAO reports that showed major deficiencies in 22 agencies in the application of requirements for financial disclosure and resolution of actual and apparent conflicts of interest, President Carter proposed remedial legislation.

The Ethics in Government Act of 1978[54] is responsive to GAO's findings and accepts most of Carter's recommendations. The act provided for the creation of an Office of Government Ethics with a director appointed by the president with the advice and consent of the Senate. The director is responsible for providing overall direction of executive branch policies related to preventing conflicts of interest by executive branch employees. It administers the financial disclosure requirements of the act, develops regulations on postemployment restrictions, issues advisory opinions, monitors agency compliance, and interprets rules and regulations concerning standards of conduct.

The act broadened financial disclosure by requiring detailed reports from high level civil service employees as well as presidential appointees. It deepened financial disclosure by requiring more extensive reporting. More specific and more demanding criteria were provided to identify and resolve conflicts of interest and the appearance thereof.

In fact, the new requirements were viewed as so stringent, particularly with regard to restrictions on executive branch officers and employees after they leave government service that many outstanding people declared their intention to resign before the act became effective. For the same reasons, individuals with superior qualifications were refusing to accept federal appointments. Consequently, the act was amended in 1979[55] to strike a better balance between the needs of the government and individual freedom with respect to financial disclosure requirements and postemployment restrictions.

Despite the 1979 changes, the law, particularly as it applies to financial disclosure, continues to be criticized by some as an obstacle to recruiting the nation's best managers; others see it as inadequate to protect the public interest with regard to conflict of interest during employment and in its postemployment restrictions. Some critics of the act appear to be unaware of the fact that there are a variety of other governmentwide and agency-specific laws and rulings that relate to the ethical conduct of federal employees. These include the criminal conflict-of-interest statutes in 18 United

States Code 201 through 209, executive orders discussed in the preceding section, comptroller general decisions, and attorney general opinions. Taken together, these "establish what constitutes a conflict of interest or the appearance of a conflict of interest. They provide the criteria for reviewing public financial disclosure reports filed under the Ethics Act."[56]

A study by Common Cause five years after passage of the Ethics in Government Act concluded that there are "some significant weaknesses in the implementation of ethics laws at the agency level." The study was based on a survey of Designated Agency Ethics Officials (DAEOs) of 50 federal agencies. Specifically, the study reported that the work of DAEOs was seriously underfunded in many agencies; the process by which DAEOs determine financial conflicts of interest is often ad hoc rather than systematic; monitoring and compliance with postemployment restrictions tends to be limited or nonexistent in many agencies; and communication between ethics officials and the Office of the Inspector General appears to be weak in most agencies.[57]

A later study by Common Cause of the Office of Government Ethics' role in investigating allegations of unethical conduct by 23 high-level Reagan administration officials led the president of Common Cause to charge that the office "has failed in one of its most basic responsibilities—to order enforcement of the law. . . . The basic question is whether the fundamental standards of conduct for public officials that have been in effect for decades are to be correctly applied or simply abandoned . . . "[58]

The absence of a strong monitoring and leadership role by the Office of Government Ethics (OGE) to prevent conflicts of interest or the appearance thereof, reflected the attitude of a former director who told GAO auditors that he views the role of the office "as that of a small legal and consulting firm providing expert opinions to its clients, the agencies."[59] The operation of the OGE under the same director came under sharp criticism for tending to be "soft on political appointees with obvious conflicts of interest and tough on career civil servants who may have committed minor transgressions." For example, career employees who violated the "appearance of impropriety" provision have been fired, whereas in the context of a political appointment, the director stated that such "appearances" do not violate the law.[60]

The chairman of the House Subcommittee on Human Resources, Committee on Post Office and Civil Service, focused on the application of the law to one high-level official. He requested GAO to "determine whether (1) Attorney General Edwin Meese III's public financial disclosure report for 1985 satisfied the requirements of the Ethics in Government Act and (2) the Department of Justice and the Office of Government Ethics properly reviewed the Attorney General's disclosure report." GAO concluded that the attorney general did *not* disclose certain assets as required by the act, and that neither Justice Department officials nor the Office of Government Ethics had taken the action required of them.[61]

The Ethics in Government Act, due to expire in 1988, was reauthorized for six years. There was no serious opposition to reauthorization. The law was clarified and the reporting, monitoring and enforcement role of the OGE were strengthened.[62]

THE INDEPENDENT COUNSEL

Abuses of the public trust by political appointees in the Nixon administration, and the president's decision to remove the special prosecutor appointed by the attorney general to investigate the *then alleged* Watergate crimes, led Congress to provide for the appointment of independent counsels as part of the 1978 Ethics in Government Act. The architects of the law sought to address the delicate task that faces our national government when it may be necessary for administration appointees in the Justice Department to decide whether to investigate and even prosecute other *high level administration appointees for criminal misconduct*, and to do so in a way that is fair and warrants the confidence of the people.

The Ethics in Government Act deals with this issue by providing that if the Justice Department receives *specific information from a reliable source* alleging that any of certain designated high government officials has committed a crime, unless preliminary investigation establishes there are no reasonable grounds to believe that further investigation or prosecution is warranted, the attorney general must request that a special panel of judges appoint an independent counsel. The Public Integrity Section of the Department of Justice is responsible for supervising the initial investigation and preparing a recommendation to the attorney general as to whether the independent counsel provisions have been triggered. If the attorney general determines that an independent counsel is not warranted, a full explanation for this conclusion must be filed with the special panel of judges. "After appointment, the independent counsel assumes 'full and independent authority to exercise all investigative and prosecutorial functions and powers of the Department of Justice, the Attorney General, and any other officer or employee of the Department of Justice,' except with respect to wiretaps. This includes the power to convene grand juries, grant immunity to witnesses, issue indictments, and 'handle all aspects of any case.' "[63]

In the two years remaining of the Carter administration after the ethics law became effective, two independent counsels were appointed to investigate two high government officials, including the president's chief of staff, Hamilton Jordan. In each case they concluded that criminal prosecution was not warranted. During the eight years of the Reagan administration, eight independent counsels were appointed to investigate 11 high government officials, including Counselor to the President and later Attorney General Edwin Meese III, former White House deputy chief of staff Michael Deaver, former assistant to the president Lyn Nofziger, former Secretary of Labor Raymond Donovan, former National Security Advisor John Poindexter, and former National Security assistant Oliver North.

As of the summer of 1988, the legal process had been completed on some of these cases and not on others. Independent counsels had concluded that further prosecution through seeking criminal indictments was not warranted in the case of Meese. Indictments were sought and obtained in the cases of Donovan, Deaver, Nofziger, Poindexter, and North. In subsequent jury trials, Donovan was acquitted; Deaver and Nofziger were convicted and sentenced to imprisonment. They appealed. The Iran-Contra judicial process starting with North and followed by Poindexter is expected to be lengthy.

The Independent Counsel statute was first authorized for only four years. With modest refinements and strong bipartisan support it was extended for another five years to 1987. Oversight hearings held in 1987 revealed some dissatisfaction with the operation of the law. The chairman of the Senate Subcommittee on Oversight of Government Management criticized the Department of Justice for "elaborate *pre*-preliminary investigations to avoid triggering the statute, missed 90-day deadlines, questionable standards for refusing to seek independent counsels . . . "[64]

In late 1987, Congress authorized the independent counsel program to continue without time limit.[65] In doing so, Congress also clarified the law in several important respects to increase the attorney general's accountability. The attorney general now has only 15 days to decide whether the information is specific and from a credible source, thus placing a cap on what the chairman of the subcommittee called "elaborate pre-preliminary investigations."

If a preliminary investigation is in order because the information is specific and from a credible source, or the attorney general was unable to reach a decision within 15 days, the preliminary investigation must commence not later than at the end of the 15-day period and it must not exceed 90 days from the date of its commencement. This change is designed to prevent an attorney general from continuing to review a matter without coming to a decision.

Another change was designed to prevent an attorney general from again closing a case before or after a preliminary investigation because the person alleged to have violated criminal law lacked the "state of mind" necessary to commit a crime. The law now provides that this "state of mind" justification is acceptable only if the attorney general has "clear and convincing evidence" to support it. The report of the conference committee on the 1987 statute states that the conferees believe it will be "a rare case in which the Attorney General will be able to meet the clear and convincing standard. . . . clear and convincing evidence will be difficult to collect because of the demanding nature of the proof necessary to establish the absence of intent, and because the Attorney General has no access during a preliminary investigation to important investigative tools such as grand juries and subpeonas." If an attorney general does conclude that there is such clear and convincing evidence, that evidence should be presented in detail in the report filed with the special court after a preliminary investigation.[66]

In a large measure, whether independent counsels can fulfill and be perceived as fulfilling the high purpose of the authorizing legislations depends on both their competence and independence from possible White House pressure. With regard to competence, the conferees agreed the special court should consider all relevant factors (investigative and trial experience, nature of case to be investigated, expertise in the law allegedly violated) and appoint the person who is most qualified to conduct the investigation and prosecution. As for independence, the person selected should have and be perceived as having the independence necessary to conduct an impartial investigation under the statute.

The conference report notes that during the Reagan administration, statements by the Department of Justice erroneously held that an independent counsel "may be fired for failing to obey *any* Presidential order—even an order which would compromise the very integrity of an independent counsel's proceedings."[67] While expressing confidence that any court reviewing the removal of such an independent counsel would reject the department's conclusion, the conferees made clear in their report that the law provides for removal only for good cause and this prohibits removals at the will of the president or the attorney general.

The fact that an independent counsel concludes that further *criminal* prosecution is not justified does *not* mean that the ethical behavior of the official is commendable. Quite to the contrary: the reports of independent counsels in such cases may reveal information which raises serious ethical questions, although not of a level to warrant criminal prosecution. (The conference committee report also provided important guidance to independent counsels with regard to referral of ethical violations discovered incidentally to their criminal investigations. Noting that one independent counsel did not refer noncriminal ethical violations to appropriate agencies in the belief that he was not authorized to do so, the report advises independent counsels to report such possible ethical violations to appropriate authorities [p. 32].)

For example, independent counsel Jacob Stein, the highly regarded Washington lawyer appointed by a panel of judges to examine allegations against Meese when he was counselor to President Reagan, stated in the preamble to his report that he "refused requests by Meese's lawyers to declare 'that the evidence does not substantiate the loose charges of moral turpitude against Mr. Meese,' and insisted that his mandate didn't allow him to 'admit an evaluation of fitness for public office or to express opinions of the type requested by Mr. Meese's counsel.' "[68]

In fact, Stein's report shows a sequence of events that leaves many readers wondering whether some people who helped Meese financially while he was counselor to the president may have in return received Meese's support in connection with their subsequent appointments to federal positions. Stein's report on some of the other allegations, which he determined do not rise to a level warranting criminal prosecution, also leaves many readers concerned about Meese's ethical propriety in those matters.

Similarly, Independent Counsel James C. McKay, appointed to investigate allegations against Meese while he served as attorney general, determined that the available admissible evidence did not warrant criminal prosecution. However, his report shows that the level of ethical behavior fell short of what might reasonably be expected from the nation's chief law enforcement officer. For example, the independent counsel determined "from the available evidence that a trier of fact would probably conclude beyond a reasonable doubt that Mr. Meese violated [law] by willfully failing to pay his income tax when due." The independent counsel decided not to prosecute because it was Meese's first such offense.[69]

The constitutionality of the independent counsel law was challenged by some of those being prosecuted as well as by the Reagan administration. A seven-to-one Supreme Court decision,[70] written by Chief Justice Rehnquist, reversed a lower court decision that declared unconstitutional the sections of the Ethics in Government Act creating the independent counsel. The Court rejected arguments that the law establishing a judicially appointed prosecutor violates the constitutional doctrine of separation of powers among the branches. With this decision, an important instrument for holding high government officials accountable remains intact and thereby helps preserve public confidence in the fairness and integrity of public officials.

ETHICS AND ADMINISTRATIVE DISCRETION

Confidence of the people in the administrative institutions of government relies heavily on *trust*—trust that the actions of officials will be in accord with the fundamental values in this pluralistic society. Ideas commonly held in the United States about what is ethical or moral come from many sources, including ancient Greek philosophers, Judeo-Christian traditions, Renaissance philosophers Montesquieu and Locke, the Declaration of Independence, the Constitution, and Supreme Court decisions.

Agency officials are often faced with ethical dilemmas. In his essay on "The Ethics of Administrative Discretion," Donald Warwick comments on dilemmas of professional integrity. "The most commonly mentioned ethical dilemmas have to do with conflicts between conscience and obedience to superiors; the use of deception, bribery, and other morally objectionable means; the uses and limits of administrative secrecy; conditions permitting or requiring 'whistle-blowing'; and the circumstances calling for resignation from public service."[71] Some public officials are insensitive to ethical concerns except if they involve a clear violation of law or prescribed rule. Of course, everything that is lawful is not ethical. Lawful administrative discretion generally leaves room for decisions that are in harmony with commonly held values.

In a decision of the Supreme Court, former Justice Felix Frankfurter said "The history of American freedom is, in no small measure, the history of procedure."[72] There is the expectation that the rules and procedures developed and applied by government officials will be in harmony with our commonly held values. Citizen confidence in government is undermined when officials try to absolve themselves of responsibility for unethical actions with such explanations as "I was just following orders"; "If I didn't do it, someone else would have"; "I had no choice."

There is the expectation that public officials will perform in a manner that demonstrates such qualities as personal integrity, commitment to the rule of law, respect for diversity of viewpoint, courage to decide in a timely way, and a concept of the public interest which leans decidedly toward administrative behavior that keeps alive and reinforces the great promises in the foundation documents of the nation—liberty, equality, justice, tranquillity, governing with the consent of the governed, freedom of speech, freedom of the press, freedom of religion, freedom of assembly, right to privacy, due process, and equal treatment under the law.

NOTES

1. 5 U.S.C., sect. 552 (1966).

2. Ramsey Clark, "Forward to Attorney General Memorandum and the Public Information Section of the Administrative Procedure Act," June 1967.

3. Samuel Archibald, "The Freedom of Information Act Revisited," *Public Administration Review*, 39 (July/August 1979): 311–17.

4. 5 U.S.C., sect. 552 (1974).

5. *Attorney General's Memorandum on the 1986 Amendments to the Freedom of Information Act*, U.S. Department of Justice, December 1987, p. 5.

6. U.S., Department of Justice, *FOIA Update*, Vol. 1. 1980.

7. Op. cit., *Attorney General's Memorandum*, pp. ii, 2–3.

8. Letter from Attorney General to Heads of All Departments and Agencies, May 5, 1977.

9. Memorandum from Attorney General to Heads of All Federal Departments and Agencies, May 4, 1981.

10. Report of the U.S. General Accounting Office, GGD–86–68, April 1986, pp. 1–4.

11. 5 U.S.C., sect. 552a (1974).

12. U.S., Congress, Senate, Governmental Affairs Committee, *Senate Report 813*, 89th Cong., 1st sess., p. 9.

13. U.S., Congress, House, Government Operations Committee, *House Report 1497*, 89th Cong., 2d sess., p. 2428.

14. U.S., Congress, House, Government Operations Committee, H98–455, November 1, 1983.

15. Report of the U.S. General Accounting Office, GGD–86–107, August 1986, p. 3.

16. Report of the U.S. General Accounting Office, GGS–88–15BR, November 1987, p. 1.

17. 92 Stat. 3641 (1979).

18. 90 Stat. 1241 (1976).

19. Washington *Post*, April 18, 1986, p. A–19.

20. Bruce Adams, "Guidelines for Sunset," *State Government* (Summer 1976).

21. U.S., Congress, Senate, Committee on Governmental Affairs, *Hearings on S–2, S–1304, Sunset Act of 1979*, June 7, 12, 13, 14; July 12, 24; September 13, 1979, 96th Cong., 1st sess.

22. 92 Stat. 1111 (1978).

23. Reorganization Plan #2 of 1978, 92 Stat. 3783 (1978).

24. Report of the U.S. General Accounting Office, GGS–88–11, November 1987, p. 2.

25. Ibid., p. 4; *Report on the Significant Actions of the Office of Personnel Management During 1983*, U.S. Merit Systems Protection Board, Washington, December 1984, p. 51.

26. A Study of U.S. Merit Systems Protection Board Appeals Decision for Fiscal Year 1986, Merit Systems Protection Board, Washington, September 1987.

27. Bernard Rosen, "Effective Continuity of Government Operations in Jeopardy," *Public Administration Review*, September/October 1983, p. 391.

28. *9th Annual Report, Federal Labor Relations Authority*, Washington, Fiscal Year 1987, Part II, Office of the General Counsel.

29. 88 S.Ct. 1731 (1968).

30. 94 S.Ct. 3187 (1975).

31. *McAuliffe* v. *City of New Bedford*, 155 Mass 216 (1892).

32. *Do Federal Employees Face Reprisal for Reporting Fraud, Waste, or Mismanagement/* Merit Systems Protection Board, 1981.

33. 92 Stat. 1101 (1978).

34. Washington *Post*, January 29, 1981, p. 1.

35. U.S., Congress, Senate, Committee on Governmental Affairs, *Report on Establishment of Office of Inspectors and Auditors General in Certain Executive Departments and Agencies*, August 8, 1978, 95th Cong., 2d sess.

36. Washington *Post*, February 2, 1981, p. A–8.

37. Statement of Milton J. Socolar, Special Assistant to the Comptroller General Before the Subcommittee on Legislation and National Security of the House Committee on Government Operations, May 17, 1988, pp. 6–7.

38. Ibid., pp. 3, 6–7.

39. Executive Order 12301, March 26, 1981.

40. *Management of the United States Government, U.S. Office of Management and Budget, Fiscal Year 1989*, p. 145.

41. Ibid., pp. 146–47.

42. Report of the U.S. General Accounting Office, OSI–88–1FS, April 1988, pp. 2–8.

43. Report to Congress on the Activities and Operations of the Public Integrity Section for 1986, U.S. Department of Justice, Criminal Division, June 1987, p. 44.

44. Ibid., pp. 27–28.

45. Ibid., p. 26.

46. Ibid., p. 12.

47. Ibid., p. 13.

48. Ibid., pp. 19–20.

49. Ibid., p. 37.

50. Ibid., p. 38.

51. "Codes of Ethics in State Government: A Nationwide Survey," *Public Personnel Management* 10 (1981): 48–58; *The Campaign Finance, Ethics, and Lobby Laws Blue Book, 1988–1989*, Council of State Governments, Table I.

52. U.S., Congress, *Codes of Ethics for Government Service: Concurrent Resolution of the United States Congress*, 85th Cong., 2d sess., July 11, 1958.

53. Executive Order 11222, May 8, 1965.

54. Public Law 95–521.

55. Public Laws 96–19 and 96–28.

56. Report of the U.S. General Accounting Office, FPCD–83–22, February 23, 1983, pp. 2–5.

57. *Bureaucratic Orphans*, Common Cause, Washington, 1984.

58. *Common Cause Magazine*, November/December 1986, p. 44.

59. Report of the U.S. General Accounting Office, FPCD–83–22, February 23, 1983, p. 6.

60. "The Office of Government Ethics, Vigilant Watchdog or Toothless Tiger?" *Government Executive*, October 1987, p. 25.

61. Report of the U.S. General Accounting Office, GGD–87–108, August 1987, pp. 1, 10–18.

62. P.L. 100–598, November 3, 1988.

63. U.S., Congress, Senate, Independent Counsel Reauthorization Act of 1987, Report of the Committee on Governmental Affairs, Report 100–123, July 24, 1987, p. 4.

64. Oversight of Independent Counsel Statute, S. Hearing 100–179, March 19, 20, 1987, p. 5.

65. Public Law 100–191, December 15, 1987.

66. Conference Report on Independent Counsel Reauthorization Act of 1987, House Report 100–452, 100th Cong., 1st sess., pp. 24–25.

67. Ibid., p. 37.

68. *Common Cause Magazine*, January/February 1985, p. 14.

69. Washington *Post*, July 19, 1988, p. A–9.

70. *Morrison, Independent Counsel* v. *Olson et al*, Slip Opinion No. 87–1279, June 29, 1988.

71. *Public Duties: The Moral Obligations of Public Officials*, eds. Fleishman, Liebman, and Moore (Cambridge: Harvard University Press, 1981), p. 93.

72. *Malinsky* v. *New York*, 324 U.S. 401 (1945).

Part III

The Future

Government bureaucracies are not out of control. Accountability policies and processes mandated by constitution, statutes, and chief executives preclude it. The significant gap between government promises and performance, however, can be further narrowed by better use of existing accountability mechanisms and some improvements in the accountability processes.

8

New Initiatives for

Improving

Accountability

Despite the number and redundancy of accountability mechanisms, the belief is prevalent among legislators, public administrators, and scholars that government bureaucracies are not as effective as they could be because of certain deficiencies in policies and processes for holding them accountable. Some go so far as to charge that government bureaucracies are out of control. Since the late 1960s, many ideas have been advanced for improving accountability. They range from more citizen involvement to educational programs on ethics and individual responsibility. This chapter focuses on areas where new initiatives are likely to generate significant improvements in accountability in the 1990s.

ACCOUNTABILITY FOR PRODUCTIVITY AND QUALITY IMPROVEMENT

With the explicit support of the president, the U.S. Office of Management and Budget initiated a major effort to improve productivity and quality of performance in the departments and agencies by providing relevant guidance and assistance and holding them accountable for achieving results.[1] The three central management agencies (Office of Management and Budget [OMB], Office of Personnel Management [OPM], and General Services Administration [GSA]), the Bureau of Labor Statistics (BLS), and the General Accounting Office (GAO) for many years had encouraged and assisted federal agencies in a variety of ways to improve productivity.

However, this new initiative constitutes the first attempt to achieve agency compliance with a comprehensive approach that focuses on "(1) quality and productivity management practices in executive-branch agencies; and . . . (2) continuous, incremental improvements in quality, timeliness and efficiency of services."[2] The emphasis is on making productivity improvement an integral part of the management process. Productivity improvement is achieved when there is "decrease in the unit costs of products or services delivered to the public, while maintaining specified standards of quality and timeliness."[3]

OMB will examine agency performance in the following areas:

Top management commitment to quality/productivity shown in practical actions (for example, top management has requested a significant increase in the employee training budget for productivity improvement skills training and made it a very high priority in its budgetary request);

Employee involvement and teamwork in problem solving and improving key services;

Quality and productivity training provided at all levels;

Elimination of barriers to productivity and quality improvement;

Employee recognition and incentive program established throughout the agency;

Customer orientation permeated every program function; and

Productivity and quality measures developed and standards set for program functions.[4]

While all of these are important, sound measurement systems and standards are essential to establishing goals, determining progress, and planning future actions. Most performance measurement systems are plagued with irrelevant and inaccurate measurement data, untimely and incorrect reporting, and inadequate managerial commitment. Without good performance data, it is virtually impossible to hold managers accountable in their major responsibilities.

By analyzing the information obtained from agencies semiannually, and by using the leverage OMB has with departments and agencies through its role as the president's agent on their budget and legislative proposals, OMB will be in a far better position to hold these organizations accountable for taking actions that improve productivity, quality, and timeliness.

PROMPT AUDIT RESOLUTION

Throughout his campaign for the presidency, Ronald Reagan talked persuasively about the need for rooting out fraud and waste in government. Nothing illustrates better the potential on this front than testimony of the comptroller general of the United States in 1981[5] (see chapter 3) indicating that billions of dollars could be saved if federal administrators would decide promptly and properly on recommendations of their own auditors for making improvements with regard to grants, contracts, subsidies, and agency operations for which they are responsible.

Since audit resolution was not then a new problem, and because it persists to a serious degree, it would be useful to highlight past efforts, along with the latest initiatives. In 1979, the comptroller general reported in detail to Congress on the problem of unresolved audit recommendations.[6] As a result, the Office of Management and Budget emphasized the problem's importance at meetings with agency heads and urged compliance with the existing instructions in its Circular A–73:

Each agency will establish policies for follow-up on audit recommendations. Timely action on recommendations by responsible management officials is an integral part of an agency's audit system, and has a direct bearing on its effectiveness. Policies will provide for designating officials responsible for follow-up, maintaining a record of the action taken on recommendations, and submitting periodic reports to agency management on action taken. When audit recommendations requiring corrective action involve more than one program, agency, or level of government, the agency making the audit should coordinate its corrective action with that of other affected organizations.[7]

Following hearings held by the House Government Operations Committee in 1979 that concluded that the above OMB policy had not been effective,[8] OMB issued a revised policy.[9] It contains more specific and more demanding requirements for audit resolution systems. At the 1979 hearings, the director of OMB acknowledged that it was necessary to go *beyond* issuing a tougher policy on audit follow-up and "integrate it with our budget review process."

Two years later, the comptroller general testified that review of audit resolution systems had not become part of the budget process. He went on to state that "Had OMB reviewed agencies' audit resolution systems, it would have learned, as we did, that agencies are not complying with Circular A–73 and that clarification is needed in its provisions to ensure: complete reporting to agency heads, applicability of the Circular to all findings, and conformity with laws and regulations of all decisions not to act on findings."[10]

Evidence of the failure to comply with the directive of the president's principal officer for management and budget is both revealing and distressing. Of 71 agencies whose audit resolution systems were examined by GAO in 1981,

40 agencies did not maintain accurate and current records of action on findings through final disposition;

37 agencies did not have adequate procedures that would assure accounting and collection controls over amounts due the government;

49 agencies did not have adequate procedures to assure that failure to act on audit recommendations, or disagreements between program managers and auditors, would be brought to the attention of the agency head or the agency head's designee;

56 agencies did not require periodic reports to the agency head on age and amounts of unresolved audit findings, and/or results of findings closed during the period;

16 agencies did not have audit resolution systems that would apply to *all* audits of agency activities, including those of contractors, subgrantees, and regulated activities;

22 agencies did not make all decisions on audit recommendations in six months with final disposition as soon as possible thereafter as required by OMB policy and the Supplemental Appropriations and Recission Act of 1980;

50 agencies did not resolve all audit findings according to law and regulation, including written justification with legal basis for decisions not to act; and

28 agencies did not have adequate procedures for coordinating corrective actions with other affected agencies or organizations.

These deficiencies help explain how agency officials could "forgive and forget error, waste, abuse, and misuse of federal funds."[11] In the light of these facts, the comptroller general proposed that OMB and heads of federal agencies take specified actions designed to strengthen policies and fix accountability in the vital area of internal audit.[12]

Both Congress and OMB acted in 1982 to improve audit resolution. For many years, the chairman of the House Government Operations Committee has been convinced that internal controls over operations and expenditures had a low priority in the agencies. "The lack of strong and effective controls has created opportunities for waste, misuse, and mismanagement, as well as fraudulent transactions," he declared at the outset of hearings which led to the Financial Integrity Act of 1982. While recognizing the importance of good judgment, competence, and ethical behavior, he expressed the need for legislation to "make Government managers responsible for their actions and accountable to the public that they serve."[13]

Congress passed the Federal Managers Financial Integrity Act (discussed in Chapter 3), which calls for prompt resolution of all audit findings and annual reports on internal control system weaknesses. OMB issued detailed instructions to federal agencies along the lines advocated by GAO.[14] Specifically, OMB directed the heads of executive departments and agencies to do the following:

Provide for appointment of a top level audit follow-up official.

Require resolution and corrective action within six months of receipt of audit recommendations.

Specify criteria for proper resolution and corrective action, including written plans and action dates where appropriate.

Maintain accurate record of the status of recommendations through the entire process of resolution and corrective action.

Provide a means to resolve major disagreements between audit organization and agency management.

Assure that resolution actions are consistent with law, regulation, and Administration policy and include written justification for decisions not agreeing with audit recommendations.

Provide for coordinating resolution and corrective action on recommendations involving more than one program, agency, or level of government.

Provide semiannual reports to the agency head on the status of all unresolved audit reports over six months old, the reasons therefor, and a timetable for their resolution.

Provide for periodic analysis of audit recommendations, resolution, and corrective action to determine trends and systemwide problems, and to recommend solutions.

Assure that performance appraisals of appropriate officials reflect effectiveness in resolving and implementing recommendations.

Provide for annual evaluations of whether the audit follow-up system results in efficient, prompt, and proper resolution and corrective action on audit recommendations.[15]

In the memorandum transmitting the above instructions, OMB told department/agency heads that they were being relied on to assure "prompt and proper resolution of all audit recommendations."[16]

There has been some improvement in audit resolutions since 1982, but more is needed. In December 1987, GAO reported to Congress on resolution of audit recommendations that "agencies do not consistently ensure effective and prompt actions." For example, "Defense as well as other agencies sometimes considered a weakness as having been corrected through the issuance of policy guidelines or plans for corrective action." GAO also reported that "corrective actions taken were not always effective," and "audit follow-up systems were not always effective."

Thus, GAO's review of 377 recommendations made by inspectors general of the Departments of Army, Air Force, and Defense, where managers and follow-up officials claimed in semiannual reports that corrective action had been completed, revealed that in 16 percent of the cases "such actions had apparently not been taken as claimed."[17] This lack of full agency compliance with OMB's directives on audit resolution also pointed up the failure of OMB to adequately oversee compliance with its requirements. The new organization and management initiatives described in the next section are designed to overcome these problems.

EFFECTIVE INTERNAL CONTROLS AND FINANCIAL MANAGEMENT

On July 23, 1987, the comptroller general of the United States, testifying before the Senate Committee on Governmental Affairs, declared that there was an urgent need to improve federal financial management in order to effectively hold federal managers accountable for their financial activities. He said: "Recent reports are replete with examples of problems ranging from an inability to account for a half billion dollars of foreign military sales deposits to an inability to manage or report on the loans and accounts owed to our government.... We can no longer afford to rely on systems and concepts that do not provide the financial information and accountability needed by the Congress, federal managers, and the public."[18]

The comptroller general proposed legislation that would include centralized financial management leadership responsible for developing and implementing a governmentwide improvement plan; corresponding financial management leadership in the agencies; and annual preparation and audit of agency and governmentwide financial statements.

The comptroller general recommended that the central leadership responsibility be placed in a new statutorily created position of Under Secretary of the Treasury for Financial Management that would be filled by a career employee. Similarly, agency chief financial officers should be career employees to provide continuity in leadership for the effort to improve financial management.

In recommending location of governmentwide leadership for financial management in Treasury, the comptroller general differed with the declared intention of OMB to establish the position in OMB, and by executive action. In favoring Treasury over OMB, he expressed concern about "OMB's historic lack of support for management activities in deference to budget responsibilities" and the fact that OMB usually has not linked management improvements to budget decisions.

He went on to say: "I am concerned about the frequent turnover in top-level positions in OMB. Recent support at OMB for financial improvements demonstrates that when someone takes an active interest progress can be made. However, the very fact that progress is dependent on who takes an interest demonstrates the tenuous position we are in. If we look at the chain of command at OMB as it relates to financial management since 1981, we find there have been two directors, two deputy directors, and four Associate Directors for Management.... Such organizational instability can have profound effects on the line agencies throughout the executive branch as they try to implement policies established by a changing group of officials."[19]

OMB did establish administratively, in July 1987, a chief financial officer to provide needed central direction and guidance for improving financial management government wide. Each agency also designated a chief financial officer in December 1987, and a council of these officers was formed to provide advice and assistance to OMB's governmentwide chief financial officer. OMB intends to develop legislation to define and provide a statutory foundation for a permanent financial officer structure in the federal government. It is intended that this organization would provide critical continuity for financial operations and improvement programs through changes of administration.[20]

Increased interest in high-level attention to internal controls is not unique to the federal government. At state and local government levels, this need is being recognized. In the private sector, top management is giving greater attention to such controls; there is a growing movement to include statements on companies' control systems in their annual reports to stockholders. All reflect the need and desire for better accountability.

CLEAR LEGISLATIVE OVERSIGHT REQUIREMENTS

The mechanisms and methods for overseeing administrative agencies available to Congress and legislative bodies in many states are formidable. The tendency of legislative bodies is to exercise their enormous oversight powers upon those administrative issues that have the potential for or have already achieved high visibility. Unfortunately, episodic micromanagement is the end product of much legislative oversight.

The comptroller general of the United States, responding to a request from Senator Patrick Leahy, advanced a far-reaching proposal for improving congressional oversight that is also relevant to state and local legislatures. The central idea is that committees of Congress would include oversight requirements when they reported authorizing legislation. These requirements would make *clear* the intent of Congress when enacting legislation by specifying the pertinent oversight issues and questions. The agency responsible for program management would be called on to furnish on an established timetable program-performance information and other evaluation data that would be responsive to the issues and questions and thereby make possible effective oversight.[21]

The comptroller general's proposal has six sequential stages. The first occurs at the time Congress enacts legislation authorizing a program. Here, Congress, through the work of authorizing committees, would take the crucial and often very difficult step of stating as precisely as possible what Congress expects the program to accomplish and what general oversight questions Congress expects the agency to answer as the program is implemented.

Stage two calls for a written policy presentation to the authorizing committees of Congress by the executive branch that describes the strategy and major actions the responsible agency will take to implement the legislated program. This presentation would identify the general types of information that the agency would collect during implementation to address the oversight questions. Congressional committees would be able to review the strategy and reporting plans. The committees could also, where needed, clarify and resolve any differences with the agencies over legislative intent concerning either results or reporting on the implementation process.

Stages three and four are to be used only when Congress wishes to exercise very stringent oversight. Stage three requires the agency to report its program design and a summary of regulations, guidelines, procedures, and *kinds* of monitoring and evaluative information that the agency will use in implementing the program. Congressional committees would review this material (more detailed than in stage two) and resolve any differences with the agency, to meet both the policy and oversight intent of Congress.

Stage four would require the agency to describe how the program is actually being carried out, based on surveys of operations made by agency evaluators. These surveys would establish whether the program is operating in accordance with applicable guidelines and regulations. Again, at this point, congressional committees would be able to clarify intent and correct any misinterpretations.

Stage five would have the agency develop specific program evaluation plans and report them to congressional committees. The reports would include a description of planned data collection, measurement analysis and related evaluative activities, and estimated costs of these processes. If the agency believed the cost is too high in relation to benefits, it would propose alternative evaluation designs. Information in the report should permit congressional committees to determine whether the program could be evaluated in a sufficiently thorough, timely, and economical manner to meet legislative and oversight needs. Congressional committees would be able to initiate necessary discussions with agencies to achieve agreement on important issues, measurements, and comparisons.

At this point in the sequential process, Congress would be reasonably certain that in accordance with legislative intent, the responsible agency had developed and begun implementing the authorized program, that the program could be evaluated in terms of specified oversight questions, within a set timetable and cost, and using agreed-upon measurements. This would lead naturally to stage six, where the agency would execute the evaluation plan and report to Congress on the results of its monitoring and evaluation activity.

While the comptroller general believed that this process would make possible effective congressional oversight without unduly burdening the members and staff of Congress, he recognized that if carried to excess, it would lead to unwarranted intrusion into executive branch responsibilities and could even delay implementation of programs. Therefore the designers of the plan did not propose that the stages be followed in every detail for every law. Rather, they advocated adoption of this concept and framework for a disciplined process to provide a climate and structure for tailoring oversight on a case-by-case basis to the nature of the program under review and the specific oversight interests of Congress.[22]

Accountability through legislative oversight would be further improved if Congress focused additional attention on GAO audits and recommendations. Some of GAO's recommendations to improve the effectiveness and efficiency of policies and programs remain unattended for long periods of time by congressional committees, as well as agencies. This continuing deficiency is reflected in a report furnished at the beginning of each congressional session by GAO to House and Senate committees on appropriations.

It summarizes the conclusions and recommendations from reports of GAO's audits and other review work previously furnished agencies and Congress—but where *satisfactory legislative or administrative actions have not been taken*. The summary is compiled to assist congressional committees in their review of agency requests for appropriations for the next fiscal year. GAO also provides committees, at their request, specific questions to be asked of agency officials in appropriation hearings on these recommendations. The 1988 GAO summary contained 1,298 recommendations, 60 of which dealt with matters that would require action by Congress.[23]

RIGOROUS SENATE CONFIRMATION

A significant weakness in the operation of our federal system of checks and balances exists in the Senate's performance on its "advice and consent" responsibility which is provided for in the U.S. Constitution, Article 2, Section 2. The committees and the full Senate proceed on the presumption that the president's nominees are qualified until proven otherwise. "Advice" from the Senate has been infrequent, and "consent" has been largely perfunctory. The result is that on numerous occasions, important policy-making and executive functions of government have been entrusted to individuals who lack the necessary qualities; little use has been made of the consent role to emphasize what Congress would hold the nominee accountable for.

A study by the Senate Committee on Governmental Affairs of the confirmation process for appointments to regulatory agencies documents the problem and recommends specific policies and procedures to improve the system. Foremost is the committee's proposal that the Senate fill an existing vacuum by establishing the following "general standards for Senate approval of regulatory nominees":

1. That by reason of background, training or experience, the nominee is affirmatively qualified for the office to which he or she is nominated.

2. That, in considering a regulatory appointment, the Senate shall consider the character and nature of the office, and the needs of the agency to which the nominee has been named.

3. That, in considering a regulatory appointment to a collegial body, the Senate shall consider the existing composition of that body and whether or not members of a single sector or group in society are too heavily represented.

4. That the nominee is committed to enforcement of the regulatory framework as established by Congress in the statutes.

5. That the nominee meets the statutory qualifications to hold the office to which he or she was nominated.[24]

The committee also proposed that the Senate establish procedures providing, as a minimum:

1. That every nominee to a regulatory agency be the subject of a public confirmation hearing with at least seven days' advance notice to the general public of the date of that hearing.

2. That committees with jurisdictions over regulatory agency appointees submit to the full Senate seven days in advance of every proposed appointment a written report containing the conclusions, recommendations, and any dissenting opinions of the committee on the nominee.

3. That the nominee agree to appear and testify, upon request, before any Congressional committee.

4. When a person is nominated to a commission, and it is also the intention of the President to designate that person chairman of that commission, the nomination papers to the Senate shall include a statement of the President's intention as far as the chairmanship designation.

5. That the President submit to the Senate nominees for regulatory vacancies at the earliest practicable time in order to avoid unnecessary and harmful lapses in commission membership.

6. That the Senate request that the President submit, as part of the nomination papers, a statement indicating the reasons for a particular selection and pointing out any relevant factors in the nominee's background or training that qualified him or her for appointment.[25]

Few committees conduct background investigations. Instead they rely upon a simple statement from the president that the nominee is fit—this is based on investigations conducted for the chief executive by the Federal Bureau of Investigation. Most but not all committees require each nominee to complete a questionnaire. The content varies with the committee. Some are very comprehensive, requesting information on education, previous employments and commitments for the future, financial disclosure, proposed remedies for potential conflicts of interest, lobbying efforts to influence legislation or administrative policy in the preceding ten-year period, and views on policies relevant to the position for which nominated.

Unfortunately, few of the committees using such questionnaires follow through with their own staff investigators to help establish a firm factual record for use by committee members in determining the fitness of the nominees, nor do all of them insist on submission of the completed questionnaires sufficiently in advance of the hearing to permit members and staff to study them and formulate appropriate questions for the hearing. These conditions led the Governmental Affairs Committee to recommend the creation of a small office whose professional staff would serve all committees of the Senate in the confirmation process by investigating nominees for regulatory agencies and making reports to the relevant committees before hearings are held.[26]

Another study of the confirmation process was conducted by Common Cause.[27] It focused on 50 of President Carter's most important nominations for top policy-making positions in the executive branch, including nine to regulatory agencies. Common Cause found that the 14 Senate committees dealing with these had a "hodgepodge of procedures and practices." While public hearings were held on 49 of the 50 nominees, only 14 nominees were required to testify under oath; and a mere seven completed questionnaires on relevant policy questions before the hearing. All nominees were approved; but there were recorded committee votes for only half, written committee reports on six, and recorded Senate votes on the same small number. These procedures and practices can hardly be construed as encouraging individual accountability on the part of either the Senators or the nominees.

In the light of these and related findings, Common Cause recommended policies and procedures for strengthening the confirmation process by providing for a full public record, time to deliberate, and affirmative standards for confirmation. Common Cause proposed that to develop a full public record, nominees be required

to complete a uniform personal and financial background questionnaire that would be published in the committee report and hearing record;

to file their tax return for recent years with the Senate—on a confidential basis if desired;

to state in writing how they will resolve potential conflicts of interest; and

to disclose their political affiliations, political contributions in last ten years, and past lobbying activities; those who ran for political office should disclose all major contributors and explain how any remaining campaign debts will be paid;

and that

nominees to major policy positions be required to respond to written questions on policy matters in advance of hearings;

the Senate establish a small office as recommended by the Senate Governmental Affairs Committee to review questionnaires completed by nominees, conduct such additional investigations as needed on the background and integrity of nominees to supplement the work of the Senate Committee;

nominees testify under oath;

committees make printed hearing records available before votes on major and controversial nominations in so far as possible;

committees prepare written substantive reports on nominations that receive their approval for major policy positions; reports should explain why the nominee is affirmatively qualified for the particular office; and that

senators' votes be recorded in committee on all nominations for policy-making positions, and on the floor for all nominations for Supreme Court, cabinet officers, regulatory commissioners, and others that are controversial.

In calling for a more deliberative process, Common Cause recommended that the Senate establish a timetable for consideration of nominees that could be suspended only by a recorded vote; that the timetable allow at least two weeks between receipt of nomination and a public hearing to permit review of background information; that nomination hearings be publicized at least a week in advance by press release and notice in the Congressional Record; that several days elapse between public hearings and committee votes to provide time for review of transcripts and reasoned deliberation; and that similar time for deliberation be provided after release of committee report and before the Senate votes.

As did the Governmental Affairs Committee, Common Cause recommended that the Senate establish affirmative standards for confirmation—that nominees be persons of high personal and professional integrity with administrative competence appropriate to the office; and that they be firmly committed to basic principles of accountability as well as to enforcing and implementing the major laws and programs within their jurisdiction. In addition, Common Cause recommended that each Senate committee periodically establish more specific standards for positions within its jurisdiction, and that the Senate should approve only those nominees who are affirmatively qualified to serve in the positions for which they were nominated.

The Senate has not established rules relating specifically to the confirmation process in committees. Senate Rule XXVI deals with committee procedures, but it remains largely irrelevant to the problems identified by the Senate Governmental Affairs Committee and Common Cause. Since the 1977 studies, few of the Senate committees have changed their own rules regarding the confirmation process. Several have improved their practices by having nominees complete more detailed questionnaires, but many of the other recommendations have not yet influenced the committees.

While the procedural improvements recommended by the Senate Governmental Affairs Committee and Common Cause are not a panacea for all problems in the confirmation process, their adoption and rigorous application would give greater meaning to "advice and consent," and strengthen the foundation for holding presidential appointees accountable.

PROTECTING WHISTLE-BLOWERS

According to surveys of federal employees conducted by the Merit Systems Protection Board (MSPB) in 1980 and 1983, the number of federal employees who felt they could *not* safely come forward with information on waste and mismanagement was increasing. In 1980, 20 percent of employees who saw such problems did not report them because of a fear of reprisal. In 1983, that figure had grown to 37 percent.[28]

As discussed in Chapter 7, the Civil Service Reform Act (CSRA) created an Office of Special Counsel. One of the special counsel's statutory responsibilities is to ensure that whistle-blowers are fairly protected by examining their allegations of reprisal and serving as the employee's advocate if the special counsel finds merit in the allegations. The special counsel serves as advocate by ordering the employing agency to investigate and report back on the substance of the allegation.

If the special counsel determines that the evidence supports the allegation of reprisal, the special counsel then continues to serve as advocate of the employee by attempting to resolve the problem informally with the agency and, failing that, by presenting the evidence of reprisal to the Merit Systems Protection Board. The latter has the authority to order corrective action by the agency and to discipline those responsible if it determines reprisals were taken against the employee for whistle-blowing.

In the years following enactment of these provisions, there have been many complaints by federal employees that the special counsel had *not* protected them from reprisals for whistle-blowing. Some charged that, without any discussion with them, the special counsel unfairly concluded in the initial examination of the allegations, that their cases lacked merit, thereby precluding directed investigation by the agency, further consideration and action by the special counsel, and decision by the MSPB. Testimony before the House Subcommittee on Civil Service showed that the Office of the Special Counsel closed one-third to one-half of all its cases without meeting with the complainant and without conducting any inquiry.[29]

Of the four individuals who have been appointed special counsel by the president, with the advice and consent of the Senate, one taught a course for federal managers on *how to fire whistle-blowers* while serving as special counsel. Another denied any responsibility to assist wronged individuals. This same special counsel was so unwilling to risk losing a case that he said he would litigate before the Merit Systems Protection Board on behalf of a whistle-blower *only* if there is "virtual certainty that the evidence provides sufficient fact to ensure success." Still another special counsel applied a very different criterion in deciding to litigate a case—"at least a reasonable likelihood of success."[30]

Until early 1989, decisions by the special counsel not to investigate or prosecute cases foreclosed the employees from personally appealing to the MSPB for decision on the merits following the process used in other employee appeals. (Employees with such assistance as they themselves engage, obtain and present evidence to an MSPB administrative law judge, who in turn recommends a decision to the board.)

The Senate report accompanying the CSRA pointed out that "protecting employees who disclose government illegality, waste, and corruption is a major step toward a more effective civil service."[31] Nine years later, the House Committee on Civil Service concluded, after examining in detail the cases of many individuals who sought assistance from the special counsel, that there is a need to "clarify the special counsel's responsibility to represent and protect whistle-blowers. . . . that the primary role of the special counsel is to represent Federal employees who claim to be the victims of prohibited personnel practices. . . . with the zeal and thoroughness of a lawyer representing a client."[32]

Whistle-blower protection bills approved in 1988 were the basis for Public Law 101–1, April 10, 1989. This by the House Post Office and Civil Service Committee[33] and by the Senate Governmental Affairs Committee[34] to deal with the problems already identified were the basis for Public Law 101–1, April 10, 1989. This legislation will enhance the value of whistle-blowing as an accountability instrument.

TRAINING IN ETHICS AND INDIVIDUAL RESPONSIBILITY

Even if all *reasonable* actions were taken to hold government bureaucracies accountable, perfection would not be achieved, nor would it, in truth, be desirable. Accountability mechanisms, processes, and commitment required to assure perfection—fully responsive, effective, efficient, mistake-and-corruption-proof execution of the laws—would have to be so comprehensive and operationally intrusive as to suffocate the initiative, decisiveness, and courage of public administrators. Since such a situation is unacceptable, the remaining safeguards must be the values and self-discipline of individual public administrators. In exercising necessary discretion to serve the public interest, administrators often reflect their personal ethics as they interpret and apply what the legislatures and courts have proclaimed. *Value-free administration is largely a myth*.

From the beginning of the Republic, political leaders have spoken out on the importance of basic values in the actions of public officials in a democratic society:

The whole art of government consists in the art of being honest. (Thomas Jefferson)

The man who debauches our public life . . . is a greater foe to our well-being as a nation than is even the defaulting cashier of a bank. . . . Without honesty popular government is a repulsive farce. (Theodore Roosevelt)

When people are dishonorable in private business, they injure only those with whom they deal or their own chances in the next world. But when there is a lack of honor in government, the morals of the whole people are poisoned. (Herbert Hoover)

The stewardship of public officers is a serious and sacred trust. (Franklin D. Roosevelt)

In world opinion and in world effectiveness, the United States is measured by the moral firmness of its public officials. (Dwight D. Eisenhower)

No President can excuse or pardon the slightest deviation from irreproachable standards of behavior on the part of any member of the executive branch. For his firmness and determination is the ultimate source of public confidence in the government of the United States. (John F. Kennedy)[35]

The Constitution, laws, and court decisions establish the basic values of our constitutional democracy. The values held by public administrators flow from this legal foundation, from their parents, teachers, religious leaders, and peers, and from other influences including the norms of the institutions in which they are employed. These values affect the policy and management choices of administrators as they recommend and implement legislation.

Stephen K. Bailey's outstanding essay on ethics and the public service[36] identifies "mental attitudes" and "moral qualities" as the essential ingredients of personal ethics in the public service. Mental attitudes bearing heavily on personal ethics are "(1) a recognition of the moral ambiguity of all men and of all public policies, (2) a recognition of the contextual forces which condition moral priorities in the public service, and (3) a recognition of the paradoxes of procedures. The essential moral qualities of the ethical public servant are (1) optimism, (2) courage, and (3) fairness tempered by charity."[37]

There are endless examples of moral ambiguity in policies and people. The achievement of worthy purposes through a particular public policy is often accompanied by predictably undesirable consequences. Personal and private considerations are rarely excluded when decisions are made; yet time and again public officials sublimate their own interests to serve the public interest better.

Bailey notes that "if a public interest is to be orbited, it must have as a part of its propulsive fuel a number of special and particular interests. A large part of the art of public service is in the capacity to harness private and personal interests to public interest causes. Those who will not traffic in personal and private interests (if such interests are themselves within the law) to the point of engaging their support on behalf of causes in which both public and private interests are served are, in terms of moral temperament, unfit for public responsibility."[38] To avoid being immobilized by these ambiguities, administrators require both optimism and courage.

The context within which value judgments are made affect the priorities given them. Conflicting loyalties, yielding on one worthy cause to prevail on another, lying to minimize damage to an activity of great public importance—all produce ethical dilemmas and strain the personal value system of the administrator. Context can appear to remove much of the "bad" from an immoral act and much of the "good" from a moral one.

As for the paradoxes of procedure, "rules, standards, procedures exist, by and large, to promote fairness, openness, depth of analysis, and accountability in the conduct of the public's business. Those who frequently bypass or shortcut established means are thereby attacking one aspect of that most precious legacy of the past: the rule of law. . . . But, alas, if procedures are the friend of deliberation and order, they are also at times the enemy of progress and dispatch. . . . For in the case of procedures, he who deviates frequently is subversive; he who never deviates at all is lost; and he who tinkers with procedures without an understanding of substantive consequences is foolish. . . . Procedural flexibility in the public interest is achieved only by the optimistic, the courageous, and the fair."[39]

Optimism is an essential moral quality for public service. An optimism born of rational hopefulness, not euphoria, one that rejects cynicism, "enables man to face ambiguity and paradox without becoming immobilized. It is essential to purposive as distinct from reactive behavior . . . true optimism is the affirmation of the worth of taking risks . . . it is the capacity to see the possibilities for good in the uncertain, the ambiguous, and the inscrutable."[40]

As noted earlier, the moral quality of courage is essential for dealing effectively with the ambiguities and paradoxes that confront the public administrator. Courage in public service is fostered by "ambition, a sense of duty, and a recognition that inaction may be quite as painful as action."[41] Courage is severely tested when administrators find that the public interest would *probably* be served better by rejecting rather than approving the special pleadings of close, long-time friends and highly regarded colleagues, or the advice of the widely recognized expert whose technical knowledge is beyond question. Obviously, the most necessary and frequent courage is the courage to decide—to act; for decisions generally attract supporters and critics, but it is the latter who are motivated to voice their views and pursue their adversaries tenaciously.

Bailey characterizes the third moral quality, fairness tempered by charity, as "perhaps the most essential" for the public service. ". . . the moral imperative to be just—to be fair—is a limited virtue without charity. Absolute justice presupposes omniscience and total disinterestedness. Public servants are always faced with making decisions based upon both imperfect information and the inarticulate insinuations of self-interest into the decisional calculus. Charity is the virtue which compensates for inadequate information and for the subtle importunities of self in making of judgments designed to be fair. Charity is not a soft virtue. To the contrary it involves the ultimate moral toughness. . . . Its exercise makes of compromise not a sinister barter but a recognition of the dignity of competing claimants."[42]

Throughout society the interest in ethics has recently reawakened, due in part to Watergate, the Iran-Contra affair, investigations by independent counsels of presidential appointees, and technological and social developments that have raised fundamental moral questions about national security, law and liberty, and life itself. Beginning in the 1970s, increased attention has been given to ethics by the professions, business, the public service, and academia. In higher education, the number of applied ethics courses has grown substantially. The purpose is to "teach students methods of ethical decision making that will equip them to deal with real life ethical dilemmas in an informed and responsible manner once they begin professional practice."[43]

Scholars in the Institute of Society, Ethics, and the Life Sciences, popularly known as the Hastings Center, assessed the state of the art of applied ethics in higher education and issued a nine-volume series of monographs in 1980.[44] They found over 1,100 courses in ethics applied to medicine, law, corporate responsibility, nursing, engineering, journalism, environment, social science research, and public policy-making. While the coverage and quality of these courses varied greatly, they all aimed to compensate for some of the narrowness of twentieth-century professional education. Moral education, the capstone of the American college curriculum in the nineteenth century, had been displaced by the curricula for the professions at whose center is the scientific method. The new applied ethics are intended to help fill the gap by causing students to examine the moral purposes of their professions.

The Hastings studies found that most colleges and universities do not *require* applied courses in ethics, and many of the courses that have been established are precariously funded and inadequately staffed. They reported that, in general, applied ethics courses have not been accepted within the academic community because of a strong fear that they will threaten freedom of choice—that they will be sources of indoctrination. Contrariwise, the director of the Hastings Center saw little cause for concern if the applied ethics courses and teachers are good. He pointed out that "Teaching methods of ethical decision making does not mean teaching one ethical approach or moral code. The aim is to liberate a student's thinking, not to restrict it."[45]

Harvard University President Derek Bok expressed similar views in commenting on recent development of college courses "designed to explore practical moral problems." He said: "In problem-oriented courses, instructors can avoid the dangers of indoctrination simply by taking care to expose their students to a variety of readings and to refrain from dictatorial methods in class discussions. The vast majority of professors understand these pedagogic principles well enough." He went on to say, "Many students who are disposed to act morally will often fail to do so because they are simply unaware of the ethical problems that lie hidden in the situations they confront. Others will not discover a moral problem until they have gotten too deeply enmeshed to extricate themselves. Through repeated discussions that seek to identify moral problems and define the issues at stake, courses in applied ethics may help students to avoid these pitfalls by sharpening and refining their powers of moral perception. . . . With the help of carefully selected readings and well directed discussions, students may learn to sort out all the arguments that bear upon ethical problems and apply them with care to concrete situations."[46]

The Hastings Center studies proposed that applied ethics courses at the undergraduate and graduate levels meet five basic goals:

1. Stimulating the moral imagination: Help students to recognize that each moral choice has repercussions for others, to understand that every human action can be seen from a moral point of view and that no decision is strictly "professional."

2. Recognizing ethical issues: Help students learn to distinguish ethical from political and economic questions in given situations.

3. Developing analytical skills: Help students learn to examine and make distinctions among large concepts such as justice, dignity, privacy, virtue, right, good, and ethical principles.

4. Eliciting a sense of moral responsibility: Help students consider what it means to take ethics seriously.

5. Tolerating and resisting disagreement and ambiguity: Help students learn that even if ethical certainty is often impossible, ethical reasoning about choices is possible.

How are competent teachers to be developed for courses with these goals? The Hastings studies recommend that applied ethics teachers be trained to teach two fields—applied ethics in a profession and a subject in that field. Teachers trained in a profession should take courses in moral philosophy, and those trained in philosophical ethics should take courses in the profession.

Applied ethics courses that meet the five goals outlined above can help public administrators develop the mental attitudes and understand the moral qualities essential to ethical public service. The environment of the public administrator requires a sharp focus on dilemmas that arise when the fundamental values of *freedom* and *order*, or *equality*, and *efficiency* are in conflict. Such training would elevate individual responsibility in the minds of public administrators as they go about their daily work of applying to specific situations the often inadequate guidance of the Constitution, laws, judicial decisions, and policies of the elected chief executive.

The aim here is not to suggest that in every administrative situation the value problems should be isolated and that they should dominate decision making, with all the ethical alternatives being explored in depth. Many values are an inherent or prescribed part of the administrative process—as, for example, "due process." Values are also reflected in many of the intuitive, "commonsense" decisions of administrators made quickly in response to fairly uncomplicated problems. However, significant ethical issues often lurk in more complex problems; and it is here that training in applied ethics can help the administrator identify and examine value issues as part of a decisions process that will best serve the public interest.

IN THE PUBLIC INTEREST

The public administrator's interpretation of the "public interest" and commitment to it form the key link in the chain for holding government bureaucracies accountable. Many laws explicitly direct the public administrator to act "in the public interest." For public administrators, coming to grips with the concept of the public interest and being willing to wrestle with the practical dilemmas that flow from it are prerequisites to fulfilling their individual responsibilities.

A popular notion that the public interest is served by denying the requests of special interests is simplistic. Many scholars and practitioners see the public interest as a compromise based on an optimum reconciliation of competing interests. Arthur Holcombe added another dimension: "Action in the public interest means an adjustment of the conflicts between special interests in such a way as best to serve the common good of the whole body of people. . . . It (the public interest) is nothing less than such an adjustment of conflicting special interests as can give the people durable confidence in the stability of the state itself."[47] That confidence can be durable only if the legitimate interests of those unable to make themselves heard—the impoverished, the inarticulate, and the unorganized—are also considered in determining the public interest. Public administrators are responsible and government bureaucracies are accountable when their power and influence are exercised in the public interest.

NOTES

1. OMB Circular A–132, April 22, 1988.
2. Ibid., p. 1.
3. Ibid., p. 1.
4. Ibid., pp. 3–5, 10–11.
5. U.S., Congress, House, Committee on Government Operations, Subcommittee on Legislation and National Security, *Statement of Comptroller General, U.S. General Accounting Office*, 97th Cong., 1st sess., May 12, 1980.
6. Statement of the Comptroller General of the United States before the House Subcommittee on Legislation and National Security, Government Operations Committee, March 21, 1979.
7. OMB Circular A–73, March 15, 1978.
8. U.S., Congress, House, Government Operations Committee, Hearings on Audit Resolution, 96th Cong., 1st sess., 1979.
9. OMB Circular A–73, November 27, 1979.
10. *Statement of Comptroller General*, 1981.

11. Report of the United States General Accounting Office, AFMD–81–27, January 23, 1981, pp. 8, 28.

12. Ibid., p. 29.

13. *Congressional Record*, February 2, 1981, p. H 282.

14. OMB Circular No. A–50 Revised, September 29, 1982.

15. Ibid., pp. 4–5.

16. "New Requirements on Audit Follow-up," Memorandum for Heads of Departments and Agencies, OMB, October 7, 1982.

17. Report of the United States General Accounting Office, AFMD–88–10, December 1987, pp. 30–32.

18. Statement of Charles A. Bowsher, Comptroller General of the United States, before the Committee on Governmental Affairs, United States Senate, July 23, 1987, p. 1.

19. Ibid., pp. 6–7.

20. *Management of the United States Government*, U.S. Office of Management and Budget, Fiscal Year 1989, p. 34.

21. *Finding Out How Programs are Working; Suggestions for Congressional Oversight*, U.S. General Accounting Office, PAD–78–3, November 22, 1977.

22. Ibid., pp. 21–22.

23. *Annual Report to the Chairman, House and Senate Committees on Appropriations*, OP–88–1, February 26, 1988.

24. U.S., Congress, Senate, Committee on Government Operations (now Committee on Governmental Affairs), *The Regulatory Appointment Process, Study on Federal Regulation*, Vol. 1, 95th Cong., 1st sess., January 1977, pp. 163–67.

25. Ibid., pp. 179–80.

26. U.S., Congress, Senate, Governmental Affairs Committee, *The Regulatory Appointment Process*, 95th Cong., 1st sess., 1977, pp. 183–85.

27. Common Cause, *The Rubber Stamp Machine*, 1977.

28. Report: Whistle-blower Protection Act of 1987, Committee on Post Office and Civil Service, U.S. House of Representatives, #100–274, August 5, 1987, p. 19.

29. Ibid., pp. 20–21.

30. Ibid., p. 22.

31. Senate Report No. 95–969, 95th Cong., 2d sess., 1978, p. 8.

32. Ibid., p. 21.

33. 100th Cong., 1st sess., H.R. 25.

34. 100th Cong., 2d sess., S. 508.

35. *Congressional Quarterly* (Spring 1974), p. 28.

36. Stephen K. Bailey, "Ethics and the Public Service," in *Public Administration and Democracy*, ed. Roscoe C. Martin (Syracuse: Syracuse University Press, 1965), pp. 283–98.

37. Ibid., pp. 285–86.

38. Ibid., p. 288.

39. Ibid., p. 292.

40. Ibid., pp. 293–94.

41. Ibid., p. 294.

42. Ibid., p. 297.

43. "Applied Ethics: A Strategy for Fostering Professional Responsibility," *Carnegie Quarterly* (Spring/Summer 1980):1.

44. Michael H. Kelly, "Legal Ethics and Legal Education,"; Clifford G. Christians, "Teaching Ethics in Journalism Education"; K. Danner Clouser, "Teaching Bioethics: Strategies, Problems, and Resources"; Charles W. Powers and David Vogal, "Ethics in the Education of Business Managers"; Robert J. Baum, "The Teaching of Ethics and Engineering Curricula"; Joel L. Fleishman and Bruce L. Payne, "Ethical Dilemmas in the Education of Policymakers"; Bernard Rosen and Arthur L. Caplan, "Ethics in the Undergraduate Curriculum"; Donald P. Warwick, "The Teaching of Ethics in the Social Sciences"; Daniel Callahan and Sissela Bok, *Ethics Teaching in Higher Education* (New York: Institute of Society, Ethics, and the Life Sciences, 1980).

45. Ibid., p. 7.

46. "Moral and Ethical Education in College: Theoretical and Practical Considerations," *Ethics; Easier Said than Done*, Vol. 1, No. 1, winter 1988, pp. 11–12.

47. Arthur N. Holcombe, *Our More Perfect Union* (Cambridge: Harvard University Press, 1950), p. 316.

9

In Retrospect

Government bureaucracies are out of control! In thousands of forums, on television and radio, in news stories and debates, that charge is made and repeated throughout the country. The occasion that prompts the charge may be:

a notorious instance of waste, fraud, incompetence, or arrogance;

a proper discretionary judgment opposed by some groups and supported by others;

an agency action that conflicts with the chief executive's philosophy but reflects the independent judgment required by law;

a general reaction to the cost of government; and/or

a part of the molding of public opinion that flows from the rhetoric of a politician running for office and using criticism of the bureaucracy as an issue on which voters can coalesce.

Regardless of the cause, the charge strikes a deep and politically rewarding chord among people who believe in freedom but whose individual lives are increasingly regulated and whose earnings pay for vast bureaucracies at the national, state, and local levels.

If a government bureaucracy is out of control, clearly it is not for any lack of means of holding it accountable. Chapters 3 through 7 identified an awesome armada of policies, mechanisms, and processes to oversee bureaucracies and cause those that do not act in the public interest to change course. Only the will to use these means may be lacking. There is a great deal of redundancy, more than enough to give citizens reasonable assurance that a bureaucracy could not get significantly out of line for any extended period. In fact, the redundancy poses a potential problem. If all existing accountability mechanisms worked as they could, they would probably hobble the bureaucracies in their essential work; administrators and their staffs would be so busy responding to queries and procedures aimed at acountability that there would be insufficient time to plan, organize, and supervise the work for which they were being held accountable.

Overcontrol encourages timidity, breeds inaction, and stimulates unnecessary conflict. For now, though, overcontrol is not the problem; the real problem in most government jurisdictions is that the accountability mechanisms are performing poorly, with little dependability and consistency. Neither systems nor authority is now at the heart of the problem. For the most part, it is *people*—on both sides of the accountability process.

EXECUTIVE COMPETENCE AND COMMITMENT TO THE PUBLIC INTEREST IS ESSENTIAL

While publicity about political appointee Max Hugel so embarrassed the Reagan administration in its first year as to cause him to resign from a key position in the Central Intelligence Agency (see Chapter 2), it is no secret that there are thousands of political appointees in national, state, and local governments who lack visible qualifications to carry out effectively major responsibilities with which they have been entrusted. Of course, many political appointees have outstanding qualifications; and few would argue with the notion that elected chief executives and their department heads should be able to bring into the executive branch a reasonable number of people of their own choice to help set policies and priorities and move the bureaucracy in the desired direction. That is part of what elections are about. There is, however, only the weakest justification to support the idea that this constitutes a license for placing significant governmental responsibilities with those political campaign workers, financial contributors, and personal friends who have little or no demonstrated competence for the positions to which they are appointed.

Nevertheless, at all levels of government this gross abuse of the public trust is tolerated with little *sustained* outcry from legislative committees, the news media, government employee unions, and various "better government" interest groups—all of which have considerable capacity to identify and publicize these situations and thereby hold our elected executives accountable. We seem to have been anesthetized by the argument that such patronage is essential to the democratic process. If the appointment of unqualified people were widely and relentlessly publicized among the voters, the political cost to a chief executive who permitted irresponsible personal and political patronage would soon exceed the benefits, and consequently the incidence of the practice would sharply diminish.

Unless competence to perform the duties of a position is an essential criterion for the selection of political appointees, there is little hope for lasting improvement in the performance of many government bureaucracies. Political appointees who are incompetent or marginally competent in their areas of responsibility will continue to terrorize career executives with unwarranted suspicions about political loyalty. They will continue partially paralyzing the rest of the bureaucracy with their inaction and poor decisions based on ignorance of programs and governmental processes, their ill-advised or illegal proposals designed to provide political benefits in the short term, and their refusal to come to grips with major problems when benefits would not be produced until after their own short tenure had ended. Throughout they will continue to complain about and try to circumvent essential requirements for accountability that have been translated into systems of administrative controls. The cost of operating the machinery of government with all this sand in the gears exceeds by many times the amount paid in salaries to unqualified appointees.

Government agencies lose their top three levels of appointees on average every two years, and several times that number of political appointees filling lesser but still important positions. No successful private enterprise could survive such frequent loss of leadership. The relatively short period political appointees are in government service precludes extensive on-the-job training. The need for a high order of competence is obvious. Career executives do provide professionalism, objectivity, competence, and continuity to help assure reasonable stability in government operations; but it is the political appointee who is responsible for capably leading the career staff.

For the federal government and many state governments, the large number of positions earmarked for political appointment is simply beyond the ability of the elected chief executive to recruit highly qualified people. A study of the presidential appointment system by a panel of the National Academy of Public Administration concluded that "The capacity no longer exists— in the White House or in the Senate—to find and assess with care the qualifications of the large number of people now needed to fill all appointed positions. The quality of governance in the United States is not improved by the enlargement of the nonprofessional workforce. It is an odd and unfortunate paradox that as government grows in technical detail and complexity, more and more leadership positions are filled by individuals who are unfamiliar with the substance of the policies they will oversee and strangers to the government environment. . . . The number of positions filled by political appointment has grown too large and must be reduced. The House Government Operations and Senate Governmental Affairs Committees should conduct a governmentwide assessment to identify and reconvert many of these positions where career executives have been replaced by political appointees."[1]

The president and Congress also need to meet better their responsibility for assuring competence at career executive levels of the federal bureaucracy. They need to face up to the problem that inadequate pay is the major reason that a majority of the career executives retire as soon as they become eligible. Most who leave are in the prime of their ability and usefulness; a national resource developed at great cost is being wasted. An archaic linkage of executive to congressional pay,[2] and the reluctance of members of Congress to raise their own pay, have resulted in unconscionable pay compression. In some instances, this affects adversely the ability of the government to recruit and retain outstanding talent in political positions. Unless Congress breaks this linkage, the drain of expertise and competence will continue and accountability within the bureaucracy will suffer.

Along with proven competence in political and career leadership positions, there is a need for understanding of, and commitment to, the public interest. Many of the numerous failures recounted in earlier chapters reflect some lack of dedication to values that enjoy wide acceptance such as honesty, integrity, fidelity, fairness, pursuit of excellence, and accountability. Preemployment investigations for political appointment need to produce information on these vital qualities. Early on-the-job orientation to the concept of public trust and special obligations of public service is essential.

As for career employees, advancement to mid-level and senior positions should depend in part on whether the above values have been demonstrated. Periodically, political and career appointees need to focus jointly on the importance of these qualities and the rule of law. It is their perceptions of the "public trust" as reflected in their actions that will have a profound effect on the behavior of the bureaucracy.

MORE OF THE BRIGHTEST AND THE BEST NEED TO BE RECRUITED AND RETAINED

At the other end of the professional and administrative hierarchy is the need for government to recruit and develop a fair share of the promising graduates from colleges and professional schools—bright young people with a strong desire for the challenge of public service. The federal government is falling behind in this competition. *Lower pay, current job market, and the negative public image* of the bureaucracy were cited as reasons students appear to be "not interested" in federal employment, according to a survey of 72 deans and placement officers. These officials were in colleges that rate high in seven curriculum areas (engineering, computer science, law, nursing, accounting, liberal arts, and public administration) that are significant recruitment sources for one or more of the ten most populous occupations in the federal government typically filled by college graduates.[3]

In presidentially appointed advisory commissions and a variety of other forums, leaders in corporate America have also expressed concern about federal pay. For example, Mobil Corporation published a paid editorial in *Time* magazine that concluded:

Federal pay scales, as we've said, have made it increasingly difficult to recruit and retain qualified people. Unless a way is found to make government careers as rewarding as those in the private sector, the American people will wind up with key people in key jobs making key decisions who are either a wealthy elite or society's less able performers. In government, as in everything else, you get what you pay for. Particularly in view of the problems facing American society, the nation can't afford less than the best.[4]

Numerous proposals for making pay more competitive have been considered by Congress; and have been approved in the form of demonstration projects; all are directed to giving employing agencies more flexibility to meet increasingly tight market conditions.

As for the negative public image cited in the survey, federal employees have always been an attractive scapegoat for politicians seeking to capitalize on citizen dissatisfaction with the taxes they pay and the purposes for which the money is used. However, the Carter and Reagan administrations engaged in denigratory criticism of the civil service to a degree unprecedented in the last 100 years.

President Carter, speaking to a group of editors and news directors on July 29, 1978, stated: "Now my biggest problems are inflation and dealing with the horrible federal bureaucracy. And the one that's been the most frustrating, I think, is the bureaucracy itself." He went on to say, "I'm a businessman. . . . When I meet around this table every week or two weeks with my Cabinet, that is the most pervasive problem that they bring to me—'We cannot manage the people who work under us.' "[5]

Some would argue that this comment tells more about those appointed by the president than those in the civil service. That aside, the president made some other unfavorable comments about the civil service that probably added to and fortified erroneous impressions already held by these newspaper and electronic media executives, and which they carried back to their readers and listeners throughout the country.

During the first two years of the Carter administration, the president's salesmen for a new civil service law traveled around the country meeting with newspaper editors and other opinion leaders to reflect Carter's perception of the "horrible federal bureaucracy" and urge their support for civil service "reform" so government could be run more like a business. The highly respected *National Journal* summed it up in one sentence: "Anti-bureaucrat rhetoric was intense during the push to pass the Civil Service Reform Act in 1978."[6]

This massive national campaign left the unjustified impression that the civil service was riddled with people who were unresponsive to national policy and political leadership because they lacked competence and/or motivation, and that only by radically changing certain policies and the central structure for personnel management would it be possible to deal with the alleged problems.

Merit system processes were often unfairly castigated as to time and cost by ignoring the reality that consistent application of process is frequently the indispensable element for assuring fairness. The systematic attempt to subvert the merit system during the Nixon administration, and the Civil Service Commission's successful investigations which ended that short-lived effort, were twisted and cited as evidence that the existing organization had been inadequate to protect the merit concept. Editors of newspapers throughout the nation were encouraged to join in the effort that created a crescendo of criticism against the then current system, criticism that moved easily and often irresponsibly from the system to the people in it. Occasional scapegoating had turned into a nationwide war on federal employees.

The notion of widespread incompetence, indolence, and irresponsibility permeating the civil service, which had been unfairly spread and vigorously cultivated to secure passage of the Civil Service Reform Act,[7] continued to flourish with a change in administration. An "overzealous" bureaucracy was blamed for everything from wanting to substitute ketchup for vegetables in school lunches to planning for expansion of secrecy in government. The fact that the responsible bureaucrats in these events were presidential appointees was largely ignored. The *Wall Street Journal* carried this item: "Baiting Bureaucrats: The White House steps up its gibes at civil servants. Reagan needles them in nearly every speech, all but calling them lazy."[8] The Washington *Post* reported that the president said some government employees may attempt to sabotage his economic program by deliberately making it appear unfair.[9] Other newspapers across the country carried the same message.

To develop strong public support for cutting federal employee retirement benefits in order to help achieve the Reagan administration's goal of reducing non-defense spending, the director of the Office of Personnel Management (OPM) issued a news release that compared federal expenditures for retirement with those for welfare.[10] It requires little imagination to understand the feelings of federal employees and the impact on their performance as they learned that their retirement benefits (to which they contributed seven and a half percent of their salaries) were being questioned and publicized in that context. In another news release also designed to generate support for reducing retirement benefits, the director of OPM cited costs to the government and stated that federal employee annuities were generally larger than those for employees in the private sector.[11] What the news release failed to mention was that when all pay and benefits are considered, federal employees are undercompensated by a significant percentage in comparison to the private sector.[12]

Federal employees at all levels deeply resented both the failure to provide the public with correct information as well as the added credibility given to the erroneous impressions that they were being overcompensated. Stoking the fires of citizen discontent about the civil service with misleading information during both the Carter and Reagan administrations has had a devastating impact on the morale of federal employees.[13] Frank Carlucci, while Chief Executive Officer (CEO) of Sears World Trade (later served as Secretary of Defense), remarked in a speech:

If I as a CEO were to say that I have loafers, laggards, and petty thieves working for me, one could hardly expect my people to perform. Nor would such talk inspire customer confidence; indeed they would wonder about us as a company and about me as a CEO. Yet that is exactly what two government CEO's—two presidents—have said.[14]

If this scapegoating is not reversed, the compelling desire for self-respect and human dignity will cause more of the best performers to leave and more of the most talented will not seek to enter public service. With the beginning of the Bush administration, there have been statements from the president with regard to the civil service which evidence an attitude quite contrary to that demonstrated by Presidents Carter and Reagan. Subsequent actions by President Bush will reveal whether a major change has occurred.

LIMITED PARTISAN POLITICAL ACTIVITY BY FEDERAL EMPLOYEES

To help hold federal employees accountable for impartial execution of the laws, not only are they prohibited by law[15] from using their official authority or influence to interfere with or affect the results of elections, they are also forbidden to take an active part in political management or campaigns. From time to time, these limits on participation of federal employees in the political process have been called an infringement on the constitutional rights of freedom of speech and freedom of assembly. That question was settled when the Supreme Court held in 1973 that it is not a violation of the constitutional rights of federal employees to prohibit them from engaging in plainly identifiable acts of political management and political campaigning.[16]

Critics of the law focus in part on its administration. They charge, with some justification, that uncertainty about the applicability of the law in a variety of situations has a chilling effect on lawful participation in political activity by federal employees and their family members. The Office of the Special Counsel has a statutory responsibility for issuing advisory opinions. The uncertainties need to be resolved by prompt and clear advisory services, and if necessary, clarifying the law.

The most intense criticism is leveled at the *denial to federal employees a right possessed by all other citizens, that is, the right to participate actively in partisan politics.* In the 100th Congress, second session, a veto-proof bipartisan majority in the U.S. House of Representatives voted to permit federal employees to participate actively in partisan politics when they are not on duty.[17] The Senate has not acted on a somewhat modified version of the House bill as this is being written. The president is committed to vetoing any bill that would permit federal employees to engage in partisan political activity.

Under current law, federal employees, like other citizens, may register and vote, assist in voter registration drives not limited to one party, express opinions about candidates and issues, participate in campaigns where none of the candidates represent a national or state political party, contribute money to a political organization or attend a political fund-raising function, wear or display badges or stickers, attend political rallies and meetings, join a political club or party, sign nominating petitions, and campaign for or against referendum questions, constitutional amendments, and local ordinances.

On the fundamental issue of permitting federal employees to engage, while off duty, in the full range of partisan political activity (campaign for partisan candidates, collect contributions, organize rallies, etc.), there is one clear consensus among supporters and opponents of this proposal. It is that any change must recognize the need for a balance between the right of federal employees to participate in the political life of this nation and the right of the public to a competent, impartial, nonpartisan, honest administration of the law. In this delicate balance, both the reality and perception are vital considerations. The *appearance* of nonpartisanship in the execution of law is essential to maintaining public confidence in the administrative institutions of government.

It is reasonable to project that whatever partisan political activity is permitted off duty would for many become the expected behavior. Those in the civil service would soon come to believe that better assignments, promotions, and bonuses depend in part on partisan political activity. Equally destructive of morale and motivation would be a growing concern that not being promoted, etc., was due to having engaged in political activity for the unsuccessful party/candidate or simply not having gotten involved at all. Subtle but effective coercion would be unavoidable. This is no way to attract and retain the high quality staff needed in the civil service.

Federal employees' involvement in partisan political activities would erode citizen confidence in the impartial administration of the laws. Many citizens would have a growing uneasiness about the objectivity of those who fought them in partisan political campaigns and who then participate in investigations or decisions that adversely affect them. This could occur in tens of thousands of situations dealing with such issues as taxes, eligibility for individual and corporate benefits, compliance with regulatory requirements, and procurement contracts. Public trust in the administrative institutions of government would be undermined to a dangerous degree.

Then there is the matter of changes in administrations from one political party to the other. Participation of civil service employees in partisan political activities would greatly increase the doubts of incoming administrations about the responsiveness of the career civil service to new political leadership. For many presidential appointees in both Democratic and Republican administrations, it has been hard to shake such doubts, even though they were almost always unjustified. Partisan political activity by career civil servants would create barriers of suspicion in political career relationships that would be insurmountable in many instances.

Some argue for less drastic changes in the law: permit federal employees off duty to engage in the full range of partisan political activity only in connection with partisan elections for local government offices. Others argue for changes in the act that would permit a full range of off-the-job partisan political activity by those federal employees whose duties do not include substantive responsibilities in any of the federal government's investigatory, regulatory, law enforcement, procurement, leasing, contracting, benefit, and employment activities. Aside from the extraordinary difficulty, if not impossibility, of making and enforcing these distinctions to prevent spillover of partisan activity in what would remain as prohibited areas, it is unrealistic to expect such distinctions to permeate the public consciousness. Instead, the public will come to believe that *all* federal employees may engage in partisan politics and that political partisanship diminishes impartiality in the execution of the laws.

UNDERSTAFFING AND ACCOUNTABILITY

Aside from providing services and benefits and assigning penalties, much of the work of government is involved with regulating in the public interest. Disposal of toxic wastes, disease-free meat and poultry products, occupational safety and health, restoration of land at abandoned mine sites, maintenance of commercial aircraft, these and thousands of other conditions in our complex, high technology society have been made subject to government regulation. Regulations have the force of law, and it is reasonable to expect that they will be enforced.

In pursuing a strategy of lowering the federal government's profile in domestic affairs and redirecting resources from non-defense to defense activities, the Reagan administration cut back its enforcement of hundreds of federal regulations. While some regulations were changed, in keeping with the new direction, more often a reduction in funds made inevitable a reduction in staff and lower levels of compliance activity. This was evident particularly in the Environmental Protection Agency, the Departments of

Agriculture, Interior, Labor, and Transportation, and the Office of Personnel Management.

Establishing agency regulations involves public notice, an opportunity for comments by interested citizens and, if the regulation is adopted, an explanation justifying content and coverage. However, decisions that lead to reduced enforcement of laws or regulations are made without public notice, without opportunity for comments, and without explanation of likely consequences. Those who could profit from noncompliance will quickly observe that it is safe to do so; many of those who would be adversely affected will learn about it only months or years later.

When government demonstrates a lack of capacity or will to enforce requirements established in the public interest, compliance drops, respect for law diminishes, and confidence in Congress and the administrative institutions declines.

There are similar considerations with regard to inspectors general, the Merit Systems Protection Board, and the Federal Labor Relations Authority—unique institutions created by Congress and the president to improve oversight. In each case, one executive branch unit oversees others in important respects. The need for such oversight has become more urgent as delegation, decentralization, and deregulation have increased.

These units have been given substantial power and independence to fulfill their responsibilities, and periodic reports are required for use in legislation and related oversight processes. Regrettably, they are understaffed for doing *well* what they are charged with doing. To realize the enormous potential benefits from these mechanisms, they must be funded adequately, and they can and must be held accountable for meeting their responsibilities. The additional cost is modest compared to the potential benefits. At stake are the rule of law and citizen confidence in government.

SHARED POWER—SHARED RESPONSIBILITY

In these areas, as well as in almost all others related to holding government bureaucracies accountable, the legislative body and the chief executive have the dominant responsibility. Legislators alone have the ultimate power to create or abolish bureaucracies, to expand or curtail their powers and responsibilities, to give "advice and consent" on who will serve as leaders, to increase or decrease staffs, to determine what they will do and, if so moved, how it will be done. With this overwhelming power goes the obligation for seeing that what the legislature decides should be done does in fact take place.

However, in our system of government with its shared powers and checks and balances, the elected chief executive has an important initiatory role and the primary operational responsibility. How well the chief executives meet these expectations depends very heavily on those they select for their immediate staff and top leadership positions in the departments and agencies. In turn, it is the ability and character of these executives that to a large extent determine whether the government bureaucracies, at all levels, are staffed with the high competence and dedication needed to serve the public interest.

Having said that, one must also recognize that all of the other forces in our democratic society that exercise power and influence in making statutory or administrative policy carry a moral obligation to keep an eye on how such policy is carried out. Responsible oversight is not as "heady" as shaping policy. Simply damning the bureaucracy when failings occur is irresponsible and unproductive. Evidence of incompetence or corruption often leads to calls for prompt dismissals or prosecutions as the solution. That may be necessary but by itself inadequate. It is the underlying causes of incompetence or corruption that must be identified and addressed.

Whatever the causes, responsible citizen groups, with the help of the news media, need to look initially to the executive but ultimately to the legislative body to determine authoritatively the facts and initiate corrective action— action which is tempered by Peter Drucker's sage advice: "If control tries to account for everything, it becomes prohibitively expensive."[18]

As we proceed along these lines, we will demonstrate a maturity for self-governance that recognizes that in our constitutional democracy *the people* are supreme and they expect those they elect to hold accountable the bureaucracies they create and sustain.

NOTES

1. *Leadership in Jeopardy: The Fraying of the Presidential Appointment System.* National Academy of Public Administration, November 1985, pp. 2–4.

2. 92 Stat. 1184 (1978). This law illustrates the decision not to permit the pay for Executive Level II to exceed that of a member of Congress.

3. *Attracting Quality Graduates to the Federal Government: A View of College Recruiting*, U.S. Merit Systems Protection Board, June 6, 1988.

4. "Less Than the Best Isn't Good Enough," *Time*, March 14, 1988, p. 6.

5. *Presidential Documents*, week ending August 4, 1978, p. 1347.

6. "Bureaucrats Under Fire," *National Journal*, September 1978, pp. 1540–41.

7. 92 Stat. 1111 (1978).

8. September 18, 1981, p. 1.

9. February 9, 1982, p. 1.

10. News Release, U.S. Office of Personnel Management, March 9, 1983.

11. News Release, U.S. Office of Personnel Management, February 22, 1983.

12. *Adjustments in Federal White-Collar Pay*, U.S., Congress, House, Committee on Post Office and Civil Service, 98th Cong., 1st sess., Committee Print 98-4, March 22, 1983; *Statement of Charles A. Bowsher, Comptroller General of the United States*, U.S., Congress, House, Subcommittee on Investigations of the Committee on Post Office and Civil Service, 98th Cong., 2d sess., May 24, 1983.

13. The preceding seven paragraphs are drawn from an essay by the author entitled "Effective Continuity of U.S. Government Operations in Jeopardy," *Public Administration Review*, September/October 1983, pp. 383–84.

14. "A Shabby Way to Treat Government Executives; The Bashing Continues," Washington *Post*, April 22, 1987, p. A–19.

15. 5 U.S. Code 1501–1508 and 7324–7327.

16. *U.S. Civil Service Commission* v. *National Association of Letter Carriers, AFL-CIO*, 413 U.S. 548 (1973).

17. H.R. 3400 (1987).

18. Peter F. Drucker, *The Effective Executive* (New York: Harper and Row, 1967), p. 84.

Selected Bibliography

Burke, John P., *Bureaucratic Responsibility*, Baltimore: Johns Hopkins Press, 1986.

Cooper, Terry, *The Responsible Administrator*, Port Washington, N.Y.: Kennekat Press, 1982.

Crane, Edgar G. Jr., *Legislative Review of Government Programs*, New York: Praeger, 1977.

Davis, Kenneth Culp, *Discretionary Justice*, Chicago: University of Illinois Press, 1976.

Fleischman, Alan et al., eds., *Public Duties: The Moral Obligations of Government Officials*, Cambridge: Harvard University Press, 1981.

Fuchs, Edward P., *President, Management, and Regulation*, Englewood Cliffs: Prentice-Hall, 1988.

Hall, Kermit, *Judicial Review in American History*, New York: Garland Publishers, 1987.

Keefe, W. J. and Ogul, M. S., *The American Legislative Process*, 6th edition, Englewood Cliffs: Prentice-Hall, 1985.

Macy, John W. and Adams, Bruce, *America's Unelected Government*, Washington: National Academy of Public Administration, 1983.

Mollenhoff, Clark R., *Investigative Reporting, From the Courthouse to the White House*, New York: MacMillan, 1981.

Mosher, Frederick C., *The GAO*, Boulder: Westview Press, 1979.

Scholozman, K. L. and Tierney, John R., *Organized Interests and American Democracy*, New York: Harper and Row, 1986.

Index

ABOUT THE AUTHOR

BERNARD ROSEN has been Distinguished Adjunct Professor in Residence at the American University School of Public Affairs since 1976. He teaches graduate courses in the politics of administration, public management, and public personnel administration. He is the author of essays published in *Public Administration Review, The Bureaucrat—The Journal for Public Managers*, and the *Washington Post.*

He was a career executive in the federal government during the administration of five presidents. From 1971 to 1975, he was Executive Director of the central personnel agency of the federal government. He served in a variety of assignments in and outside Washington, including membership on numerous interagency groups established by the Executive Office of the President to deal with organization, management, and productivity problems. He is a Fellow of the National Academy of Public Administration and a member of the American Society for Public Administration (on its National Council for three years) and the International Personnel Management Association.

Rosen has received numerous awards in recognition of outstanding service. A member of Phi Beta Kappa, he did undergraduate work in Political Science at the University of Alabama and graduate work in Public Administration at the Universities of Alabama and Illinois.

DEC - 7 1990

DEC 1 5 1990

MAY - 9 1991